THE SOUL OF THINGS

THE SOUL OF THINGS

Psychometric Experiments for Re-living History

WILLIAM DENTON

Introduction by Colin Wilson

THE AQUARIAN PRESS
Wellingborough, Northamptonshire

First published 1863
This Edition 1988

© The Aquarian Press 1988

British Library Cataloguing in Publication Data

Denton, William
The soul of things: psychometric
experiments for re-living history. — 9th
ed. — (The Colin Wilson library of the
paranormal).
1. Psychometry (Occult sciences)
I. Title   II. Series
133.8   BF1286

ISBN 0-85030-707-4

*The Aquarian Press is part of the
Thorsons Publishing Group,
Wellingborough, Northamptonshire, NN8 2RQ, England*

Printed in Great Britain by
Woolnough Bookbinding Limited,
Irthlingborough, Northamptonshire

1 3 5 7 9 10 8 6 4 2

INTRODUCTION

In my opinion, this is one of the most important books in the history of psychical research, and its neglect for more than a century is nothing less than a tragedy. It is also — as its new readers will discover — one of the most exciting books ever written. The simplest way to explain what it is all about is to quote a paragraph that appeared in the *Saturday Review* about 1870:

'Something new has turned up in the wonderful spiritualist world. It is called Psychometry, and means a certain power possessed by people who are termed psychometers, which enables them, when any piece of matter is placed in contact with them, to see all that has ever happened to that piece of matter ... So far as is yet known, almost all psychometers are American ladies. The greatest are Mrs Denton, wife of Mr Denton, a lecturer on geology at Boston, US; Mrs Cridge of Pennsylvania; and Mrs Lucielle Do Viel, of Pultneyville, Wayne Co., N.Y., — "a lady who, on examining a specimen psychometrically, not only goes to the spot from which the specimen was obtained, but has the sensation of travelling while doing so", and who may possibly have had this gift allotted to her by the kindness of nature as some compensation for her extraordinary name.'

That paragraph is basically accurate except that 'psychometers' (we prefer to call them psychometrists) are not a special group of people with special powers; Denton was convinced that all human beings possess such powers, and that it is merely a question of developing them. He believed, in short, that we all possess the gift of 'time travel'.

For the beginning of this strange story we must go back to the year 1843, when a newly qualified doctor named Joseph Rhodes Buchanan met an archbishop of the Episcopal Church named Leonidas Polk. They discussed Buchanan's interest in phrenology — the belief that the human personality reveals itself through 'bumps' on the skull — and Buchanan mentioned his belief that he had located the 'region of sensibility' in the brain, which governs all man's finer perceptions. The archbishop intrigued him by asserting that he himself had a rather peculiar faculty — the ability to detect brass with his fingertips alone. Even in the dark, he could distinguish brass from other metals because it produced an unpleasant metallic taste in his mouth.

To Buchanan, this made good sense. The tongue has the power to detect brass because its nerves are sensitive to taste. But the same must be true of *all* our nerves, even those in the finger ends — although obviously they are far less sensitive. The archbishop allowed Buchanan to feel his 'bumps', and Buchanan was delighted to discover that his 'bump of sensitivity' was highly developed, verifying that his nerves were abnormally sensitive.

Buchanan decided to experiment with his students at the Eclectic Medical Institute in Cincinatti, Ohio. He tried wrapping various chemicals and metals in brown paper, and asking the students if they could detect them with their fingertips. Many of them were amazingly successful, and again Buchanan discovered that these had a well-developed 'bump' of sensibility. (Phrenology is now dismissed as nonsense, but Buchanan's results suggest that there *may* be something in it worth investigating.)

One of Buchanan's best 'sensitives' was a man named Charles Inman, and it was while experimenting with Inman that Buchanan made his most amazing discovery. He asked Inman to hold sealed letters and try to 'sense' the characters of the writers. Inman's character readings were incredibly accurate. He was even able to sense the mood of the letter writers — whether they happened to be feeling depressed or cheerful as they wrote. But how could *that* be explained scientifically? Simple, said Buchanan. Our nerves detect things because they give off an electrical vibration called the nerve aura. But this aura also leaves its imprints on the things it comes into contact with — like a smell. Sensitives like Inman are simply human bloodhounds, who can 'pick up' these normally undetectable smells.

It was Buchanan who decided to call this faculty 'psychometry' — meaning 'soul (or mind) measurement'. He published articles about it in his *Journal of Man* (started in 1849), and later brought all his results together in a remarkable work called *Manual of Psychometry*, optimistically subtitled 'The Dawn of a New Civilisation', published in 1885.

The work should have become a classic and led to a new branch of scientific investigation. Unfortunately, there had been a tremendous change of public opinion between 1849 and 1885, due to the emergence of the cult called 'spiritualism', whose starting point had been the amazing 'poltergeist' disturbances in the house of the Fox family in 1848 and '49. Buchanan was, in fact, a spiritualist — although he had been a student of psychometry seven years before spiritualism was even heard of. So the scientists and the medical profession dismissed his 'discoveries' as superstitious rubbish. Buchanan died in California a few days before the arrival of the new century, his work virtually forgotten.

But Buchanan had at least one warm supporter: an Englishman named William Denton, the author of the present work. And, as this book makes clear, there were some ways in which the pupil surpassed his master. Denton had been born in Darlington, Yorkshire, in 1823 — so he was nine years younger than Buchanan — and after his conversion to Methodism at sixteen, he became a popular Temperance lecturer. He came to America at the age of 25, and spent some time in Cincinatti, where Buchanan had founded his medical institute. I have not been able to determine whether Buchanan and Denton became friends, but it seems highly likely. Denton married a lady from Cincinatti named Elizabeth Foote, and moved with her to Dayton, Ohio, where he became principal of a school. In 1849, he read Buchanan's original paper on psychometry in the *Journal of Man*, and was greatly excited by it. The great love of Denton's life was geology, and in 1853 he began a series of experiments designed to find out whether the faculty of 'psychometry' would work with geological specimens.

Now this idea may sound absurd and unscientific; for after all, a piece of rock has not had a chance to pick up the 'nerve aura' which, according to Buchanan, is the scientific basis of psychometry. But then, Buchanan had been forced to modify his own views when he made the disconcerting discovery that Charles Inman could also pick up information from photographs — not just studio daguerreotypes, which have probably been handled by the sitter, but even from newspaper photographs, which have been turned out in their thousand by a printing press. Buchanan could only explain this bewildering observation by assuming that the personality of the sitter somehow imprints itself on the photograph, and that a 'sensitive' can somehow 'read' this information.

So Denton decided it would be worth seeing what happened if he presented his 'sensitives' with geological specimens wrapped up in brown paper. His sister-in-law Anne Cridge was an excellent sensitive. So Denton presented her with a piece of limestone from Kansas, on the Missouri River. He response was interesting: 'It seems to me that there is a deep hole here. Oh, what shells! Small shells; so many. I see water; it looks like a river running along. What a high hill, almost perpendicular; it seems as if the water had cut it in two; it is not so high on the other side. The hill is covered with sand and gravel.' Denton's memory of the spot where he had found the limestone suggested that this was an accurate description. It seemed a good beginning.

The next experiment with Anne Cridge was spectacular. He handed her a fragment of volcanic lava from Kilauea, on Hawaii, wrapped in paper. Mrs Cridge had an impression of an ocean with ships on it, and could tell she was looking at an island. Then she saw 'an ocean of fire pouring over a precipice and boiling as it pours. I see it flow into the ocean and the water boil intensely'. The lava had been ejected in the eruption of 1840, when the American navy had been in Hawaii, so even the vision of ships was accurate.

A modern scientist would object, of course, that Denton's experimental precautions were inadequate — that he might have provided Anne with enough unconscious clues to enable her to identify the specimen. But Denton himself was aware of this possibility. He even took into account another possibility — that a picture might have been conveyed directly from his mind to hers. (The word telepathy was not invented for another twenty years, when it was coined by F. W. H. Myers.) So he put several specimens in brown paper, then mixed them up thoroughly so even he had no idea of which was which. He handed his wife one of them, and she had a vision of a volcano with molten lava. 'It must be lava', she said, and she was correct.

There would be no point in describing more of these fascinating experiments, since the reader can study them for himself. We shall see how a fragment of dinosaur bone brought a vision of a prehistoric beach, how a mastodon's tooth brought a vision of a huge, unwieldy creature with heavy legs, how a fragment of chamois horn produced a description of the Alps, a Cuban fossil brought a description of a tropical island, a rock from Niagara produced a vision of a foaming torrent of water, a glacial pebble gave an impression of being submerged in an immense depth of water . . . But one experiment *is* worth pointing out. Denton handed his wife a fragment of mosaic pavement from the villa of the Roman orator Cicero, and was disappointed when she described rows of helmeted soldiers and a fleshy faced

man with an air of command; this was not in the least like
Cicero, who was tall and thin. By 1888, when he came to
republish the book, Denton had discovered that the previous
owner of Cicero's house had been the dictator Sulla, who *did*
correspond accurately to Mrs Denton's description. We could
hardly ask for better proof that his wife's 'visions' were not
influenced by her husband's expectations.

This first volume of *The Soul of Things* appeared in Boston
(where Denton had become a lecturer in geology) in 1863, and
was later published in London under the title *Nature's
Secrets, or Psychometric Researches*. It is complete in itself,
which is why I have chosen to include it in this 'Library of
the Paranormal'. Later, Denton added two more volumes,
and re-published all three in 1888. The second volume is
largely concerned with experiments in which his son
Sherman acted as the psychometrist, and contains some
important and fascinating material — including some more
remarkably accurate insights into Pompeii (some account
of which will also be found in the present volume, pp. 178-91).
But it adds nothing to what has already been said in Volume
One.

Volume Three is an entirely different matter, and — it must
be confessed — provides plenty of ammunition for the
sceptic. By this time, Denton had decided to ask his
psychometrists to make an attempt to 'project' themselves
to the planets. He had already made the discovery that they
could look at a map, and then 'project' themselves to the
places on it. It is a faculty known as 'travelling clairvoyance',
and has been widely studied by modern psychical
researchers. (At Stanford University, Ingo Swann
demonstrated remarkable abilities to project himself to
other places and describe what is going on there.) But what
Sherman Denton and Anne Cridge produced when they
'travelled' to outer space was mostly bad science fiction. The
book has a frontispiece of a 'map of Jupiter' which includes
a city, and continues with descriptions of visits to Venus,
Mars and Jupiter. Venus has giant trees shaped like toad-
stools and full of sweet jelly, and an animal that was half fish

and half muskrat. Mars had men with four fingers and blond hair, and possessed an elaborate civilisation; Jupiter was full of blue eyed blondes who were lighter than air and had plaits down to their waists like Valkyries. The sun was a molten ball of lava which had hardened to a crust in places.

It is hardly necessary to excuse this nonsense by pointing out that 'travelling clairvoyance' is *not* the same thing as psychometry. (Sherman would undoubtedly have been more accurate if he had been allowed to hold a piece of rock from the moon or Mars.) But it *is* worth pointing out the interesting parallel case of Emanuel Swedenborg, the eighteenth century Swedish mystic whose 'second sight' was undoubtedly genuine — for example, in July 1759, he was able to tell guests at a party in Gothenburg that a great fire had broken out in Stockholm, three hundred miles away, and to describe what was happening with incredible accuracy. Yet Swedenborg also wrote an account of his visits to the planets, which his disciples took for literal truth, with savage giants, weird animals and a variety of peculiar humanoid creatures. One commentator has attempted to justify these by suggesting that Swedenborg's visions were supposed to be symbolic parables. It is far more likely that Swedenborg's method of obtaining his visions — in a semi-dream state — produced a nightmare phantasmagoria which was merely a product of his unconscious mind. The same undoubtedly applies to that embarrassing third volume of *The Soul of Things*, which it would be kinder to forget.

Sadly, Denton died in 1883, at the age of 59 — before the definitive republication of this book. His work, like Buchanan's, was subjected to a great deal of derision — not least because he was known as a defender of Darwin's theories, his geological studies having convinced him that the earth was a great deal more than six thousand years old, as the Creationists insisted. His work, like Buchanan's, was almost immediately forgotten, and the present reissue is the first since 1888. Buchanan, as we have seen, died in 1899.

But this was not the end of psychometry, as I have pointed out in my history of the subject, *The Psychic Detectives*. The

Society for Psychical Research — founded in 1882, the year before Denton's death — paid little attention to the subject, possibly embarrassed that the irrepressible Madame Blavatsky had incorporated the ideas of Denton and Buchanan into her system of 'Theosophy', in which the whole history of the universe is inscribed in the 'Akashic records' and is available to clairvoyant vision. (Her disciple Rudolf Steiner went into incredible detail in his own descriptions of the remote past, including Atlantis and Lemuria.) Yet in the 1920s, the French version of the Society for Psychical Research — the Metapsychic Institute — began to conduct some careful and scientific research into psychometry, and established once and for all that the faculty really exists — that Buchanan's 'telescope into the past' was not a figment of his imagination. In 1921, a group of people were testing a clairvoyant at the Metapsychic Institute and someone passed her a letter. A novelist called Pascal Forthuny, who was sceptical about such matters, grabbed it, pressed it to his forehead, and proceeded to improvise 'nonsense'. 'Ah yes, I see a crime, a murder.' He was rather shaken when he discovered that the letter was from the murderer Landru, then on trial for the murder of eleven women. He tried again with some other object, and was equally successful. Soon even he was convinced this was no fluke. Dr Eugene Osty, one of the most conscientious of psychical investigators, studied Forthuny's powers; his book on Forthuny was published in the following year. So was his great work *The Supernormal Faculties in Man*, which is full of carefully observed cases of psychometry, and which establishes beyond all reasonable doubt that a skilled psychometrist can produce precise, detailed information about material objects. In one particularly impressive case, his 'psychic', Mme Morel, was able to locate the body of an old man who had collapsed and died somewhere in two thousand acres of woodland, simply by holding a scarf that belonged to him.

This in itself raises a baffling problem. The old man's scarf had been left at home when he set out on that final walk — so how could it have 'recorded' where he died? We have to presuppose some other 'link'. And the moment we do that, we have abandoned Buchanan's comfortingly scientific 'bloodhound' theory... But then, we have already, in effect, abandoned the bloodhound theory if we can accept that Mrs Denton could identify a pebble from under the sea, or a piece of meteorite, by 'reading' its history.

There have been many other impressive cases of psychometry recorded by sceptical enquirers. Before the First World War, an architect named Frederick Bligh Bond was asked to excavate the ruins of Glastonbury Abbey; with the aid of a psychometrist, he was able to locate two 'lost' chapels. But here again, psychometry seems to spill over into 'spiritualism', for much of this incredibly accurate information was given by an entity that claimed to be a long-dead monk.

At about the same time, a German doctor named Gustav Pagenstecher tried hypnosis on a patient suffering from insomnia, Signora Maria Reyes de Zierold, and discovered, to his bewilderment, that she developed psychometric powers when in a trance; with her eyes closed she could identify any object and describe its history. The long series of tests conducted on her by the American Society for Psychical Research have become classics in their field. And in the 1930s, a Russian named Stefan Ossowiecki demonstrated in a series of rigorous tests that he possessed the secret of a 'telescope into the past' — again and again historical experts were able to confirm the remarkable accuracy of his 'readings' of prehistoric objects and the cultures from which they came.

When Buchanan and Denton launched the 'science' of psychometry, both were convinced that they had made a discovery that would profoundly affect the course of human history — for if they were correct, there would be nothing to prevent historians from 'revisiting' the scene of every great event in history. Today, most people have never even heard of psychometry. But not long before his death, Buchanan declared that during the course of the twentieth century, he would be remembered as the 'herald of a coming illumination'. And there is still time for his prophecy to be fulfilled. It is even possible that the republication of this book could be the beginning of its fulfilment . . .

COLIN WILSON

"Enter into the soul of things."

Wordsworth

PREFACE.

THERE is a wide realm lying between the known physical and the comparatively unknown spiritual, — a realm as yet almost entirely unexplored. Mesmeric experimenters have been pioneers in exploring one portion of it, Reichenbach and Buchanan in other portions, while in this volume, we record our experience in travelling over a part of this little known, but exceedingly interesting and important region.

Facts are constantly presenting themselves, that no philosophy explains; and as the most obvious phenomena are the first to be brought within the domain of science, because their explanation lies nearer the surface, so what remain necessarily lie deeper, are the results of the operation of subtler forces, and their existence is more likely in consequence to be denied by those whose belief is bounded by what their senses supply, or what can be inferred therefrom. But he who knows most of Nature, he who is most reverently her lover, will be least likely to set up his knowledge as a boundary beyond which fact and philosophy may never advance. The higher we rise, the wider the circle of the unknown stretches around us; while Destiny with uplifted finger beckons us on.

It has been suggested by some persons who have read portions of the manuscript of this volume, that many of the statements made are too strange to be believed, and that, by their publication, we subject ourselves to very severe criticism. So far as the conclusions drawn from the facts presented are concerned, I am willing they should receive all that criticism can bestow; for the facts, I am not responsible, nor am I concerned about their reception; and if any one chooses to do battle with them, he is welcome to the fruits of his victory. When a fact comes, I am prepared to welcome it; and I envy not those who discard a truth because Fashion has not set her seal upon it.

This work is, I feel, the merest introduction to one of the widest and most important fields in which the soul of man ever labored; and I trust that it will have the effect of inducing men of intellect and means to investigate and teach, though they should pull down all the theoretical scaffolding that we have erected.

W. D.

BOSTON, JUNE, 1863.

———————

IN presenting this third edition of the Soul of Things to the public, I have only to say that its statements are such as time and further experiments have but strengthened. The recent discoveries of fossils in the Laurentian rocks, of the animal origin of petroleum, which is now generally acknowledged, and the light thrown upon the condition of the early men of Europe since the first edition was published, strengthen much in it that was received with distrust, and render it highly probable that the further revelations of science will demonstrate the truth of what, in this volume, may still be regarded by some as wild and improbable.

W. D.

BOSTON, Feb. 21, 1866.

CONTENTS.

PART I.

PSYCHOMETRIC RESEARCHES AND DISCOVERIES.

CHAPTER I.

PICTURES ON THE RETINA AND BRAIN.

CHAPTER II.

PICTURES ON SURROUNDING OBJECTS.

CHAPTER III.

PSYCHOMETRY.

CHAPTER IV.

EXPERIMENTS.

CHAPTER V.

REMARKABLE PHENOMENA EXPLAINED.

CHAPTER VI.

UTILITY OF PSYCHOMETRY.

CHAPTER VII.

MYSTERIES REVEALED.

CHAPTER VIII.

CONCLUSION.

PART II.

QUESTIONS, CONSIDERATIONS, AND SUGGESTIONS.

VIII   CONTENTS.

PART I.

PSYCHOMETRIC RESEARCHES AND
DISCOVERIES.

BY WILLIAM DENTON.

"On the hardest adamant some footprint of us is stamped in; the last rear of the host will read traces of the earliest van." — *Carlyle.*

"The air is one vast library, on whose pages are forever written all that man has ever said, or woman whispered." — *Prof. Babbage.*

"In Nature's infinite book of mystery I have a little read." — *Shakspeare.*

THE SOUL OF THINGS.

CHAPTER I.

PICTURES ON THE RETINA AND BRAIN.

By looking into the eye of an individual beholding a landscape, we can see therein a picture of the fields, houses, trees, and objects generally that come within the range of his vision. This is because rays of light proceeding from these objects pass to the retina of the eye, and there form images or pictures of them. Nothing is apparent to ordinary vision until it is painted upon this window of the soul.

The pictures so made and seen are not as evanescent as they are generally supposed to be. They seem to pass from the retina of the eye into the brain, and are there indelibly impressed upon its substance; and under certain conditions they can be brought before the gaze years afterward, with as great distinctness as the beholder was conscious of at the time the objects themselves were presented to the sight.

Thus Sir Isaac Newton, in a letter to Locke, says: "I looked a very little while upon the sun in the looking-glass with my right eye, and then turned my eyes into a dark corner of my chamber and winked, to ob-

serve the impression made, and the circle of colors
which encompassed it, and how they decayed by degrees, and at last vanished.   Intending my fancy upon
them to see their last appearance, I found, to my
amazement, that they began to return, and by little
and little to become as lively and vivid as when I had
newly looked upon the sun.   But when I ceased to
intend my fancy upon them they vanished again. After
this, I found that as often as I went into the dark and
intended my mind upon them, as when a man looks
earnestly to see anything which is difficult to be seen,
I could make the phantasm return without looking any
more upon the sun; and the oftener I made it return,
the more easily I could make it return again.   And at
length by repeating this, without looking any more
upon the sun, I made such an impression on my eye
that, if I looked upon the clouds, or a book, or any
bright object, I saw upon it a round, bright spot of
light like the sun. . . . And now in a few hours' time
I had brought my eyes to such a pass, that I could
look upon no bright object with either eye but I saw
the sun before me, so that I durst neither write nor
read; but to recover the use of my eyes I shut myself up in my chamber, made dark, for three days
together, and used all means to divert my imagination
from the sun.   For if I thought upon him I presently
saw his picture, though I was in the dark. . . . For
some months after, the spectrum of the sun began to
return as often as I began to meditate upon the phenomena, even though I lay in bed at midnight with
my curtains drawn." *

* Brewster's Life of Newton, p. 237

There are probably but few persons that perceive such impressions as readily and vividly as Newton did this of the sun; but I think there are facts sufficient to show that all persons retain these impressions in a latent form, though the conditions favorable for their manifestation may not be present. Were experiments instituted for the purpose of testing the duration of visual impressions, as in the following, the result would be surprising to most persons. "Dr. Darwin says, ' I covered a paper about four inches square with yellow, and, with a pen filled with a blue color, wrote upon the middle of it the word BANKS in capitals, and, sitting with my back to the sun, fixed my eyes for a minute on the centre of the letter N in the word. After shutting my eyes, and shading them somewhat with my hand, the word was distinctly seen in the spectrum, in yellow colors on a blue ground; and then, on opening my eyes on a yellowish wall, at twenty feet distance, the magnified name of BANKS appeared on the wall written in golden characters.' "* In this case the word was seen with closed eyes, though in a different color from that in which it was written. The reason that blue was seen in place of yellow, and yellow instead of blue, probably arose from the fact that when we look for a long while upon one color, the eye becomes unable for some time to perceive that color, and we see, in the place of it, its complementary color. Blue and yellow being complementary colors, the one was seen in place of the other.

"Dr. Ferriar mentions of himself that when about the age of fourteen, if he had been viewing any inter-

* Abercrombie's Intellectual Philosophy.

esting object in the course of the day, as a romantic ruin, a fine seat, or a review of troops, so soon as evening came, if he had occasion to go into a dark room, the whole scene was brought before him with a brilliancy equal to what it possessed in daylight, and remained visible for some minutes." In these cases, the impressions do not seem to have been retained long after the objects were presented to the eye; and it might be supposed that the impression made upon the *retina* was so strong, that the pictures were retained there for a time and gradually faded away; but in the cases that I shall now bring forward, it will be seen that this explanation is altogether insufficient to account for the facts presented.

Persons who have become blind are very naturally more observing of such visions, as well as more liable to their presentation; and we have, therefore, many well-authenticated instances of persons, who, having become blind, could at times see the objects on which their eyes had previously rested, with all the vividness of reality.

"Dr. Samuel Willard, of Deerfield, Mass., has for the last twenty-five years been completely blind, and for twelve years previous had only been able to distinguish large objects indistinctly; but even now, when closeted in his room, visions of the green fields and sunny slopes of the Connecticut valley appear to him as really as when he gazed upon them with his eyes which for so long a period have admitted no light. He denies that this is imagination, but regards it as an exhibition of one of the mysterious modes by which the mind may hold communication with the outer world without the aid of the senses." * The imagination possesses no such power as some persons attribute to it, and Dr. Willard very properly refused to recognize this phenomenon as its offspring. But if he can only see what his eyes had previously gazed upon, it is not, I think, as he supposes, an exhibition of a mode by which the mind may hold communication with the outer world without the aid of the senses, for the sense of vision had first to be employed to obtain these pictures; but it is an exhibition of a power by which the scenes taken into the mind by the sense of vision become again visible, — scenes no one of 'which, apparently, is ever lost or obliterated.

The case of Niebuhr, the celebrated Danish traveller, much resembles this. "When old, blind, and so infirm that he was able only to be carried from his bed to his chair, he used to describe to his friends the scenes which he had visited in his early days with wonderful minuteness and vivacity. When they expressed their astonishment, he told them that as he lay in his bed, all visible objects shut out, the pictures of what he had seen in the East continually floated before his mind's eye, so that it was no wonder he could speak of them as if he had seen them yesterday. With like vividness the deep, intense sky of Asia, with its brilliant and twinkling host of stars, which he had so often gazed at by night, or its lofty vault of blue by day, was reflected in the hours of stillness and darkness on his inmost soul." †

That these images are really imprinted upon the brain, in many cases at least, and not merely upon the

* American Encyclopedia, Vol. III. p. 357.   † Intellectual Philosophy, p. 100.

retina of the eye, there is the best of evidence. Müller, the German physiologist, informs us that a remarkable case was observed by Lincke, in which the extirpation of the eye was followed by the appearance of luminous figures before the orbit as long as the inflammation consequent on the operation endured.

"A Jewess who had been for a long time blind became insane. Her illusions were of the sight, and she was constantly haunted by strange visions. After her death it was ascertained that the two optic nerves, from the part at which they are united within the head (which anatomists call their commissure) to their termination in the retina, were shrunk and wasted, so that they must have been wholly incapable of performing their functions." * In these cases it must be evident that the pictures seen were not impressed on the retina, and in the latter case we can hardly conceive the power to behold them to reside in the optic nerve; the pictures must have been impressed upon the brain, and the excitement of inflammation in the one case, and of insanity in the other, rendered them visible.

Many persons, when attacked by fever, or diseases accompanied with fever, have had presented to them scenes that they had beheld years before, and which in some cases they had entirely forgotten. Mr. Macnish gives the following interesting account of a vision thus seen by himself: "In March, 1829, during an attack of fever, accompanied with violent action in the brain, I experienced illusions of a very peculiar kind. They did not appear except when the eyes were shut or the room perfectly dark; and this was one of the

* Brodie's Psychologic Inquiries, p. 86.

most distressing things connected with my illness; for
it obliged me either to keep my eyes open, or to admit
more light into the chamber than they could well tol-
erate.

"One night, when the fever was at its height, I had
a splendid vision of a theatre, in the arena of which
Ducrow, the celebrated equestrian, was performing.
On this occasion everything was gay, bright and beautiful. I was broad awake, my eyes were closed, and
yet I saw with perfect distinctness the whole scene
going on in the theatre — Ducrow performing his wonders of horsemanship, and the assembled multitude,
among whom I recognized several intimate friends —
in short, the whole process of the entertainment, as
clearly as if I were present at it.   When I opened my
eyes the whole scene vanished like the enchanted palace of the necromancer; when I closed them, it as
instantly returned. . . . This theatrical vision continued for about five hours." *   It is evident, from his
account, that Mr. Macnish had seen just such a performance as this; the inimitable painter, Light, had
drawn it in the eye, complete in every feature, and
thence it had been transferred to the brain.   During
the paroxysm of the fever, the curtain was drawn that
ordinarily conceals such pictures from our gaze, and
there it hung, as bright and beautiful as on the day of
its execution.   The wonder is, not that such pictures
are seen, but that they are so seldom seen, or, being
seen, are so little noticed.

Hugh Miller, when young, attended theatre in Edinburgh. "The scenery," he says, "made no favorable

* Combe's Phrenology, p. 352.

impression upon me; but fourteen years after, when
the whole seemed to have passed out of my memory,
I was lying ill of small-pox, which, though a good deal
modified, apparently, by the vaccination of a long an-
terior period, was accompanied by such a degree of
fever that for two days together one delirious image
continued to succeed another in the troubled senso-
rium, as scene succeeds scene in the box of an itinerant showman. As is not uncommon, however, in
such cases, though ill enough to be haunted by the
images, I was yet well enough to know that they were
idle unrealities, the mere effect of indisposition, and
even sufficiently collected to take an interest in watching them as they arose, and in striving to determine
whether they were linked together by the ordinary
associative ties. I found, however, that they were
wholly independent of each other. Curious to know
whether the will exerted any power over them, I set
myself to try whether I could not conjure up a death's
head as one of the series; but what rose instead was
a cheerful parlor fire, bearing atop a tea-kettle; and as
the picture faded and then vanished, it was succeeded
by a gorgeous cataract, in which the white foam, at
first strongly relieved against the dark rock over which
it fell, soon exhibited a deep tinge of sulphurous blue,
and then came dashing down in one frightful sheet of
blood. The great singularity of the vision served to
freshen recollection, and I detected in the strange cataract every line and tint of the waterfall in the incan-
tation scene in 'Der Freischutz,' which I had witnessed
in the Theatre Royal of Edinburgh, with certainly no
very particular interest, so long before.

"There are, I suspect, provinces in the philosophy of mind into which the metaphysicians have not yet entered. Of that accessible storehouse, in which the memories of past events lie arranged and taped up, they appear to know a good deal; but of a mysterious cabinet of daguerreotype pictures, of which, though fast locked up on ordinary occasions, disease sometimes flings the door ajar, they seem to know nothing." *

As reasonably might the Ptolemaic astronomer have supposed that he had discovered the boundaries of the material universe, as for the metaphysician to suppose that he has traversed and bounded the mental universe, which seems to be as infinite as space itself.

"At the Leeds meeting of the British Association, Prof. Stevelly narrated the following anecdote: At the close of the last college session he had been in weak health, and had gone to his brother-in-law's seat in the country for a few weeks. While there, he had become greatly interested in the economy and habits of the bees. 'One morning, soon after breakfast, the servant came in to say that one of the hives was just beginning to swarm. The morning was a beautifully clear sunny one, and I stood gazing at the insects, as they appeared projected against the bright sky, rapidly and uneasily coursing hither and thither in most curious yet regular confusion, the drones making a humming noise much louder and sharper than the workers, from whom also they were easily distinguished by their size, but all appearing much larger in their rapid flights than their true size. In the evening, as it grew dark, I again went out to see the bee-hive, into which the swarm

* My Schools and Schoolmasters, p. 332.

had been collected, removed to its stand. Soon after I was much surprised to see, as I thought, multitudes of large flies coursing about the air. I mentioned it to my sister-in-law, who said I must be mistaken, as she had never seen an evening in which so few flies were abroad. Soon after, when I retired to my chamber, and knelt to my prayers before going to my rest, I was surprised to see coursing backward and forward, between me and the wall, what I now recognized as the swarm of bees, the drones quite easily distinguishable from the workers, and all in rapid whirling motion, as in the morning. This scene continued to be present to me as long as I remained awake, and occasionally when I awoke in the night; nor had it entirely faded away by the next night, although much less vivid. This was the first instance I had ever seen of moving impressions having become permanently impressed upon the retina, nor can I give the slightest guess at the *modus operandi* of the nerve.'" *

These visions, or re-visions as they may be termed, are not unknown to persons who are in sound mind and good health; and I find with some they are so common, they never regard them as at all wonderful, supposing that all persons are conscious of them. In companies of five or six persons, I have sometimes found two, and at other times three, who often see ordinary objects with the eyes closed, especially such as have frequently come before them during the day. I have just received a letter from a lady, in which she says: "Since strawberries began to ripen, or rather since I began to pick them, I can see nothing

---

* Physiology of Common Life, by G. H. Lewes, Vol. II. p. 283.

else: they are before me whenever I close my eyes."
Müller, to whom I have referred, says: " Any one
who can watch the changes which take place in himself, at the time when sleep is coming on, will sometimes be able to perceive the images distinctly in the
eyes. On waking, too, in a dark room, it sometimes
happens that images of landscapes and similar objects
still float before the eyes. Aristotle, Spinoza, and still
more recently Gruithuisen, have made this observation.
I have myself also very frequently seen these phan-
tasms, but am now less liable to them than formerly."

Generally these visions are seen with the eyes
closed, and the observer has no power to produce or
destroy them; at other times they are seen with the
eyes open, and can be produced at will. " A painter
who inherited much of the patronage of Sir Joshua
Reynolds, and believed himself to possess a talent
superior to his, was so fully engaged that he told me,
that he had painted three hundred large and small
portraits in one year. The fact appeared physically
impossible, but the secret of his rapidity and astonishing success was this: he required but one sitting of
his model. I watched him paint a portrait in miniature
in eight hours, of a gentleman whom I well knew; it
was carefully done, and the resemblance was perfect.
I begged him to detail to me his method of procedure,
and he related what follows: ' When a sitter came I
looked attentively on him for half an hour, sketching
from time to time on the canvas. I did not require a
longer sitting. I removed the canvas and passed to
another person. When I wished to continue the first
portrait, I recalled the man to my mind. I placed him

on the chair, where I perceived him as distinctly as if he were really there, and, I may add, in form and color more decided and brilliant. I looked from time to time at the imaginary figure, and went on painting, occasionally stopping to examine the picture, exactly as though the original were before me; whenever I looked toward the chair I saw the man.

"'This method made me very popular, and as I always caught the resemblance, the sitters were delighted that I spared them the annoying sittings of other painters. In this way I laid by much money for myself and my children.'" *

Combe, in the same valuable work on Phrenology, gives another instance of an individual in sound health, who was liable to the presentation of visions of objects that he had previously beheld. He says: "Several years ago I saw a person in the West of Scotland who was liable to spectral illusions. He was then thirty-eight years of age, in sound health, remarkably intelligent, and by no means liable to extravagance either in his statements or ideas. He mentioned that there was almost constantly present to his mind the appearance of a carpet in motion, and spotted with figures. On visiting Glasgow, he saw a large log of wood, mounted on two axles and four wheels, passing along the street; and on returning home, the apparition of the timber and its vehicle, with the horses and driver, stood before him in the dimensions and hues of actual existence.

"On another occasion he saw a funeral pass by the end of Queen Street, in Glasgow, and for some time afterward, whenever he shut his eyes or was in dark-

* Combe's Phrenology, p. 238.

ness, the procession moved before his mind as distinctly as it had previously done before his eyes. These are merely a few instances, out of many, of beings and objects which he had seen reappearing to his fancy. He was not conscious of the appearance of any object which he had not previously seen; and he was rarely, or almost never, troubled with these visions when actual existences were before his eyes in broad daylight; but at all times they appeared to a greater or less extent when his eyes were shut or darkness prevailed. He mentioned that this peculiarity had descended to his son."

I know a family in which mother, daughter, and granddaughter all possess this peculiarity. "Spectral illusion" is, however, an improper name to designate that by, which is simply re-vision, or the retention of what has been seen, and its presentation to some interior organ of vision, that human beings evidently possess.

Dr. Kitto says, "I retain a clear impression or image of everything at which I ever looked, although the coloring of that impression is necessarily vivid in proportion to the degree of interest with which the object was regarded. I find this faculty of much use and solace to me. By its aid I can live again at will in the midst of any scene or circumstances by which I have been once surrounded. By a voluntary act of mind I can in a moment conjure up the whole of any one out of the innumerable scenes in which the slightest interest has at any time been felt by me." *

From these facts it is evident, that the pictures

* Body and Mind, Dr George Moore, p. 206.

taken in by the eye on ordinary occasions, are, in some
individuals at least, wonderfully enduring; after many
years retaining all the perfection of detail and beauty
of coloring with which they were originally invested.
And there is good reason to believe that this is the
case with all persons; the pictures are retained, though
conditions may not be favorable for their manifestation.
If Hugh Miller and Dr. Macnish had never been attacked by disease, could they have credited the existence in the mind of the pictures which they saw? So
the mass of mankind dream not of the existence in
their own minds of all they ever saw; there notwithstanding, and only waiting till the veil shall be removed. There is the little cradle in which we were
rocked, and the faces that bent over it; the oak under
whose branches we played and whose acorns were our
treasures. The old school-house is there, and the portrait of every boy and girl that sat in it with us.
There hang all the landscapes we ever beheld; their
numberless hills, streams, fields, trees, beasts and birds;
in all lights and shades, from early morn to dewy eve;
in all seasons, when Winter spreads his snowy mantle
to hide his nakedness, and when Summer sits smiling
at the beautiful prospect. In that gallery are all the
men and women we ever saw; the hurrying crowd that
swept past us in New York, Boston, or London—none
went so swiftly but he left his portrait. No beggar
but carries about with him pictures, that outnumber
and outvie all that art has made since the day of its
birth, — pictures better colored than Titian's, more
original than Raphael's, more beautiful than Guido's,
and more natural than Hogarth's. In sleep we some-

times wander through this soul's picture-gallery, and catch glimpses of its beauty; but of its grandeur and perfection we have not even dreamed.

Wild as the statement may seem, I have no doubt that our minds receive and retain impressions of what is transpiring around us, even when we are unconscious at the time of what is taking place. "A boy, whose case is given by Dr. Abercrombie, was obliged at the age of five years to have his skull trepanned, it having been fractured by a fall from a window. He was of course quite insensible at the time, and after his recovery had no recollection either of the accident or the operation. But when a grown man, fourteen years after, he was attacked with fever; and during the consequent delirium he astonished his mother with an account of the operation, describing minute particulars, even to the dress worn by the surgeon, all which his mother knew to be correct. He never alluded to it in his after life." * The probability of this will become more apparent as we proceed.

* Lecture by W. J. Fox.

CHAPTER II.

THE rays of light, proceeding from objects in the light, have the power of forming pictures on othei bodies, as well as on the retina of the eye. If the body be sufficiently opaque and polished, we can readily see them, as in an ordinary mirror, or a polished plate of metal, or water; as we observe in the river the trees that grow by its margin; and although when the object is removed no picture is visible, there is good reason to believe that the picture thus formed is nearly, if not entirely, as enduring as the substance on which it is formed.

We visit a daguerrean room and sit before the camera; while thus sitting our picture is formed on a prepared silver plate, and while we sit it is distinctly visible upon it; it is taken out of the camera, and now, nothing whatever can be seen; a searching microscopic investigation discovers no line; but, on a suitable application, the image appears as if by magic. It is no more there, now that it is visible, than it was before; all that has been done is to make that visible which as really existed on the plate before, or no application could have revealed it. If the process of making these images visible had never been discovered, who could have believed that an image was formed upon a

26

plate under such circumstances, and lay sleeping there till art should awaken it?

If the silvered plate had not been previously made sensitive, some will say, the image of the sitter would never have been retained; but facts prove that this is incorrect.   G. H. Lewes says, "If a wafer be laid on a surface of polished metal, which is then breathed upon, and if, when the moisture of the breath has evaporated, the wafer be shaken off, we shall find that the whole polished surface is not as it was before, although our senses can detect no difference; for if we breathe again upon it, the surface will be moist everywhere, except on the spot previously sheltered by the wafer, which will now appear as a spectral image upon the surface.   Again and again we breathe, and the moisture evaporates, but still the spectral wafer reappears.   This experiment *succeeds after the lapse of many months,* if the metal be carefully put aside where its surface cannot be disturbed."   On trying a similar experiment, I have repeatedly brushed the surface of the polished plate with a camel's hair brush, and yet, on breathing upon it, the image of a coin previously laid upon it was distinctly visible.

"If a sheet of paper on which a key has been laid, be exposed for some minutes to the sunshine, and then instantaneously viewed in the dark, the key being removed, a fading spectre of the key will be visible. Let this paper be put aside *for many months* where nothing can disturb it, and then in darkness be laid upon a plate of hot metal, the spectre of the key will again appear.

"In the case of bodies more highly phosphorescent

than paper, the spectres of many different objects which may have been laid on in succession will, on warming, emerge in their proper order."

"If a screen cut in a pattern be held over a polished metallic surface at a small distance, and the whole breathed on, after the vapor has evaporated so that no trace is left upon the surface, the pattern comes out when it is breathed on again."

These are facts whose truth can be readily tested. Here there is no previous preparation beyond that of producing the polished surface, and yet images are formed, even without contact. And where the surface of a body is unpolished, there is no doubt that pictures are still formed upon it, though the difficulty of making them visible is greatly increased. Thus Sir David Brewster, whose authority on this subject cannot be questioned, says, "All bodies throw off emanations in greater or less size and with greater or less velocities; these particles enter more or less into the pores of solid and fluid bodies, sometimes resting upon their surface, and *sometimes permeating them altogether.* These emanations, when feeble, show themselves in images; when stronger, in chemical changes; when stronger still, in their action on the olfactory nerves; and when thrown off most copiously and rapidly, in heat affecting the nerves of touch; in photographic action, dissevering and recombining the elements of nature; and in phosphorescent and luminous emanations, exciting the retina and producing vision."

These emanations of which he speaks are passing from all bodies by night as well as day, and have the power of transferring the appearances of objects

to others in their vicinity, not merely upon their surfaces, but even into their interiors, so that the roughness of a body can be no hindrance to its reception of
these pictures.

Niepce de St. Victor, "having exposed to the sun
for a quarter of an hour an engraving which had been
kept several days in the dark, applied it to a sheet
of sensitive paper, and after four hours' contact *in the
dark* he obtained a negative picture of the engraving.
If the distance between the engraving and the paper
is one-eighth of an inch, or if a film of collodion or
gelatine is interposed, the picture will still be obtained." *

More recent experiments show that the previous
exposure to the sunshine is unnecessary. "The impression of an engraving was made by laying it face
downward on a silver plate iodized, and placing an
amalgamated copper plate upon it; it was left in darkness fifteen hours, when an impression of the engraving had been made on the amalgamated plate through
the paper." † The same may be done, it is said, on
plates of iron, zinc, or copper. "An iodized silver
plate was placed *in darkness* with a coil of string on
it, and with a polished silver plate suspended one-
eighth of an inch above it; after four hours they were
exposed to the vapors of mercury, which became uni-
formly deposited on the iodized plate; but on the silver one there was a sharp image of the string; so that
the image was formed in the dark, and even without
contact." †

* See Annuals of Scientific Discovery from 1858.
† Mrs. Somerville's Connection of the Physical Sciences, p. 237.

That photographic impressions are not confined to the mere surfaces on which they are visible, is evident. Every daguerreotypist knows the difficulty there is in effacing impressions from a plate; for after polishing a plate once used, and using it again, the image of the former sitter, to the chagrin of the artist, will frequently reappear. After a photographic impression upon a plate has been to all appearance wholly removed by polishing, so that another image could be taken upon it without the reappearance of the former, repeated discharges of electricity will reproduce the impression, showing that it had sunk into the substance of the plate to a considerable depth. And since .this is the case, it must be evident that the roughness of a body is no hindrance to the formation of pictures upon or within it; for the condition of the surface can make no difference in the capability of the interior to receive impressions.

The rapidity with which photographic impressions may be made is shown by the following experiment: "A wheel was made by Mr. Talbot to revolve as rapidly as a combination of multiplying wheels could make it fly; and when lit by an electric flash its photograph was taken, and in it every spoke was distinctly visible as if the wheel had been at perfect rest, though the duration of the illuminating spark, according to the experiments of Prof. Wheatstone, is only one-millionth of a second." *

Apply these indisputable facts, and in the world around us radiant forces are passing from all objects to all objects in their vicinity, and during every mo-

* Annual of Scientific Discovery for 1860, p. 162.

ment of the day and night are daguerreotyping the appearances of each upon the other; the images thus made, not merely resting upon the surface, but sinking into the interior of them; there held with astonishing tenacity, and only waiting for a suitable application to reveal themselves to the inquiring gaze. You cannot, then, enter a room by night or day, but you leave on going out your portrait behind you. You cannot lift your hand, or wink your eye, or the wind stir a hair of your head, but each movement is infallibly registered for coming ages. The pane of glass in the window, the brick in the wall, and the paving-stone in the street, catch the pictures of all passers-by, and faithfully preserve them. Not a leaf waves, not an insect crawls, not a ripple moves, but each motion is recorded by a thousand faithful scribes in infallible and indelible scripture.

This is just as true of all past time. From the first dawn of light upon this infant globe, when round its cradle the steamy curtains hung, to this moment, Nature has been busy photographing every moment. What a picture-gallery is hers! There are the heaving crust, as the fiery tides pass under it; the belching volcanoes, the glaring lava torrents, the condensing waters, the rushing floods, and the terrible struggles of the early stormy times; the watery ex-panse unshored; the new-born naked islands peeping above the waves; the first infusorial points, too small to leave a fossil trace behind them; and the earliest fucoids that clung to the wave-washed rock. Every radiate and mollusc of the Silurian era, every ganoid of the Devonian, has sat for its portrait, and here it is. Not a

leaf that grew in the Carboniferous forests, not a beetle
that crawled, nor frog that hopped; not a monster of
the Oolite, nor beast of the Tertiary, wanting. There
are grand panoramas of the past, containing all that
man ever did, — the first rude savages of the world,
their hunts, their wars, their progress; the history of
all nations and peoples from the cradle to the grave.
" They may be there," says the cool reader, " but how
shall we be able to see them? None but a madman
would dream of such a thing."

It would be strange if Nature admitted no mortal
to her matchless galleries; if, after employing myriads
of artists in drawing the waking and sleeping world,
she should permit no human eye to behold her instructive pictures. To catch a shadow, was once the acme
of the impossible; now, country lads, with a camera
for a trap, do it in almost every little village. And
this is in appearance no greater impossibility than that
was once regarded. There is nothing more difficult
than to tell what can not be done; and many wise
men have made themselves foolish prophets in attempting it.

I know of no chemical application that can make
visible to ordinary observers these pictures with which
all objects abound; but in some individuals the brain
is sufficiently sensitive to perceive them when it is
brought into proximity to the objects on which they
are impressed.

CHAPTER III.

THIS discovery was made in consequence of reading of Dr. Buchanan's researches and discoveries in another department of this great field; and some account of his discoveries is necessary in order to the understanding of this. In 1849 he writes: "About nine years since, in conversation with Bishop ——, of the Episcopal Church, he informed me that his own sensibility was so acute, that if he should by accident touch a piece of brass, even in the night, when he could not see what he touched, he immediately felt the influence through his system, and could recognize the offensive metallic taste."* This remark would have led to nothing farther, had it been related to many, but in this case the right thing was told to the right man; and he commenced a series of experiments, placing metals of various kinds into the hands of persons of great sensibility, and in this way found that there was a number who possessed the power of naming metals, without any knowledge but that which was communicated in this way by touch. As the experiments were continued, it was found that other substances could thus affect sensitive individuals. "Sugar, salt, pepper, acids, and other substances of a de

---

* Buchanan's Journal of Man, Vol. I. p. 51.

cided taste, made so distinct an impression that each could be recognized and named, by many of those upon whom the experiment was performed. These experiments were carefully performed; the substance either concealed from sight, or enveloped in paper, and sometimes no person present knew what substance was being tested until the close of the experiment. Out of a class of one hundred and thirty students at the Eclectic Medical College, Cincinnati, forty-three of them signed a declaration that when various medicines were enveloped in paper, so as to be unknown to them, by holding them in their hands from five to twenty minutes, the distinct effects were produced upon them similar to those which would have been produced by the action of the same medicines administered in the ordinary way. Dr. Buchanan adds that "when an emetic was the subject of the experiment, the individual was able to avoid vomiting only by suspending the experiment." *

After proceeding thus far, he thought that sensitive persons might be affected by contact with living beings in a similar manner; and this conjecture he found abundantly verified by experiment. Persons of highly impressible constitution could, by placing the hand on different portions of the head and body, "experience at each point a distinct effect, corresponding to the peculiar vital functions of the part. Nor was contact absolutely necessary. Highly sensitive persons coming into the presence of diseased individuals, recognized the disease, and were able at once to locate it."

Without giving all the steps taken by Dr. Buchanan

* Journal of Man, Vol. I., page 54.

in his researches, it may be sufficient to say that about two years after making his first discoveries, he found individuals so sensitive that the influence communicated by the writer to a letter could be recognized by them, when the letter was placed in contact with the forehead, and in some cases the character and habits of the individual writing the letter could be thus given with wonderful accuracy.

This will doubtless seem to some too marvellous for belief; but the evidence on this subject is now overwhelming. I know numbers of persons who by taking a letter in the hand, or placing it on the forehead, without seeing the writing, or having the slightest idea of the writer, can describe his character with as great, or greater accuracy than his most intimate friends. Any person desirous of testing this can readily do so.

On reading the statements of Dr. Buchanan, I resolved to see what portion of them I could verify by experiment. My sister, Anne Denton Cridge, being highly impressible, was able, in a short time, to read character from letters readily; and what was still more wonderful to us, and at the same time inexplicable, was, that at times *she saw and described the writers* of letters she was examining, and their surroundings, telling, at times, even the color of hair and eyes correctly.

After testing this thoroughly by numerous experiments, being intensely interested in geology and paleontology, it occurred to me that perhaps something might be done by psychometry — the term given by Dr. Buchanan to the power by which character was described by contact with persons, or from letters — in these departments of science. If there could be impressed upon a letter the image of the writer and his surroundings during the brief space of time that the paper was subjected to their influence, — and this was the conclusion I eventually arrived at, — why could not rocks receive impressions of surrounding objects, some of which they have been in the immediate neighborhood of for years, and why could they not communicate these in a similar manner to sensitive persons; thus giving us the clue to the conditions of the earth and its inhabitants during the vast eras of the past?

I accordingly commenced, some ten years ago, a series of experiments with mineral and fossil specimens and archeological remains, and was delighted to find that without possessing any previous knowledge of the specimen, or even seeing it, the history of its time passed before the gaze of the seer like a grand panoramic view; sometimes almost with the rapidity of lightning, and at other times so slowly and distinctly that it could be described as readily as an ordinary scene. The specimen to be examined was generally placed upon the forehead, and held there during the examination; but this was not absolutely necessary, some psychometers being able to see when holding a specimen in the hand.

The result of some of the experiments, made at various times, I give in the words of the psychometer at the time. In some cases the phraseology has been slightly changed, the idea never; and generally the exact words are given.

CHAPTER IV.

EXPERIMENTS.

Our earliest experiments were by no means as satisfactory as they subsequently became; the power of the psychometer increasing as the experiments continued. Many of these are presented, because they show the manifestation of this power as we first became acquainted with it.

EXPERIMENT I.

Piece of limestone, full of small fossil shells, from Quindaro, Kansas, a small town on the Missouri River.

Examined by my sister, Mrs. Cridge. Specimen unseen, and nothing known by her regarding it.

"It seems to me there is a deep hole here. Oh, what shells! small shells; so many. I see water; it looks like a river running along. What a high hill! almost perpendicular; it seems as if the water had cut it in two; it is not so high on the other side. The hill is covered with sand and gravel."

In this case the present condition of the place, where I obtained the specimen, was given, and, as far as I am acquainted with the spot, it is a very accurate description. This piece of rock had taken in the pictures of the turbid Missouri that swept past it, the hill that hung over it, and the country in general around it, and, to the eye of the psychometer, they became apparently as plainly visible as to a spectator on the spot.

EXPERIMENT II.

Piece of quartz from Panama.

Examined by my wife, Mrs. Denton. Saw it, but knew nothing respecting it.

"I see what looks like a monstrous insect. Its body is covered with shelly rings, and its head is furnished with antennæ that are nearly a foot long. It stands with its head against a rock that looks like this. I see an enormous snake coiled up among wild, wiry grass. The climate of the country seems to be much warmer than this; the vegetation is tropical."

The animal seen was probably a land crustacean of some kind. The whole of the vision is evidently in harmony with the tropical condition of the country, from which the specimen was obtained.

EXPERIMENT III.

Fragment of lava from Kilauea, on Hawaii, one of the Sandwich Islands.

Mrs. Cridge. Specimen unseen by her. She had no idea of what it was, nor did she know that I possessed any such specimen.

"I see the ocean, and ships sailing on it. This must be an island, for the water is all around.

"Now I am turned from where I saw the vessels, and am looking at something most terrific. It seems as if an ocean of fire was pouring over a precipice, and boiling as it pours. The sight permeates my

whole being, or the terror which it inspires. I see it
flow into the ocean, and the water boils intensely. I
seem to be standing on one side of it."

The feeling of terror, produced by the sight, did not
entirely pass off for an hour. It seemed to be as great
as if she had actually stood upon the spot, and beheld
the whole as an ordinary spectator.

Those who have read Mr. Coan's account of the
eruption of Kilauea, in 1840, will see the accuracy of
the description. The specimen of lava examined,
which was not larger than a hazel-nut, was, I understood, ejected from Kilauea, during that eruption,
when, as Mr. Coan says, " a river of fused minerals, of
the breadth of Niagara, and of a gory red, fell in one
emblazoned sheet, one raging torrent, into the ocean."

There can be no guess-work about such a description as this. I am well satisfied that my sister had not
the most remote idea of what the substance was that
she was trying, until the vision was presented to her
view, nor indeed then; and it will be seen, in experiments that I shall present, that my knowledge had
nothing to do with calling up these images before her.

EXPERIMENT IV.

I wrapped a number of specimens of various kinds
in separate papers, and Mrs. Denton took one, neither
of us knowing anything respecting it. She said, —

" The first thing I see is a volcano, or what I take to
be one. An elevation of considerable height appears
before me, and down its side flows a torrent of melted
matter. though torrent does not convey the idea; it is
broad and shallow, and moves, not rapidly, like water,

but creeps slowly along. Now I see another stream pour over the top of the first, and the whole side of the mountain is covered. This second flow moves much more rapidly than the first. This specimen must be lava."

On examination it proved. to be a piece of brick-colored lava, picked up on the banks of the Upper Missouri, where it is common; having been washed down probably from the Rocky Mountain region.

We have the means, then, by this wondrous power, of calling up and examining in minute detail the volcanic eruptions of all time, provided we can obtain specimens of their products; — see Teneriffe's mighty crater when covered with glowing lava, and its surging waves beat madly against the black, craggy precipices that gird them; — read the story of Vesuvius, — that fiery old man of the mountain, — from the time that he was a screaming baby. Etna's history, written by his own finger, before the reed was fashioned or the papyrus prepared, will be read by coming savans, and his ruddy page shall shed new light on many dark and mysterious subjects.

EXPERIMENT V.

Fossil fish-bone found near Painesville, in a bone bed, of, probably, about the same age as the Hamilton group of the Devonian formation.

Mrs. Foote. Had no idea of what it was.

"I see clouds of steam rising from the side of a hill, and on one side a large ledge of blue rocks.

"I now see something long and dark that looks like a fish; there seems to be a large hump or bunch near the head. I should think it is ten or twelve feet long, — perhaps not quite so long as that. I see now that there is no hump on its head. What I thought so is a rock that hangs over near its head. High rocks hang over the water, and trees grow on them. East of me is what seems to be the lake or ocean. I can see the bottom of the water; it consists of sand and gravel. What a most beautiful place! It seems so much so that it appears artificial."

Some may think it strange that trees should be spoken of as growing during this period; yet, I think, there is little doubt that the earth supported a luxuriant vegetation even before this period; not as much so as during the succeeding Carboniferous period, but luxuriant compared with the flora of our temperate zone at this time. In the very bone-bed from which the specimen was taken, I found the impression of a tree nearly a foot in diameter.

EXPERIMENT VI.

Same specimen.

Mrs. Denton. Had no knowledge of it, or of the previous examination.

"I see a point of land extending into a large body of water. The water looks to me like a lake. It hardly seems large enough for the ocean. I can see along the shore for miles. There is a singular-looking object in the water, about eight or ten feet long; and, from just below the head, it tapers the whole length nearly to a point. It has a skin without scales, like a cat-fish. I see it dive obliquely down, fasten itself at the bottom, and then wave its body to and fro. This is a large fish. It has six fins; two pectoral, two ventral, one caudal, and one anal. Its eyes and mouth are large. It has no teeth, but a hard, sharp, bony gum. It sucks its prey, and when doing so, the opening of the mouth is nearly round; but when closed, there are corners on each side."

She now became fatigued; but the examination was continued on the following day.

"Now I see the skeleton of it within the body. There is a large bony plate below the head, and to it other bones are fastened in some way. The back-bone at the upper part is as large as my wrist, but not one-third as thick laterally as vertically; but near the tail the vertebræ are nearly circular.

"I see roe within it. The eggs are quite large, but the layers are thin; there are two of them, one lower than the other. The lower one is the more developed.

"I catch a glimpse of a singular animal. The body seems roundish, but it is at such a distance, as well as in the water, that I cannot describe it minutely. The upper part is out of the water, and seems spread out like a sail, and the wind blows the animal along. It is so gauzy that I can see the light through it; but there are dark lines that look like ribs supporting it; and between the upright ribs are horizontal ones, jointed in the middle, that fold up in a very singular fashion, closing completely like a fan, when the animal wishes to sink. I see eight or ten of them now near each other."

There is considerable difference between the two descriptions, just as there would be in the descriptions of any scene, given by two independent observers. The scene in both cases is the shore of a large body of water; both see a large fish, and nearly agree as to its length. It is, in both cases, the principal object seen, the bone of a fish being the subject of examination, but neither person having any idea of it. What remarkable coincidences indeed, if this were mere guess-work, or chance. It might have been a piece of chert from a lead mine, shale from a coal mine, a fragment of a mastodon's tooth, or bone from some existing fish or beast. No mere ordinary sensation could have distinguished it from these; yet, here, without a hint or question, the conditions present themselves to two independent observers, that, I think, paleontologists will at least consider probably existed during the period when the fossil under consideration was a part of a living organism.

What a peep into the Devonian times this gives us. Trees adorn the land; the water, in places, at least, is clear enough to see the gravelly bottom; large fishes are basking in it, and genuine Nautilidæ, undreamed of by the naturalist, are floating upon the placid waters.

What myriads of organic forms must have lived, with bodies that could not under any circumstances be preserved as fossils: jelly-fish, radiates of infinitely diversified forms; mollusks, destitute of shells, or having shells too fragile for preservation. Of all these, the ordinary paleontologist knows no more than the historian knows of nations that flourished before letters were invented, or than the ancient astronomers knew of planets invisible to the naked eye. As the telescope came to the assistance of the astronomer, and gave him more correct conceptions of known celestial

bodies, and revealed to his gaze the otherwise invisible worlds of space, so this psychometric power will
shed new light upon many extinct animals and plants
of which we have some knowledge, and reveal to us
innumerable organic forms of whose existence, without
its assistance, we should be as ignorant as the world
was of the existence of Uranus and her moons before
the telescope was invented.

EXPERIMENT VII.

Calcareous tufa from the Temple of Neptune, Pæs-
tum, twelve miles from Mount Vesuvius.

Mrs. Denton. Specimen unseen, and nothing known
by her regarding it.

"I see near me deep ravines and high hills. Some
of the hills appear destitute of vegetation and look
rocky and naked. Others in the distance are worn
down and appear covered with verdure, and a mellow
light shines over the country. At the foot of a mountain, which looks to me like a volcano, are a few houses
having the appearance of a village; but they vanish
almost instantly. That mountain *is* a volcano. I see
smoke and vapor mingled issuing from it, and it
spreads over so as to hide the view from me in that
direction. The sea is behind me. That mountain and
its ejections are more strikingly visible than anything
else. Around here is a great waste, as if the country
had been covered by eruptions from the mountain,
making a dark brown surface which is above the original level of the country."

Why was not the temple seen? it may be asked. I
do not know; but if the experiment had been contin

ued or renewed, I think it is probable that it would have been. Vesuvius seems, for the time being, to have overshadowed everything.

Striated block of limestone, Grand River, Painesville, Ohio.

Mrs. Denton. Saw the specimen, and may have had some idea of its nature.

"I see a mountain ridge of ice, gorgeous, magnificent, and yet terrible. The ridge has a sharp edge with deep notches in it. The sides are ragged. The whole mass seems moving slowly along. I can hear it grind and scrape as it passes over the rock. I believe it must be in water; it certainly could not move on land in that way. The lower part *is* in water." (Turned the specimen over.) "I see no water on this side, but great spires of ice rise very high."

Nothing can seem much stranger than that the grinding sound of a moving glacier which passed over the country ages ago should have been communicated to, and retained by, an imbedded boulder, so as to be heard by a person to-day; and yet I am as well assured of its truth, as I am of anything that has not come within the sphere of my own sensation. If light can impress itself upon objects so that they retain its influence for centuries; if radiant forces, proceeding from objects in the dark, can form pictures of those bodies upon contiguous bodies, — and these facts science recognizes, — why may not the waves of sound register themselves so as to perpetuate their existence, and give that explanation to the ear that the eye of the psychometer demands, as the life-like panorama passes before it?

That sounds are registered in the human brain is evident; and so thoroughly is this done that they can be heard by the individual years afterward, and, what is most surprising, with even more than their original clearness and force.

Dr. Macnish, in his statement of the illusions to which he was subjected during an attack of fever referred to in page 16, says, "But though by closing my eyes I could thus dissipate the spectacle, I found it impossible to get rid of the accompanying music. This was the grand march in the opera of Aladdin, and was performed by the orchestra with more superb and imposing effect, and with greater loudness, than I had ever heard it before; it was executed, indeed, with tremendous energy. This air I tried every effort to dissipate, by forcibly endeavoring to call other tunes to mind, but it was in vain. However completely the vision might be dispelled, the music remained in spite of every effort to banish it."

The air played at the theatre was no more lost than the scene displayed; and under the peculiar conditions produced by the fever, it was executed with even greater effect than before. The outward ear probably heard not, but the inward ear heard more intensely than it was possible for the outward ear to do.

A blind man, mentioned by Dr. Macnish, was subject to illusions of sound; "for he often had the consciousness of hearing music so strongly impressed upon him that it was with difficulty his friends could convince him it was purely ideal."

"In October, 1833, a woman, aged twenty-eight, born in Piedmont, went to a village ball; she danced during three days in a sort of frenzy, and afterwards heard without cessation the melodies which had charmed her. They were Montferrines, and each gave place successively to the other. This continued until she died."*

Probably she was diseased, and her disease produced such a condition of the brain that the melodies existing there could be heard. Disease possesses no power to make sights or sounds; they are in the brain, and all that disease does is, occasionally to produce the conditions by which they shall become manifest to the individual. Facts indicate that what we once hear, however carelessly, becomes indelibly impressed upon the mind, so that under extraordinary conditions it may be repeated with all the accuracy with which it was originally impressed. One step farther, and we have the impression made on material objects retained, then revealed to human consciousness, as in many of these experiments.

Dr. Abercrombie, who deserves credit for recording many strange and valuable facts, relates the following: "A girl aged seven years, an orphan of the lowest rank, residing in the house of a farmer, by whom she was employed in attending cattle, was accustomed to sleep in an apartment separated by a very thin partition from one which was frequently occupied by an itinerant fiddler. This person was a musician of very considerable skill, and often spent a part of the night in performing pieces of a refined description; but his

* De Boismont on Hallucinations, p. 316.

performance was not taken notice of by the child, except as a disagreeable noise. After a residence of six months in this family she fell into bad health, and was removed to the house of a benevolent lady, where, on her recovery, after a protracted illness, she was employed as a servant. Some years after she came to reside with this lady, the most beautiful music was often heard in the house during the night, which excited no small interest and wonder in the family, and many a waking hour was spent in endeavors to discover the invisible minstrel. At length the sound was traced to the sleeping-room of the girl, who was found fast asleep, but uttering from her lips a sound exactly resembling the sweetest tones of a small violin. On farther observation it was found that, after being about two hours in bed, she became restless and began to mutter to herself; she then uttered sounds precisely resembling the tuning of a violin, and at length, after some prelude, dashed off into an elaborate piece of music, which she performed in a clear and accurate manner, and with a sound exactly resembling the most delicate modulation of the instrument, and then began exactly where she had stopped in the most correct manner. These paroxysms recurred at regular intervals, ranging from one to fourteen and even twenty nights, and they were generally followed by a degree of fever and pain over various parts of the body. When awake she showed no kind of turn for music."

As nothing we see is ever effaced, so nothing we hear ever dies out. Not only is there a wonderful cabinet in the mind containing pictures of all we ever saw, but there is also a storehouse of latent sounds containing all we ever heard. The lullaby sung by our cradle, the patter of the rain upon the roof, the sighing of the wind, the roll of the thunder, the dash of the falling water, the murmur of affection, the oath of the inebriate, the hymn in the church, the song at the concert, the words of wisdom and folly, the whisper of love, — all are faithfully registered. And our experiments have convinced me of what is still more difficult to believe, that all sounds register themselves on all objects within their influence, and that these phonotypes, as they may be termed, are almost, if not entirely, as enduring as the objects themselves. Philosophers tell us that "the slightest movement of the smallest body, in the remotest region, produces results which are perpetual, which diffuse themselves through all space, and which, though they may be metamorphosed, cannot be destroyed." * These experiments demonstrate, to a great extent, the accuracy of this statement.

If we could become at once cognizant of all the sounds that are locked up in the objects surrounding us, or in our own brains, what a din would be presented to our ears. Occasionally individuals seem to pass into this interior world of sounds, to their great astonishment. "A farmer in the neighborhood of Edinburgh, accustomed to drink freely, was invited to the funeral of a friend. He took a dram before he left home, and another at the house of his deceased friend. He had some of his acquaintances to dinner, with whom he continued to carouse until late at night. On the following morning he heard five hundred people

* Buckle's History of Civilization, Vol. II., p. 384.

talking at once. He compared what he heard to the confusion of tongues at Babel." * The surgeon bled him, and in two days he was cured.

As our experiments proceeded, the power of recognizing sounds increased, though it never became as active as the power of vision.

Incredible as it may appear, all forces that operate upon bodies leave their impress upon them just as indelibly as the radiant forces. Or, in other words, what we call insensible matter receives the impression of whatever force is applied to it, treasures it up, and can impart it to a sufficiently sensitive individual. A pebble, that has been rolled to and fro by the waves, retains the rolling sensation communicated to it, and with such tenacity that the heat of a furnace does not cause it to relinquish that hold. Thus every body retains, not only all that light and sound have communicated to it, but all that motion has impressed upon it; and the autobiography of the meanest boulder by the roadside would fill more volumes than all our libraries contain. The nail retains the impression made upon it by hammering, the clay by grinding, the brick by burning, the wool of the cloth, every step of the torturing process by which it was transferred from the back of the sheep to the back of the man.

Hence it is, probably, that all fossil remains of animals are imbued with the feelings of the animals of which they formed a part, and, under their influence, the psychometer, for the time being, feels all that was felt by them; and thus the characteristic actions of

* Diseases of the Brain and Mind, Winslow, p. 310.

monsters that have been extinct for millions of years can be accurately realized and described. This branch of psychometry may be termed psychopathy; and I find that generally, in examining specimens, seeing and feeling go together; though some psychometers only see, while others feel most readily the influence of a specimen, but can see nothing.

EXPERIMENT IX.

Pebble of Trenton limestone, with glacial scratches upon its surface, picked up near Lyons, Wayne county, New York.

Mrs. Denton. Specimen unseen and unknown.

"I feel as if I were below an immense body of water, — so deep that I cannot see down through it, and yet it seems as if I could see upward through it for miles. Now I am going, going, and there is something above me, I cannot tell what. It is pushing me on. It is above and around me. It must be ice; I am frozen in. The motion of the mass I am in is not uniform; it pitches forward, then halts and pitches again, then goes grinding, pressing, and crushing along, a mountain mass.

"All is dark. Now, I see a tinge of crimson, mixed with purple. What can it be? How beautiful! I feel water again, as if I were drenched with it." (What kind of water is it?) "It is not rain. It seems like a mixture of fresh and salt water; a little while the one and then the other. I see lights before me, apparently reflected from rising vapors. They are finer and more broken than those I saw before, and reflect the colors of the rainbow.

"What an awful chasm we are approaching; we cannot cross it without being dashed to pieces I am sure.
I say we, because I feel completely distinct from the
mass that moves me.   There is that chasm again!   It
is terrific!   We are going right to it, dashing most
recklessly.   We shall never get out or across.   (Pause.)
That is most astonishing.   I felt desperate as we approached the brink, but it was full of water, and we
floated across.   I wonder if that is not the lake?   so
deep and so broad.   Why did I not see the water?
The first I knew, I felt the sensation of floating.   Now
we are aground.   All around us is shallow water, except a few islands, which are not high enough to be
dry.

"Now, I see ice before me over a wide field.   There
are thousands of spires melting gradually away.   There
is a flood all over the country, but the water is not
very deep.   There is a shallow sea this side of the
chasm, except a little spot of land here and there, and
that is completely water-soaked.

"There are five icebergs in sight, some of them as
high as mountains ; they are anchored ; the sight is in-
describably grand.   There is another at my right that
has a tall spire and a large mass for a body.   It is rocking, and I believe will tip over yet.   It is rounded at
the base.   There is a current in the water that dis-
turbs it."

What a fine picture of the latter part of the drift
period in North America, when a sheet of ice covered a
large part of Canada and British America, from Lake
Ontario, which was then probably an arm of the ocean,
to the Arctic regions; as at the present time a glacial

sheet covers northwestern Greenland. On comes the icy mass toward the south, the only direction in which motion is possible, because the only direction in which the ice can melt, and room be found for the mass constantly increasing by falling snows. On it comes, bearing with it the rocks that it tears off in its passage, slides into this arm of the sea that we have supposed to occupy the place of Lake Ontario, thus forms icebergs, which float southward till they strand on what is now the northern part of the State of New York, and leave their rocky burdens to form the boulders that are so common over the face of that country.

How often, on looking at some gray old boulder, we have wished it could relate its history, and tell us what had passed before and around it during its eventful career. Little did we dream of the possibility of that, and more than that. These "hard heads" are wise heads, too, in a sense, and much they can teach us when we are prepared to learn. They are "chiels takin' notes," indifferent spectators though they appear, and what they report may be depended upon as true. What is described by the psychometer is but a small portion of what is presented. At times, one panoramic view after another is unfolded in too rapid succession for the most meagre description.

I know the explanation that some will offer to account for these marvels. The self-confident biologist says, "I know well how it is done; I can make my subjects see anything that I have in my mind. I imagine a snake, a crocodile, a volcano, and they are seen at once by my subjects; and this is done in the same manner." He is mistaken, however. I have repeatedly tried to influence the minds of psychometers, when making examinations, and at all times without avail. Many specimens have been examined when no one knew what they were, and yet the results were quite as accurate as at any other time; indeed, in almost every case, statements have been made and ideas advanced of which we had not previously the most distant thought. Take the following example: —

EXPERIMENT X.

Out of a number of minerals and fossils lying upon the table, Mrs. Denton, with closed eyes, picked up one, no one knowing its character.

"I am in the ocean, deep under the water. I can see a long way, for the water is clear. There are millions of minute coral polyps busily at work. I am looking down upon them. I observe one kind of coral that is very peculiar; it is a foot in diameter at the bottom, and rises in terraces to the top, where it is much smaller. I should judge this specimen to be coral, or something worked over by coral, though it feels nothing like it."

On examination it proved to be a piece of flat coral about an inch long and an eighth of an inch in thickness, from the Niagara group of the Silurian formation, at Lockport, N. Y. This is a specimen of various experiments tried in a somewhat similar manner and with like results, conclusively demonstrating that the biological explanation is an incorrect one.

EXPERIMENT XI.

A small fragment of the enamel of a mastodon's tooth, cut off so that it might not be recognized, being about one-twentieth of an inch in thickness, and three-tenths of an inch in diameter.   The tooth was dug, by miners in search of lead, out of a crevice thirty feet beneath the surface, near Hazel Green, Wisconsin.

Mrs. Denton. She did not see it, and had no idea of what it was.

"My impression is that it is a part of some monstrous animal, probably a part of a tooth. I feel like a perfect monster, with heavy legs, unwieldy head, and very large body. I go down to a shallow stream to drink. (I can hardly speak, my jaws are so heavy.) I feel like getting down on all fours.

"What a noise comes through the wood! I have an impulse to answer it. My ears are very large and leathery, and I can almost fancy they flap my face as I move my head. There are some older ones than I. (It seems so out of keeping to be talking with these heavy jaws.) They are dark brown, as if they had been completely tanned. There is one old fellow, with large tusks, that looks very tough. I see several young ones; in fact, there's a whole herd.

"My upper lip moves strangely. I can flap it up. It seems strange to me how it is done.

"There is a plant growing here higher than my head; it is nearly as thick as my wrist, very juicy, sweet and tender, something like green corn in taste, but sweeter." (Is that the taste it would have to a human being?) "Oh, no" (appearance of disgust on the countenance); "it is sickish, and very unpleasant."

The complete identification at times of the psychometer with the thing psychometrized, or the animal with whose influence it is imbued, is one of the remarkable facts developed by our experiments, and it throws light upon some of the most mysterious depart-ments of nature. Some forms of insanity appear to present a condition produced by intense sensitiveness, resulting in the overpowering of the mind by sur-rounding influences, so that the individual ceases to be himself, and becomes the tool for those influences unconsciously to use; the individual supplying the power, but the influences directing and spending it, instead of the will of the individual.

Some manifestations considered to be spiritual come under this head, and may be readily accounted for in this way. You cannot walk into and out of a room without leaving a portion of your influence in that room, which will continue as long as the bricks and mortar endure. You cannot sit upon a chair but the chair receives from you that which can convey to some sensitive persons the idea of your presence and your mental peculiarities. Hence our houses — made of brick, from clay over which the Indian passed and re-passed; with their letters from hundreds of persons, some living, some dead; with objects in them handled at some time by men of many races; arrow-heads made by Indians, tea fingered by Chinese, coffee and cotton by negroes, ivory-handled knives and forks, the ivory of which passed through the hands of Samoides and Russ; abounding with impressions made by persons who have visited them—are conventions of unseen in-fluences representing thousands of diverse individuals, the sphere of which sensitive persons can and fre-quently do recognize, and are affected by, without being aware of the source from which it proceeds. I

say not this from any desire to throw discredit upon
the fact of present communication between the spirit-
world and our own, for this I know to be absolutely so;
but it will be found, as Science marches on with her
hosts, and conquers the dark realm where ghosts and
witches and fairies have revelled for ages, that much
which is supposed to come from another world is the
offspring of our own.

EXPERIMENT XII.

In the summer of 1861, I obtained a small fragment
from a slab containing the impression of two toes of
one of the bird-like tracks from the Connecticut Valley. It was but a mere speck, not more than a quarter of an inch long and one-twentieth of an inch thick;
but it was quite large enough to tell some wonderful
tales of a remarkable time.

Mrs. Denton. Specimen not seen, and not a word
had ever been uttered in reference to my possession
of it, and since we were in the Far West at the time
of the examination, she could have had no idea of its
original whereabouts.

"There is some magnetism about this. I have a
glimpse of a long, broad, flat place, frequently washed
by water; it is sufficiently rolling, however, to prevent
the water from remaining upon it. Whether it is the
edge of the sea or not I cannot tell, but there lies
before me a large body of water.

"I begin to get the outline of objects moving, some
on this flat and some among bushes that grow near
there. One that I see attracts my attention much by
its great singularity; it is without exception the

strangest-looking being I ever saw. (When I go back so far, there is a difficulty in seeing objects at a distance, which I think is owing to the thick, heavy atmosphere of those early times.) One of these animals is right before me now; it has a rather long, small neck. A second one appears with a flat head and a neck tapering rapidly to it. The first one has a flattish head; from that there is an angle to the back, and then another to the tail. As it moves, its back rises and falls, and it looks as if the arch of the back assisted in propelling it. Now I see three other backs, but no other part. (I had a glimpse just then of a turtle.) That animal I saw puzzles me; it seems to be deficient in legs, though I cannot see them distinctly. It goes very easily, though its motion is so singular. Its legs are short, and the angles of the body are not far from the ground. It moves with a good deal of rapidity. It has flat-looking feet, wide enough for it to balance itself upon. It has just two feet. There! I know what it is now. It is that two-footed reptile I have read about. From foot to foot it measures, I should think, about four feet."

Second examination, made two days after, from a larger portion of the same slab.

"Its head very much resembles in form the head of a snake, and its neck is long and gracefully arched. Its scapula is long, extending on each side of the neck a little beyond its articulation with the humerus, which appears to be on the under side. At first I thought the scapula projected beyond the articulation, but I believe now that it is a bone united to it by a joint, and connected with other bones, that elevate what look like wings on each side of its body. Lifting its fore foot it can sit upon its hind foot, assisted by the tail; then, giving a spring, pass through the air for quite a distance. It does not seem to move its wings during the transit, but they act like parachutes, in its descent, and it comes gently down.

"I cannot see any teeth; but in the place of them appears to be a bony gum. It is carnivorous, and feeds upon fish and reptiles. I can taste how sweet they were to it. It had a motion of its head among the weeds in the water like that of a duck. There is something about it that resembles the opossum, but whether it is marsupial or not I cannot say."

Some time after this, many specimens from various localities having been examined in the intervening time, we tried another fragment of a slab from the same locality, Mrs. D. as before knowing nothing of the nature of the specimen.

"I see an animal that approaches the mammal in appearance more closely than those animals I saw some time ago. It has claws, and is digging or scratching in the earth. Its long tail, with a bunch on the end of it, is elevated. It has a long body, and is a quadruped. It is somewhat reptilian in appearance, and yet it seems to be a mammal. It is carnivorous and very savage."

If minute fragments can yield so much to the psychometer, what may we not expect when the quarries of the Connecticut valley are interrogated; when the pictures preserved in its slabs are copied by psychometric artists, and its wonderful menageries of ornithoid lizards and sauroid mammals are brought before us for inspection?

Some two years afterwards, having obtained a larger specimen in Albany, which was taken from the same locality, Mrs. D. examined it as before.

"I see the bed of a stream that is partly dry. It is broad, and sometimes rises high. The banks here are low and sloping. There is rock on the other side.

"I am farther south and southeast now. I see an extensive tract of low, even ground. It seems naked, and looks as if washed by water sufficiently to prevent the growth of vegetation upon it. I see the appearances of bodies moving through the air, but they are partly hidden. That low, flat ground seems to be connected with the river, and there seems to be a mingling of salt and fresh water here."

"I see multitudes of objects. They swarm around me; there are fishes among them; they change rapidly. What strange-looking animals there are here! This seems to be the shore of the ocean, covered by the tide and then left bare.

"One animal I see with a very long neck; it has wings, but does not look like a bird; the wings are bat-like; but the animal is, I think, a reptile. There are many of them here, and they look like those I saw in Chicago, with a specimen from the Connecticut valley. They have exactly the same appearance.

"I see another animal with feathered wings, but they are the coarsest-looking feathers I ever saw. One is very near me; it is lightish-colored, with a reddish tinge. There are many among weeds that grow in stagnant water, of which there is a large body between here and the main land. The head and neck are reptilian in form; the mouth is large, and the jaws are very different from the bill of a bird. I see one drinking; but it does not raise its head to swallow as a bird does. It sits up like a bird, but has a slimy appearance, notwithstanding its feathers, which are thin and wide apart; they look stiff and unfinished. The barbs on the shaft are widely separated, and the feathers look something like those of a drowned bird. I see some of these animals in the air; their wings are thick near the body, and gradually become thinner toward the edges, where they are membranous.

"Here is a large monster that looks as if it might devour all these; but it is sluggish in its movements. It is a reptile, with a head like a crocodile, but larger. It has enormous jaws, large eyes, small neck, and broad shoulders. It is looking at the other animals, and crawling softly toward them. It has a sly look. It is crested with an edge of thick points all along the back. (I feel as if I should be swallowed alive, with so many rapacious monsters around me.)

"I see another animal, with a tail of great length, that curls round and round just like a snake. It looks like the body of a serpent joined to the body of a lizard. It may be five or six feet long; but the body is not more than two feet. I believe it could draw the head in and dart it out for some distance. It seems like a link between the lizard and the serpent. Its tail winds and unwinds rapidly, sometimes in the air, and sometimes on the ground.

" The only thought manifested here is, on the one hand, to devour, and, on the other, to escape being devoured."

These descriptions will be appreciated by those who have made the sandstones of the Connecticut valley and their footprints a matter of study. They give a life-like, and, I doubt not, accurate picture of the time when the valley of the Connecticut resembled the Bristol Channel or the Bay of Fundy, having rivers pouring in large bodies of muddy water, and high tides, which deposited sediment over wide areas on each side; and these left baking in the sunshine until the return tide. Over this surface crept, crawled, wriggled and stalked the strange organic forms of this time, — slimy reptiles, and more slimy worms, walking fishes, and rude reptilian birds, foot-prints of which are so numerous in various portions of the valley.

EXPERIMENT XIV.

Whalebone walking-cane.

Mrs. Denton knew it was a walking-cane, but, having no opportunity of examining it, supposed very naturally that it was a wooden one.

"I feel as if I am a monster. There is nothing of a tree about it, and it is useless for me to go any farther." (With great difficulty she was induced to continue the experiment.) "I feel like vomiting. Now I want to plunge into the water." (Convulsive shuddering.) "I believe I am going into a fit. My jaws are large enough to take down a house at a gulp. I know now what this is, — it is whalebone. I see the inside of the whale's mouth. It has no teeth; it has a slimy look; but I only get a glimpse of it. Now I see the whole animal. What an awful-looking creature!"

This identification of the psychometer with the animal psychometrized is at times so complete as to compel the suspension of the experiment, the influence produced sometimes affecting the person for hours.

EXPERIMENT XV.

When lecturing in Oswego, N. Y., the high school was burnt down, and I picked from its ruins a small piece of brick, which I handed to Mrs. Denton for examination, she supposing it to be a piece of rock.

" I feel as if all was in commotion, and I was moving with tremendous force, and flying into ten thousand pieces. It seems as if I could not go with sufficient rapidity.

" It makes me nervous. There is fire about it. It is horrible. It produces a terrific feeling. It is a piece of brick, I am certain. There is such confusion about it I cannot see anything, though I know there is fire about it. I feel like leaping down."

Some may suppose that some of these remarks were in reply to leading questions; but such was not the case. In most instances not a word was said; and in others, the questions asked have been merely in reference to what was not fully explained.

In these last two experiments it will be seen that the substance was eventually named; and, in many experiments that we have tried, the substance is often correctly named in an instant, though nothing was known of it except psychometrically.

I am not sufficiently acquainted with the history of

the brick from which the specimen was taken to tell whether the account given is correct in every particular; but it must be evident to any one that the feelings experienced were much in harmony with what the clay generally passes through in being formed into brick. It seems a little singular that the heat of the fire had not obliterated the sense of the motion to which the clay had been previously subjected, but many experiments have convinced us that intense heat does not destroy even the pictorial impressions that have been made upon bodies.

EXPERIMENT XVI.

Many years ago I gave to Mrs. Cridge for examination a specimen of the residuum of cannel coal, she not seeing the specimen or knowing anything of its history.

"It is coal. I seem to be at the bottom of a mine. What a mass of coal! It seems soft, and the bed is about as thick as the height of this room."

In other experiments, made with metals melted from the ores, I have met with similar results. I have not a doubt that fossiliferous rocks which have been so highly metamorphosed that all organic traces are invisible, may be made to yield impressions to the psychometer, and a wide and important geological field will be rescued, to the great benefit of future explorers, and the perfection of the geologic record. I think it will yet be found that many rocks, regarded as belonging to the non-fossiliferous groups, are rich in organic influences.

EXPERIMENT XVII.

Fragment of fossil shell from Carboniferous formation, Iowa.

Mrs. Denton. Neither she nor I knew what it was till after the examination.

"I see something that resembles a star-fish in form, though it differs from all living ones that I have seen. It is round, and has four long arms or tentacles, and shorter ones between. The shorter ones seem to be used for locomotion, and the longer ones for prehension. The long ones are the most pointed; the small ones are flatter, and more like feet. The mouth is in the centre. The long arms are ringed or jointed, so that the animal can bend them rapidly, and convey food to the mouth. Each long arm has two points at the end.

"I see another animal moving through the water. It has a head nearly as large as the body; the body tapers to the tail. It does not move with fins or true feet either, but with a webbed apparatus of some kind, apparently between a fin and a foot."

In this case the shell, or the mollusk originally occupying it, was not seen at all, but animals that probably inhabited the ocean at the same time, and whose influence was received by the shell, and preserved for ages after it became fossil.

The star-fish described, resembles the ophiura, or serpent-like star-fish, one species of which Professor Sedgwick found in the lower Silurian, and other forms occur in the more recent formations. The animal seen moving through the water was probably one of those extinct forms of which the geologist may never know, unless it be by the investigations of future psychometers.

EXPERIMENT XVIII.

It was naturally to be expected, if there was any

truth in psychometry, that animals would be seen of which the geologist knows nothing, for the number that the geologist knows is necessarily but a small portion of the mighty host that has existed. The air seems to have had tenants long before geology recognizes their existence.

Bone from Tully limestone, near Seneca Lake.

Mrs. Denton. Specimen unseen, and nothing known regarding it.

"I see a long, smooth beach. It is before me, for I seem to be on the water. It extends for a great distance, and gently rises as it recedes from the water. On that beach are quadrupeds of some kind. One is large, heavy, thick-skinned, dark-colored, and thick-necked; the flesh is not fibrous, but soft. Its head is broad, and horns rise up from its nose. I see another with a long neck, and a head nearly as large as a sheep's, but in appearance like that of a snake, though it is a quadruped. Both look reptilian.

"What a beautiful place this is! I see a large rock completely covered with beautifully green moss. The rock is craggy, but all green, and the water at times sweeps over it. There are many large objects in the air, but they do not seem to be birds."

Second examination, a month afterward. Specimen unrecognized.

"I see something that looks like a fish with spines on both sides and nearly round it. It seems short, compared with its breadth, for a fish.

"I see part of another animal in shallow water, with its body hid among the water-weeds, that look like long moss, but differ from all I ever saw before. The back of that animal is now visible to me. It has what looks like ears, but I cannot tell whether they are or not. They are in the same situation, and lie back on the body for a considerable distance. It has sharp-looking eyes. There are a great many of these animals, and they have a very strange appearance. What I took for ears must be folded wings; I can see between them and the head, though they are attached on the upper side. The wing is membranous, but I cannot describe it, it differs so much from anything I know. It is ribbed. The animal looks more like a reptile than a fish, though I cannot see the whole distinctly."

The Tully limestone is one of the representatives of the Devonian formation, in the State of New York; it lies immediately above the Hamilton group, so widely distributed and so well known. That the air was occupied by flying animals so early is a very startling idea, when we remember that the earliest remains of birds that have been found are in the Cretaceous, or Chalk formation, certainly formed millions of years after the deposition of the Tully limestone. If the air was tenanted thus early, we may presume that it was occupied by successive forms, as the earth was during the time intervening between the Devonian and Cretaceous periods, and if so, what an evidence we have of the imperfection of the record that geology gives us of organic existences. We have but fairly made a beginning in the study of ancient life-forms.

These are the earliest psychometric evidences that we have had of the existence of reptiles, though they may have lived long prior to this; for our ignorance should never be made the boundary of knowledge.

EXPERIMENT XIX.

Stones falling from the heavens, commonly known as meteoric stones, have always excited considerable attention. "They are," says Humboldt, "the only means by which we can be brought in possible contact with that which is foreign to our own planet." Some years ago, a farmer near Painesville, Ohio, informed me of a singular stone on his farm, that looked, as he said, like iron ore. On arriving at the spot, I found a dark, boulder-like mass, weighing eighteen hundred and fifteen pounds, covered with a dense crust, from one-fourth of an inch to three-eighths of an inch in thickness. On breaking off portions, its peculiar appearance seemed to indicate its meteoric character. I carried off small fragments of it, and had some of them tried psychometrically; one by Mrs. Foote, who had no conception of what it was, nor that I had any such specimens in my possession.

"I seem to be travelling away, away, through nothing, right forward. I see what looks like clouds and something sparkling like stars; but there seems to be a mist between me and that. How curious that is! it carries my eyes right up; every other specimen has taken my eyes right down."

What could be more descriptive of the path of an aerolite—"away, away, through nothing, right forward"? In reference to her last statement, she said that her eyeballs were rolled upward in opposition to her own will.

Whence come these singular visitors? Are they ejected from lunar volcanoes? Are they formed in the upper regions of the atmosphere? Are they small planets of a similar class to those circulating between the orbits of Mars and Jupiter? or are they fragments of rings once surrounding the earth, as the rings of Saturn surround that planet? I think our experiments throw some light upon this dark subject, though much remains yet to be done.

EXPERIMENT XX.

A few days after the last examination, I tried Mrs. Foote with another fragment of the supposed meteorite, under similar conditions.

"It carries my eyes right up. I see an appearance of misty light. I seem to go miles and miles very quickly, up and up. Streams of light come from the right, a great way off. I see something sparkling,— a huge body like a mountain. Between me and that is a broad road, that glitters like diamonds. To the right of that I see a large round body that I can see through, and yet there is substance to it. The sun is rising behind that mountain, or a sparkling light is shining at a vast distance."

EXPERIMENT XXI.

I gave the same specimen to Mrs. Denton, who knew nothing of it, nor of the previous examinations.

"This seems to have been moved. I see it turning rapidly on its axis, and little flakes or cinders flying from it, which it leaves behind, like a tail. As it moves it changes its shape." (Turned the specimen over.) "I see what looks like a vein of metal, and through it I see what appear like joints; it is curved. From this vein streaks of light pass off like the beard from a head of wheat.

"Now I see a temple, built of wood, and in it a rock with three points. It is about three feet to the highest point. I am reminded of the Aztec temples."

Aerolites have been objects of worship in many countries. At Emesa, in Syria, the sun was worshipped under the form of a black stone, reported to have fallen from heaven. Pliny mentions a stone which fell at Abydos, and was worshipped at that place. The holy Kaaba of Mecca, and the great stone of the pyramid of Cholula, in Mexico, have all the same history. It is possible that this Painesville aerolite had answered for a god to some race that preceded the Indians in Ohio. I had never thought of it previous to this examination, but a subsequent one made me think it more probable.

EXPERIMENT XXII.

Another fragment of the same.

Mrs. Foote. Conditions as before.

"I see thousands of persons moving along. What a multitude! They are marching in rows; a few are standing still. How strange they look! Beyond them there seems to be a city, with trees set out in beautiful rows. The people are in different companies; some look dark and others light. One company is busy stooping over, as if they were digging. By the side of that company is a ledge of rock, and from that a smoke is rising, one cloud after another. The company digging are bare-headed; they have dark skins, but are not negroes. Now I see a river, and away off is a range of rocks, covered with moss, ferns, and bushes. The rocks taper off in height as I go down the river, and there is a level plain, with woods in the distance. Farther down on the right is a city. There is something round it, posts and high work, that seem made to protect it. I see buildings and people; the buildings are small." (What are they made of?) "Don't look like boards at all; most of them seem plastered, or mud-bedaubed. It looks nothing like our cities. One building that I see is very large, and a great many people are coming and going near there, some walking and others riding." (What are they riding on?) "Not horses, but animals much smaller; I do not know what. Some of the streets are very dirty, others clean. From the city I can see out into the country; there is a fine, broad highway." (In reply to a question,) "The large building is not high, but covers considerable ground. The roof goes up to a peak, but it looks nothing like our buildings; it resembles most a huge tent. People are riding on strange-looking things, drawn by animals that look more like sheep than anything else, though they are not sheep, for they are larger and of a darker color, and hold up their heads like deer. The vehicles look like old boxes mounted on two wheels."

That a race of comparatively civilized people, living in cities, and employing beasts of burden, ever existed in Northern Ohio, will seem like a very strange story to some persons; yet those who are familiar with the remains of mounds and fortifications that are scattered over the surface of Ohio and the Western States generally, may regard it as possible that such a people, as Mrs. Foote saw, once lived in Ohio, who, being startled by the descent of an enormous aerolite, had made it an object of religious worship, and it had thus become impressed with the scenes described.

That Indians should have employed animals as beasts of burden will appear strange, to those only who are unacquainted with their history. When the Spaniards first invaded Peru and Chili, they found the llama in common use as a beast of burden. Augustin de Zerate, in 1544, thus describes the llama in Peru: "In places where there is no snow the natives want water, and to supply this they fill the skins of sheep with water and make other living sheep carry them; for it must be remarked these sheep of Peru are large enough to serve as beasts of burden. They can carry about one hundred pounds, or more, and the Spaniards used to ride them, and they would go four or five leagues a day." Captain G. Shelvocke says of them, "The heads of these animals are small in proportion to their bodies, and are somewhat in shape between the head of the horse and that of the sheep. Their necks are long. They walk holding up their heads with wonderful gravity."

These animals are found both brown and white; but the white are most common. The llama was not, however, found by the Spaniards in North America, but it is quite possible that at a much earlier period it may have been, having perished, as the camel and horse had perished, that we know to have existed in North America during the Tertiary period.

EXPERIMENT XXIII.

The first opportunity I had of trying what was *known* to be an aerolite, was in June, 1861. It was a small fragment broken from a specimen in the possession of Rev. W. B. Cristopher, of Galena, Ill. As before, the examiner neither saw nor knew anything of the specimen, and as we were trying experiments with mundane specimens under like conditions, almost every day, that could not be distinguished from this by touch, there was little probability of the peculiar character of this being in any way guessed. The specimen was very black, heavy, and somewhat lustrous. From the appearance of it, it probably consisted of iron and nickel, as meteoric stones generally do.

Mrs. Denton.

"This seems to have had something done to it. I am at the foot of a mountain or high hill. I can easily see into the inside of it, but with difficulty the outside. I know not how to describe what I see. Here are different kinds of metal, and beautiful objects that look like gems. I see a great deep chasm; what a terrible depth! It must have been dreadfully disturbed.

"I see a hilly country now. The landscape is beautiful, delightful. All is at perfect rest, like a calm, summer's day. The climate seems to be that of continual spring, without the heat of the tropics, or the cold of this climate."

EXPERIMENT XXIV.

Ten days afterward I broke a small portion from the above specimen, and tried it again as before.

"I see a mountain of rock, with iron-like network all through it. It looks like meteoric iron. (This must be a piece of the specimen I tried the other day.) I see different colors in the rock that look like the reflection of brilliant gems. It is, however, merely light reflected from the iron.

"There seems to be a great deal of electrical light in this. In proportion as I move this specimen from my forehead, the mountain increases in visible size. It looks ragged. The iron seems quite distinct."

EXPERIMENT XXV.

More than a year afterward I gave this specimen to Mrs. Foote, she having no idea of its character. She held it in her right hand.

"This is curious. There is nothing at all to be seen, and I feel as if I was in the air; no, not in the air, either, but in nothing, — no place. I am utterly unable to describe it; it seems up, however. I feel as though I was rising, and my eyes are carried up; but I look around in vain; there is nothing to be seen.

"I see clouds now, but nothing else. They are so close to me that I seem in them. My head, and neck, and eyes, are affected. My eyes are carried up, and I cannot roll them down.

"Now the clouds appear lighter and lighter, and look as though the sunlight would burst through them. As the clouds separate, I can see a star or two, and then the moon instead of the sun. The moon seems near, and looks coarse and rough, and paler and larger in size than I ever saw it before.

"What a strange feeling comes over me. Seems as if I am going right to the moon, and it looks as if it was coming on to me. It affects me terribly."

She was too much affected to continue the experiment longer. Had this aerolite, at some period of its

history, come within the sphere of the moon's attraction, and had its velocity so increased that its increased centrifugal force had carried it off into space
again, whence, drawn by the superior attractive force
of the earth, it had fallen, and its planetary career
ended forever? Large fire-balls have been seen approaching the earth, and then flying off again apparently in this very manner.

EXPERIMENT XXVI.

Another meteoric specimen I obtained of Professor
McChesney, Chicago. It was a small fragment of
meteoric iron, and was tried as before.

Mrs. Denton.

"I am a very large — a monstrous beast. Others
are near me that are different. My proportions are
huge. I seem to be among trees. (I do not believe I
can get at the true influence of the specimen.)

"I see a great rock that goes up like a mountain. I
feel like flying, going, going. What a high rock that
is! I am at the foot of it. (I cannot make this agree
with the other.) There is a slope off to a tract of low
land in the distance; it looks marshy. I do not feel
at home up here; I am too awkward and clumsy. I
am rising through the air to the top of the rock.
(That certainly cannot be right; the two do not agree
at all.) Is it a fossil?" (No.) "That rock looks
like a great broken mass. There are bodies in it that
shine so as to dazzle my eyes. I cannot tell what
they are. Now I have that moving feeling again. I
know what this is now; it is a piece of an aerolite.
The slope or inclined plain that I saw is covered with

short, green vegetation, differing from all I have ever seen. It looks more like moss than grass, though I never saw anything covered with moss to such an extent. The soil in which it grows seems very thin.

"That is strange! I seem to have come to the 'jumping-off place.' The sky is overhead, and almost under my feet. There is a ledge of bare rock of great height, and miles in length, and, looking down at an angle of about thirty-five degrees, I see the sky below."

This specimen, previous to examination, had been wrapped up in a paper with a fragment of the tooth of a mastodon, and had apparently imbibed considerable of its influence, and to this, in my opinion, strange as it may seem, was owing the difficulty that Mrs. D. had in obtaining the true influence of the specimen.

Facts that have come before us during examinations since made, have convinced me of what I then surmised, — the transference, at times, of psychometric impressions from one specimen to another. I have sometimes thought that where specimens have no striking history of their own, they more readily receive impressions from neighboring specimens.

EXPERIMENT XXVII.

Two months after this, Dr. Bartlett, of Aurora, Ill., gave me a piece of rock, looking somewhat like a light lava, supposed to be of meteoric origin. It was one of a number of pieces that were found upon his farm, west of Waukegan, Ill., covering the ground over an oval space, at one end of which, where the fall had apparently taken place, they had sunk deeply into the ground.　The doctor thinks the aerolite, before 'its fall, must have been as large, at least, as a flour-barrel.

Mrs. Denton.　Conditions as before.

"Feel as if I were away down at the bottom of the sea.　I can see about twenty feet around me ; not very distinctly though, for the water is not clear.　I hear it roaring above me.

"I am near a cliff that presents a perpendicular face to me ; whether it rises above the water or not I cannot tell.　I occupy the same position with regard to the high cliff that I did before with a meteoric specimen [Experiment 26] ; the only difference being that I am now in water and do not see that long, green slope.　I cannot help thinking that this is the same place, and this specimen must be meteoric.

"I am now rising, and everything around me is rising at the same time.　I have a nervous feeling in connection with it, as a person might be supposed to have during an earthquake.　I rise and sink, rise and sink, though never as low as before.　I feel as if there would be a collision before long.　There is a bright stream of light now, right before me.　What can that mean ?　It flashes upon my vision every moment, and produces great terror.　All seems strange and terri-ble.　There are two streams of bright light, which I seem to see through a dense fog.

"Now I am moving with great velocity and tremen-dous force, and then there comes a terrible crash.　All is confusion.　I do not think the concussion took place on this earth.　I see enormous rocks, like moun-tains for size, shattered and piled one on another.　I have seen nothing like it for magnificence and sub

limity. The rocks are absolutely naked. What a pit!
I can see down a vast distance; it is horribly deep.

"Now I am down, and miles of rock are above me.
This is chaos. I see water pouring down like a torrent
among the naked rocks." (In reply to a question,)
"There was heat before the concussion, and heaving
rolling, sinking, and rocking before moving through the
air.

"I have travelled for many miles over the surface of
that world, for world it is, with plains and seas.

"I see a road between two cliffs; it is natural, of
course, and near it is a low ridge, covered with green
vegetation; the soil is exceeding thin."

Many experiments are yet needed to bring order
out of this apparent chaos. Our experiments indicate
that meteorites were once portions of a world, or of
worlds, shattered by some terrible concussion intc
fragments; that these worlds, or at least one of them,
had an atmosphere surrounding it, and large bodies of
water upon it, and vegetation apparently in the condition of that of our own planet about the close of the
Silurian period.

EXPERIMENT XXVIII.

In July, 1860, there was an eclipse of the moon, visible in Lockport, New York, where we then were. It
occurred to me that a psychometric examination of
the moon might be made by the psychometer sitting
where the lunar light could fall upon the forehead.
The event seemed to justify the conjecture; and, although we have tried no other experiments in connec
tion with celestial bodies, I have no doubt whatever
that the astronomer will eventually derive as much as

sistance from psychometry as the geologist is likely to do.

Mrs. Denton.

"I feel a sensation of intense dryness; everything is dry, hot, and crisp. What a rough, ragged, rocky scene of desolation this is, everywhere. It is absolutely terrible; it affects my whole system. Near the edge of the moon which lies toward the sun, I see an enormous crater, miles in diameter, and at the bottom is a lake of lava; it is red, and I see it in slow motion. It is remarkable how it keeps its place in the basin that encloses it, which seems miles deep, with craggy rocks on every side." ("Why does it seem remarkable," I said, "that it should keep its place in this basin? I should think it would be the most natural thing in the world." She replied, "I am looking up, and it seems as if it should pour out.") "I have a view of the moon's crust, and compared with the earth's it seems a mere shell, enclosing the liquid lava.

"The electrical condition of the moon seems to me to be disturbed by the eclipse, and that disturbance is reflected to the earth and back again; but I cannot properly describe it. The disturbance in the electrical condition of the moon and earth seems to be reciprocal; a tremulous vibration is produced that seems unusual."

It is a common idea that the moon is cold, and poets have long sung of the "cold, inconstant moon;" but, if this psychometric observation may be relied on, it is by no means as cold as we may have supposed. A body like the moon, destitute of water and an atmosphere, must part with its heat slowly; and it would not be at all surprising if our little attendant planet had a very warm heart, after all.

Sir William Herschel discovered, with his great reflecting telescope, on the dark part of the new moon, what he conceived to be the flames of an active volcano. Since his time, various persons have seen luminous spots upon the moon, which favor the idea of present igneous activity upon its surface.

According to Humboldt, "Melloni was fortunate enough to observe, by means of a lens of three feet in diameter, the most satisfactory indications of an elevation of temperature during different changes of the moon."[*] In this case, I suppose the heat would be attributed to reflection from the sun, but it may be owing to heat radiated from the substance of the moon itself.

EXPERIMENT XXIX.

Some of the bodies, of which the aerolites are fragments, appear to have resembled the moon in the absence of water, for Mrs. Denton remarked on trying one specimen subsequently:—

"This has a great deal of the lunar feeling. I am in a region of rocks, all dry. I do not feel the heat of the moon, but the dryness is similar, as if all water were absent. I see large masses of rock, with veins of iron all through them, forming quite a net-work, with here and there large, pure masses of iron."

EXPERIMENT XXX.

I have a small stalactite, which I obtained in a cave, about a mile and a half west of Salem, Indiana. I put this into the hands of Mrs. Cridge, when her eyes were

[*] Cosmos, Vol. IV. p. 143.

closed, and requested her to examine it psychometrically. She supposed, from the feeling, that it was an orthoceras, of which I had many specimens, and which it resembles.

"I see pieces of rock hanging down; they look like icicles, as if they had been formed by the droppings of the rock. I don't understand it, for the rock seems quite hard. I feel cold, and as if water were dropping on my head."

EXPERIMENT XXXI.

Many months after this I gave the same specimen to Mrs. U. Taylor, of Lockport, New York, whom I found to be a good natural psychometer. She supposed it to be a part of some animal.

"I go straight along a road; there is water near, and a cave, into which I enter. I see two persons going in with lights. Stalactites hang from the top all over. The two stand looking up. It is so damp and cold, it fairly makes me feel chilly. It is a large, roundish place. Off at a distance seem places where you can go still farther, but I cannot go; it makes me shudder. Now I go to the right; there is a basin of water; and to the left, room after room. Stalactites hang down like curtains, and shine most beautifully."

The accuracy of this description surprised me, accustomed as I was to the faithfulness of the psychometric pictures. The road to the cave is along the western bank of the western branch of Blue River, Indiana; and out of the cave, which is a "large, roundish place," a small stream issues. When I obtained the stalactite, I was in company with another gentleman, and each carried a candle; but as the cave had

been repeatedly visited by parties with candles, I do
not presume that we were the parties she saw. A
few hundred yards from the mouth the cave branches.
There is a basin of water in the body of it, and rooms
on the left with stalactites, as described.

EXPERIMENT XXXII.

I have a small fragment of fibrous gypsum, which
was obtained in the Mammoth Cave, Kentucky. This
I gave to Mrs. Denton for examination; she saw it,
but knew nothing of its history, and supposed it to be
a piece of asbestos, which it somewhat resembles.

"You must have had this given to you. The place
I see does not look like this region. I see a bench
with rocks upon it resembling this specimen. Back
of this bench I see a hill with soil and vegetation on
it. The rocks I saw seem to have been placed there
by artificial means. Now I see a curved wall arching
over head; the rocks that lie around seem to have
come from an open place near there. Farther on, the
rocks are perpendicular.

"I am in a cave that I have seen represented in
books, I am almost sure. It is very extensive. (I am
not in good condition for examining, or I could see
much better.) It has been visited a good deal, for I
perceive artificial light; that is, light differing from the
light that the rocks give out, by which I see objects
under ground. There are parts of the cave, however,
that have been but little visited. I notice one room
that has been visited a great deal, and visitors must
have remained and talked in it.

"At one place I see steps going up, and a rock juts

out a long way; it looks fearful. I judge this place is more extensive than it is known to be. All the rooms near the entrance seem to have been visited; this I know by the artificial light in them. Where that is, I cannot see as distinctly; it makes *itself* visible, rather than the objects around.

"There is a cave below this that is more magnificent than the other, much more so. It has not been visited, I think. It is surpassingly beautiful. It looks like a palace built to embody the idea of beauty. There is something that shines like a sun, raying out light all around; I cannot tell what it is. I cannot think of this as a cave; it is a gorgeous palace. I see a beautiful curtain-like partition between two rooms, with ridges and deep flutings. I notice one long hall with two walls, about three feet high, running the whole length of it; they look very singular here, for they have quite an artificial appearance. What a splendid place this would be to live in; only there is a cool, damp feeling about it. I know not how to get out of this labyrinth.

"There is a pit down, down much deeper. It goes into another cave by a winding way. What monstrous rocks! The cave near the surface is but a baby compared with these giant caves below. I thought that was a great cave, but what a poor pigmy by the side of these! This cave is partitioned off, in every direction, into long, fine rooms, with entrances from one to another, generally having high ceilings, though they are not all of the same height. There are grand long halls opening into the entrance where I came down. I wonder if it is not dangerous. If those rocks were to fall, how could one get out? I don't know what it means, but I have a sense of animal influence. All at once I am on the surface."

I then informed her that the specimen was from the Mammoth Cave. She said, "Is there water in the Mammoth Cave? for I saw streams of water in it, but did not notice them particularly, there was so much else to see."

I have never visited the Mammoth Cave; but those who have will, I think, acknowledge the accuracy of the descriptions of the known parts of the cave. The truth of the statements with regard to the unknown portions future explorers may yet determine. The animal influence felt was probably owing to the fossils contained in the Mountain Limestone, in which the Mammoth Cave has been hollowed out, by the action of underground streams for ages.

One thing the reader will notice in this, as well as in some other examinations, that the psychometer seemed to be at the spot and travelling over the ground. When our experiments first commenced, pictures connected with the history of the specimen passed before the gaze of the psychometer, like a panoramic view, she being a mere passive spectator. After some time these pictures could be to a certain extent controlled, their progress arrested or hurried at will, till at length the psychometer seemed to travel to the spot where the specimen came from, and describe it as a living person would who beheld it with the natural eye. Not only was this done with regard to present time, but with regard to all past time. All past to the psychometer seemed to become present;

all that had been was found to exist, and could be examined as thoroughly, almost, as the present around us.

It would seem that rays of light are passing from all objects continually, which are invisible to the eye, as a general rule, and can pass readily through some substances, if not all, which are opaque to ordinary light. These rays seem to be able to pass at once to the brain of sensitive persons and give the sensation of vision, without the intervention of the eye as an organ. Ordinary light is too coarse for such a refined organ as the brain to receive without the intervention of another organ, which receives it and then introduces it to the brain. But for this refined light the brain needs no such go-between, but it passes at once through the portals and is admitted into the inner chamber of the soul. Some of the lower animals seem to perceive objects, although they are totally blind, and, in some cases, do not even possess the visual organs. We find in most large caves blind animals, such as beetles, millipeds, crawfish, etc.; but although they possess none of the ordinary power of vision, they yet move away from the light of the explorer's torch, just as similar animals out of doors when they see a coming individual. Eyes are unnecessary to these cave tenants, and in process of time they are withdrawn; but they possess what answers the purpose to them in their underground existence equally as well; otherwise they would certainly cease to exist.

In the fresh-water polyp the whole body is sensitive to the influence of light, for it turns to it; and that this is owing to the sensitiveness of the whole body, is evident from the fact that, if cut in two, both parts equally seek the light.

"The *monas sulphuraria, stentor niger,* and the *actiniæ,* seek the light, but change their position if exposed to the full glare of the sun, and sink beneath the surface, before any part of their bodies comes in contact with the atmosphere. *Veretillum cynomorium* (a species of zoöphyte) seeks the darkest spots and folds itself together if brought within the influence of the light. In all these animals the power of sight, or rather the sense of perception, is spread over the whole surface of the body."*

Bats, that spend their lives in twilight or darkness, appear to possess this interior vision to a wonderful extent. Experiments made by Spallanzani, and repeated by eminent philosophic naturalists, demonstrate that the bat, when blinded, regulates its motions in the same manner as when it has full possession of its eyes. "Completely blinded bats were not in the slightest degree obstructed in their motions. They flew about by night or by day with their wonted ease and rapidity, avoiding all obstacles which lay, or were intentionally placed in their way, as dextrously as if in full possession of their sight. They turned round at the right time when they approached a wall, rested in a convenient situation when fatigued, and struck against nothing. The experiments were multiplied and varied in the most ingenious manner. A room was filled with thin twigs; in another, silken threads were suspended from the roof, and preserved in the same position and

* Thompson's Passions of Animals.

at the same distance from each other by means of small weights attached to them. The bat, though deprived of its eyes, flew through the intervals of these threads, as well as of the twigs, without touching them; and when the intervals were too small, it drew its wings more closely together. In another room a net was placed, having occasional irregular spaces for the bat to fly through, the net being so arranged as to form a small labyrinth. But the blind bat was not to be deceived. In proportion as the difficulties were increased, the dexterity of the animal was augmented. When it flew over the upper extremity of the net and seemed imprisoned between it and the wall, it was frequently observed to make its escape most dextrously. When fatigued by its high flights, it still flew rapidly along the ground, among tables, chairs, and sofas; yet avoided touching anything with its wings. Even in the open air its flight was as prompt, easy, and secure as in close rooms; and in both situations, altogether similar to that of its associates who had the use of their eyes."*

Any animal living in darkness during a continued existence, would, in my opinion, receive visual impressions in the same way; still more, animals whose ancestors had existed in a similar manner for ages, the power increasing with continued use, as transmitted for many generations.

It is not surprising that human beings should possess a power which is thus shared in by many animals, some of which are quite low in the scale of existence.

Harriet Martineau tells us of an old lady who had

---

* Chambers's Edinburgh Journal, Vol. IV., p. 293.

been blind from her birth, and yet saw in her sleep; and, when in her waking state, described the color of the clothing of individuals correctly.

Most blind persons exhibit such phenomena to a greater or less extent, according to the sensitiveness of the individual and the length of time during which the power has been cultivated. The case of the blind Yorkshire surveyor is familiar to most persons, and, in his case, the possession of vision, without the use of eyes, seems most evident.

Somnambulists who read and write with eyes closed, and sometimes bandaged, who in dark nights walk along the roofs of buildings and narrow walls, and perform various feats which other individuals could only do in the light of day, bear evidence to the possession of this faculty, that we are now considering, in man. For this subtle light to which I have referred is never obscured; it is always day with it, and, to those who perceive by its instrumentality, the darkest midnight is light and clear as the sunniest noon.

Clairvoyance is but the exercise of the same power by an individual in a somewhat different condition. If this subtle light can pass through a brick wall, the brick wall can be as readily seen through, by the person who sees by its instrumentality, as we can see through a pane of glass. To the clairvoyant, therefore, all things are transparent as air, because they are pervious to the light by which he sees; the rays proceeding from objects passing directly through the transparent skull — transparent to this light — to the brain.

Facts which philosophers have sneered at, and phenomena which they have denied, will eventually be accepted, and found to be in harmony with refined forces of matter with which they are as yet unacquainted.

I have recently become acquainted with Mrs. Lucielle do Viel, of Pultneyville, Wayne Co., N. Y., a lady who, on examining a specimen psychometrically, not only goes to the spot from which the specimen was obtained, but has the sensation of travelling while doing so, and frequently sees towns, ships, rivers, seas, etc., as she passes along to her destination. She informs me that she has seen objects with her eyes closed, from infancy, and frequently heard sounds that were inaudible to all but herself. After picking berries or gathing cl estnuts, on lying down to sleep, she saw them in great abundance, and often wished she could have the privilege of gathering what was so plainly visible. When young, she frequently told her friends what she saw; but, being laughed at and called visionary, she ceased to be communicative in reference to these visions. Previous to my trying her with the following specimens, she had never done anything of the kind, nor heard of its being done. I simply requested her to tell me what she saw and felt. The following experiments were made, she having no knowledge whatever of the specimen previous to its examination. She is more familiar with the French language than with English, and hence had more difficulty than another would have had in describing what appeared to her.

After trying her with two specimens of but ordinary interest, I gave her the specimen of hornstone brought from the Mount of Olives, an examination of which is recorded in experiment 66.

"I am going back, back, — over the water I glide along, but I see no vessels. Now, I am on shore; and see stones and rocky hills. There are large and small stones scattered all around, with moss among them. It is too stony for trees. What a long way off this is! There is water near where I am now, and a little grass, and small bushes. I see a basin of water; it is a lake, I judge.

"There does not seem to be many people. The land is so poor, I judge, they could not raise enough to eat. I see a forest a long way off.

"I see an ancient place now; how old-fashioned it is! Old houses almost down; arched gates and windows; how curious they look! Now I see people. Is that Spain?" (No.) "There is something growing on that rocky mountain; a few trees. They are not very tall, but thick and bushy. I should judge they were fig trees; but the leaves look like the olive.

"I have seen people like these; but I cannot tell where. The women wear turbans and pantaloons; and men and women are much alike. I see cattle, but they look different from ours. Farther back I see horses, sheep, and goats.

"I see a great palace. It is very beautiful. It looks like a Roman Catholic church. That is what it is. I see images, the cross, candlesticks, and an image of the Virgin. It is a very large place. Women are kneeling, and men walking on their tip-toes, as if they were afraid of disturbing something. Back of that palace I see a high mountain that lies to the north, I judge. Now I see ruins, — large stones lying round that have fallen down. Some are in heaps, and some are scattered; they seem too large for men ever to handle."

After supper, a second examination was made of the same specimen.

" It seems just as it did before. I'm going over the water again. I guess I'm crossing the Red Sea, it looks so red and dark. I see no vessel. Now I'm on shore. It is dreadful far. I see rocky little hills, heaps of stones, and large, flat stones lying by the wayside. The roads are narrow and crooked; they look like paths. I notice a large hill; it is all stone though, except a few small trees, which can hardly find root.

" Now I see a city, with high stone walls and large iron gates. The wall is thick and high. Two men are watching at the gate; they look like Jews. I wonder if they will let me in. Now I come to that temple and go in again. There is the crucifix at the altar, the images, and the women praying. It is a splendid place. Now I see another nice temple, not so large as the first. There are Greek letters on the outside; I cannot read them. I see many houses; they look curious; some are in ruins, and some are nice-looking places.

" I am on a mountain now; and there is another mountain on the opposite side, with olive trees and fig trees all the way. I see a garden, and water in a kind of basin. I have seen a description of this place, I know. Is not this Jerusalem? The mountain I stood on was Mount Moriah, and that opposite the Mount of Olives."

Who does not see that what was stated is true of Jerusalem and its vicinity, and of no other place? I found, on visiting her house subsequently, a work on Palestine, by means of which she had become familiar with Jerusalem and its vicinity, and hence the readiness with which she identified what she saw, which, at first, very much surprised me.

EXPERIMENT XXXIV.

Fibrous gypsum, Mammoth Cave.

"I am travelling south now. I see the soldiers' camp and tents. There are mountains around there, back and back. I see a cave; it looks white, like marble. What curious things on shelves, or what look like shelves, — vases, cups, candles, and candle-sticks, all in stone. There is a natural seat all round there.

"I see a spring; how clear the water is. There are fine statues, horses, camels, everything one can think of, almost, in stone.

"What a pretty place *this* is; it glitters like gold. What makes it shine so? Now I see water falling into a kind of basin down there. I see the appearance of curtains. That water pours into another basin below again."

This specimen is the one that was the subject of Experiment 32, and was obtained from the Mammoth Cave some years ago, at a time when there were no camps or soldiers in the neighborhood; so that it appears she saw the locality at the very time the examination was made, a time when, as I afterward learned, our soldiers were in the immediate vicinity.

I have a small black pearl, given me by Captain Loper, who brought it from the Gulf of California. This I gave to Mrs. do Viel for examination, who did not see it, but supposed, as she afterward told me, that it was a small bean, which in shape it much resembles.

"I am travelling a long way again; I think southeast. I see a man on his knees, digging and scraping with his hands. He has something like a basket on a stick, which he puts into the water and dips out, and then scrapes with his hands in the dirt. It is not much inhabited here. It is either between points or islands, where this man is at work getting things." (What is he getting?) " Stones, or something valuable, for he is very choice of them, selecting them with great care. (Oh, but it is a long way from here!) As near as I can see, he is getting pearls. He scrapes into this vessel, full of holes ; the water runs through, and he selects out of what remains at the bottom. They may be diamonds for aught that I know ; they shine very bright. He puts them into a little bag, after he picks them out.

" Back from him there is a large building, but it looks as if no one lived there. I see goats ; they are the only animals that I can find. I see trees and vines. That sea-shore is splendid. What clean, nice sand ! "

In this experiment she apparertly travels to the spot, but whether she saw what was occurring at the time, or what had occurred at the time the pearl under examination was gathered, it is impossible to say. The lower part of the Gulf of California is the place

where pearls are obtained, and the land in that neighborhood is very sparsely populated, or, as she described
it, " not much inhabited."

EXPERIMENT XXXVI.

A small fragment of Table Rock, Niagara.

" I am in a place where I see stony land. I travelled west from here. I see a stony mountain ahead
of me. This came from a rock at that mountain. It
is settled all around there, and there are forests back
from the villages. Some parts of the village look well,
but it is nothing particular as a whole. The people I
see look like our people. I see several places where
water runs down the side of the mountain. I see something clear and white in the rocks; it looks like silver."
(Look around, down below.) " I see two or three huts
and arbors, and some rabbits. There is a cave that
goes under that mountain. I am curious to see it. I
see bones on the ground that look like human, and a
beast's head of some kind." (Turned the specimen
over.)

" Now I see a kind of smoke, — it may be a cloud of
some kind; it goes right up. It is more toward the
middle than the cave. I see no fire, — once in a while
a little spark. That smoke does not spread; it goes
straight up.

" I am looking down now in the mountain. It is a
deep hole. There is something down there boiling up,
boiling up all the time, and the smoke comes from
that. Is that a hot spring?" (No.) " What makes it
boil so? It makes just such a noise as the lake does.
How it roars! It is louder than the lake. It sounds

just like a torrent." (Go across to the mountain on
the other side.) " That is a small one, not so high as
the one I was on before. Can that be a volcano? I
hear it roar off here. There are no inhabitants here.
It is very rough. There is a river that goes right
round, — yes, all the way. It has a very pretty shore,
but it is not very deep. There are two or three small
villages round there. The people seem to fish a good
deal.

" That river has a very rapid current; it looks stony
in places, and the water boils right up. What makes
it smoke so? It runs right under that big mountain.
There is a place under the mountain where it runs
just as it does above, and boils right up; that is what
makes the smoke. On the other side the water de-
scends into a deep hole; it seems like a whirlpool
down there. Under that water is a place where I can
go. The stones are flat under there. The water
pours over my head. There is an arch of stone over
me. The stone is white in places. It is right under
the mountain where I see this. I can go a long way
under that arch, and as far as I go the water is. It
seems as if the water was engulfed as fast as it fell.
I wonder where it comes from? The water makes
that smoke; it looks like a rain-cloud or mist. It rises
right up through that hole in the mountain, and when
the sun shines it sparkles, and that is what I took for
sparks.

" I am on top of the mountain again, and looking
over the water. There is a great, big cataract. The
water goes down with tremendous force, and that
makes it go up like smoke. What monstrous stones

there are near that cataract,—many as big as this house. That is a terrible whirlpool; the water goes round like a wheel. It is so strong it carries the fish up with it. Near the cataract is a large, square face of stone, and that is what the water falls over. That stone comes over, something like a piazza, and the water falls over it. There is quite a space behind the water; it looks like a long tunnel. What a tremendous body of water! What force! I never saw any cataract like this before."

She travelled in the right direction, and seemed to be at the spot in a few moments; but her vision seems to have been very much circumscribed, so that she could only describe what was in the immediate vicinity of where she seemed to be. She had never been at Niagara personally, or she would doubtless have recognized the spot. Any one who has been there, must see the exceeding accuracy of her description, which evidently none but an eye-witness could give. The white substance she saw in the rocks on two occasions is a very pure variety of gypsum, as white as chalk, which is worked up by persons at the Falls into ornaments and sold to visitors.

On crossing the mountain she seems to have gone over to Goat Island, for she sees the river " goes right round," and from there, right under the cataract itself, where there is an arch of stone above, and the water pours right over her head. She then passes to the Canadian side, and sees the cataract in its grandeur, which she seems to have been unable to do before, and beholds, with keener vision than ordinary visitors, that long tunnel, as she likens it to, which all visitors

know exists between the descending sheet and the
wall of rock behind it, along which many persons ven-
ture daily, accompanied by guides.

EXPERIMENT XXXVII.

Sulphuret of iron from the Marsden lead, west of
Galena, Ill. (Thought it was a stone.)

"I am going over Niagara River. I see the cataract
and suspension bridge. I am travelling west. I see
a place dug out of the earth where this came from. I
see something there that looks whiter than copper,
and a good many people are digging it. It is a good
way off west. Back of here there is a town or city,
and a body of water and vessels." (The Mississippi is
about three miles west of there, and Dubuque, Iowa,
perhaps seven or eight miles.) "I see horses and
wagons that carry the stuff away.

"Now I see a place where they melt it; there is a
great furnace. It looks like lead. There are many
people at work; I never saw anything like it before.

"They have axes under ground there for cutting it
out. I see them pick out white stones and lay to one
side.

"Now I see them shipping it in a vessel — they un-
load it from wagons — it is in bars.

"They have dug quite deep, and there are two or
three ladders in different holes. As they go down they
dig away under and very wide — thirty or forty feet, I
should think. They have lights down there, and very
long ladders to go up and down. The men are hack-
ing into the wall; they are almost as black as negroes.
They haul the stuff out in buckets from one hole to

another. It is very damp and cold in there. How
the wall shines! There is very clear water there."

The accuracy of this whole description is marvellous. The Marsden lead is the richest known in the
neighborhood of Galena, and is worked about five
miles west of that city. The mine is the deepest in
that region; and the inflow of water, which is very
pure, is so great, that an engine is kept constantly
employed in pumping it out. There are several holes,
as she stated, furnished with ladders; and in the principal one they have dug "away under," for the roof
of the mine dips at an angle of about fifty or fifty-five
degrees. The wall glistens much more than is common in lead mines, on account of the great abundance
of crystallized sulphuret of iron.

When at the mines she seems to have come into
rapport with the lines of travel to and from it; along
one she goes to the smelting furnace, and from there
to Galena, where the lead is shipped on board vessels,
in bars, as she states, and then returns on the other
again to the mines, to continue her explorations.

The only statement that she made in reference to it
that is open to criticism is the one in which she says,
"They haul the stuff out in buckets from one hole to
another." If my remembrance of it is accurate, the
ore is drawn up in buckets by the steam-engine that
pumps the water out, by a very crooked passage, it is
true, and this may have led her to describe it as going
from one hole to another.

EXPERIMENT XXXVIII.

Piece of chamois horn, from Switzerland. It was but
a small fragment, and no person by feeling could have

imagined its character; and as she did not see it, evi
dently the remarkable power that she possesses could
alone give her the clue to the surroundings of the animal of which it was once a part.

"I am travelling south-east now, I think. I pass
over many places that I have done before. I see
many soldiers and cannon, but I go over them. Now
I am on the sea-coast, and here are all kinds of shells.

"I go farther back into the wilderness. I see prairies
and dark-colored hills. I go farther back to the mountain land. There are large mountains; I see one higher
than any I ever saw before. I see a splendid city a
little way off.

"I see little caves here and there that seem to have
been dug for shelter. The rocks are dark, and so is
the soil. I see goats or deer climbing up. There are
numbers of animals running round me, some goats and
some deer. The horns of the goats arch over back,
but the deer's horns are bushy. Streams run down
from the mountain-side and make gullies; the water is
clear, and they look beautiful.

"I went into one of those caves; they are dens for
wild animals. Nuts grow on that mountain — some
look like hazels — they are not ripe. They are very
sour — I tasted them; they make the water run out
of my mouth.

"It is a splendid country all round here. I'll go
into that city and see how it looks. Some buildings
are of white marble, and others of dark stone. The
people are swarthy, but they dress a good deal like
our people. They have a stern look. I see a Roman
Catholic church; there is a cross on the top. I see

other churches. There are many mules in that country — more than horses. I can see the whole city.
On the other side is a body of water, and a very extensive wilderness in the distance."

Here we have the mountainous region of the Alps,
where the chamois dwells, the caves in which wild
animals shelter, the animals themselves, with their
horns arching back, — though she supposed them to be
a peculiar kind of goat, — and, generally, what we
should behold if visiting the region in proper person.

EXPERIMENT XXXIX.

Conglomerate from Eagle River, near where it empties into Lake Superior.

"I am going west of here. I pass over Niagara,
where I was before. I pass rocks and over woods and
waters, and now I am close by a lake and a wilderness.
That is a pretty shore. It is a nice place all around —
quite a wilderness back. I see a creek that runs
through the wilderness and empties into the lake. It
makes quite a ripple over the stones as it goes down.
Those are beautiful trees — oak, I think, white oak. I
am close to the edge of the creek, and but a little
way from the lake.

"A little way back there are inhabitants. I see
farms, and log houses, and saw-mills. They take wood
to the lake. (That creek is narrow.) They are not
all Yankees there. I see different kinds of people —
some French. That is a great place for timber. That
water is deep enough for vessels to come in. I see
one at the wharf now taking in wood."

This description of the place from which I obtained

the specimen is correct, I believe, in nearly every particular. I obtained it from the rocky bank of Eagle River, about 300 yards back from Lake Superior, and within the bounds of Eagle River village, where the water "makes quite a ripple over the stones as it goes." The creek runs through a wilderness and empties into the lake, which has at that point a beautiful pebbly shore. There is a wharf near the place, and vessels call, in going up and coming down the lake. I am not certain that she is correct about the kind of trees in the neighborhood, which, I think, are principally small pines.

EXPERIMENT XI.

Glacier-scratched pebble, Palmyra, New York.

"This draws me down. There are many stones where this came from; I see numbers of them. It did not come very far. You got this close by, a little south of here; not very far from Pultneyville. You did not pick it up for its beauty, but to see if any one could tell where it came from. There is a bed of this stone where it came from, — different layers, one above another. I see a village; there is nothing remarkable about it."

These examinations were made at Pultneyville, on the shore of Lake Ontario; and Palmyra, where I obtained the specimen, is sixteen miles south of Pultneyville. She had never been at Palmyra, and hence did not recognize the place, which she appears to have seen psychometrically.

Some persons may think that out of a multitude of examinations I have chosen just the few that had in them something remarkable, but this is not the case. My time was limited, and Mrs. do Viel's family duties prevented her trying as many experiments as she otherwise would. She examined, in all, thirteen specimens, and out of the thirteen I have presented eight. The rest were probably just as correct, but I have not yet been able to verify them as fully as I could wish.

This lady had no idea that she possessed any such power, till she tried a specimen that I gave her, and she expressed the greatest delight at the wonderful things that she was thus enabled to see. She seemed less fatigued by it than any psychometer that I ever saw, owing probably to her robust physical constitution.

Of what great utility this department of psychometry may become! All drift may be tracked by the future geologist to the place of its dispersion; and where that drift contains portions of the precious metals, the vein from which they were borne may readily be discovered. A simple, cheap and efficient telegraph line may be established between the most distant places on the earth, that may be worked as rapidly as a person can read. In short, the uses of this power are innumerable, and such as only the great future can develop.

I am strongly inclined to believe that if we detach a rock from its parent bed, wherever it may be carried, there is a line of connection extending from that rock to the bed from which it was derived, and that along that line something (call it soul, spirit, or mind, I know not what term would be most appropriate) passes from the psychometer to the place, and sees objects as they at present exist. When a psychometer examines a specimen of rock from a building, some-times the quarry is first visited where the rock was obtained, and then the building; and at other times the building is first visited, and then the quarry.

If psychometers only wandered over places as they exist at the present time, which appears to be the case with Mrs. do Viel, such an explanation would be quite sufficient for all cases; but when they wander, as they appear to do, through the streets of cities, which they find in their prime, though they have been but heaps of ruins for centuries, when they skim over wide continents, containing strange mountain chains and long-perished rivers; roam through trackless for-ests alive with extinct mammals, and visit the ocean-caves of early geologic periods, very different must be the explanation of this. Can it be that all the Si-lurian period — its thermal oceans, its shelly beaches, its foggy skies, all its tenants of water and rock, and the diversified surface and changing conditions of the globe and its inhabitants during its vast continuance — is locked up in the fragment of limestone, whose interior is viewed by the psychometer? I am some-times inclined to think that the universe is contained in every pebble, and it only needs the all-compelling soul to call it forth. Time will explain all.

EXPERIMENT XLI.

There is a remarkable gulf, north of the town of Lockport, New York, evidently produced by a branch of the Niagara river, which, at some distant period, flowed over the ridge there, and cut its way back for more than a mile. At the present time there is a small creek flowing through it, which empties into Lake Ontario a few miles below.   There is a mineral spring at the bottom of the gulf, and some one had dug out the rock in its neighborhood in order to deepen it.   I carried away a block of it to Lockport, and broke out *from the centre* of it a small piece, which, up to that time, had never seen the light.   I wrapped it in two thicknesses of paper, and then presented it to Mrs. Taylor for examination, she having at the time, I am positive, no knowledge of it whatever.   She was silent for some time, but at length said: —

"I find great difficulty in fixing my mind upon it. I am on the edge of a cliff; below me there is a deep ravine, with a little stream running through it, off to the lake.   I go across a rocky, uneven piece of ground, and see trees and grass; trees grow on the side of the ravine.   I see you hammering among the rocks."

The description is accurate in every particular. Is a man exaggerating when he says the paving-stones can see, and tell what they see?   Images of external objects in their vicinity are impressed even upon their interiors; images that will continue as long as the stones themselves endure.

EXPERIMENT XLII.

When seeking for fossils in the bed of the Wyandotte River in Kansas, some years ago, I found a piece of petrified bone, apparently a portion of the leg-bone of some monstrous mammal; and near it a piece of the enamel of a tooth, looking somewhat like the side of a mastodon's tooth.   This was examined by Mrs. Den-

ton, she as usual neither seeing it nor knowing anything of its supposed character.

"I see a very large and singular-looking animal,
great beyond anything that I ever conceived a quadruped to be. Its huge legs are wide apart; the hind
legs considerably larger than the fore legs. The head
is large, and must be very heavy; it moves from side
to side. There is a kind of marsh where plants grow,
and there it goes to eat.

"It seems as if I could describe the whole of the
internal organs of the animal. The bones are large,
and the marrow seems monstrous. The skin is very
thick. The nose comes down a long way and widens
out, and the animal seems to have had the power of
lengthening its neck at will."

EXPERIMENT XLIII.

The fragment of tooth was also examined by Mrs.
Cridge, under like conditions. I had carefully kept
both specimens from observation previous to these experiments, in order to have a satisfactory result.

"I can see many animals that are large, but I see
them too indistinctly to describe them. One is a large
animal with horns, which lie back toward the shoulder.
It has a very long head, and is about the size of a
horse, but differs from all animals that I have seen.

"A river appears before me, and a swamp, and a
thicket connecting the swamp and river. There is
one very large animal near there, a walking stack of
flesh. What curious legs! They are spread out and
look very heavy, but look short compared with the
size of the animal; the ankle joint seems to come right

down on the ground. It has a very long neck. The
fore feet are unlike the hind feet. It eats branches of
trees. It has the power of drawing in and sending
out its neck. The head seems small compared with
the size of the body." (In reply to a question:) " I
think it has a trunk, but it is shorter than an elephant's ; it seems to smell by it. It is very wide at the
end and open. There ! I see the animal roll it over
and over, and place it on the top of the head.

" I see another animal, light-colored and scaly, covered with a suit of armor; it has quite a long tail. It
has a long head, and horns laid back upon it. The
back is covered with regular, sharp protuberances;
underneath it is of a brown color. It is quite harmless, living upon herbs. I can see it nibbling. Its
teeth seem to be quite sharp."

It appears evident that both saw the same animal,
though the descriptions differ somewhat. One sees a
marsh where plants grow; the other sees a swamp and
a thicket. Both see a very large quadruped; both
notice that its legs are wide apart, though they speak
of it in somewhat different language, and both observe
a difference between its fore and hind feet. One sees
that it possesses a trunk, which the other does not
appear to observe until the question is asked whether
it has or not ; but both state that it is wide at the end,
which is very different, as every one knows, from the
shape of the elephant's proboscis. Let it be remembered, that neither person knew that the specimen examined was a part of any animal, and that these remarkable coincidences were brought out, not by hints given
or leading questions asked, but by presenting the

specimen, which certainly could convey no idea to ordinary touch of its nature, and then leaving all to be educed by its pyschometric examination alone.

From pyschometric examinations, made at various times, I believe that many huge animals existed in North America during the Tertiary period, allied to the mastodon and megatherium, and some that appear to have been links between the pachydermata and edentata; the descriptions given agreeing partly with the one and partly with the other.

From the appearance of the cervical vertebræ, in the engraving of the skeleton of the megatherium, given in Dr. Buckland's Bridgewater Treatise on Geology, it seems very probable that it had the power of protruding the head, thus enabling it to reach distant branches without moving its ponderous body. The vertebræ of the neck seem to be concave on their upper surfaces, and convex on their lower, fitting into each other, as one cup of a set fits into another; so that they could be removed a considerable distance apart without danger of dislocation.

The animal seen encased in armor was probably allied to the Armadillo family, many of which, of gigantic size, with shells like turtles, existed on the American continent during the Tertiary period.

EXPERIMENT XLIV.

At Chagrin Falls, Cuyahoga Co., Ohio, there is, in a sandstone quarry, a layer about three inches thick, on which are found, over the whole surface, the impression of rain-drops; corresponding casts of them being found on the under surface of the overlying layer. Occasionally, fossil fish with heterocercal tails have been found in the same layer as the rain-drops. The rock is a member of the Devonian formation. Mrs. Denton, without seeing it or knowing anything regarding it, placed a small piece of one of the slabs, containing the impressions of rain-drops, upon her forehead, and said : —

"I see a zigzag flash of lightning; it divided before it reached the earth. Now I am in a shower, and feel as if drenched by rain. This must be the impression of rain-drops."

How strange that the electric flash which darted to the earth millions of years ago, should still be visible, and the rain that followed it still be felt !

EXPERIMENT XLV.

When travelling through Texas, several years ago, I found in Henderson County a creek, the bed of which contained innumerable fragments of silicified wood, some of them of rare beauty; and in the vicinity, I saw bodies of trees, two and three feet in diameter, and many feet in length, changed into solid flint. One of the small pieces that I brought home with me, was the subject of this experiment, which was made as before.

"I see water and trees, some standing and others lying. The water is peculiar; it has some property in it that produces a feeling of incrustation, on putting the hands into it. It is very warm ; a hot steam rises from it. It has a saltish taste, but there seems to be some alkali in it. It looks clear, except on the top, where a kind of crust floats upon the surface. The water

flows over a small cascade into a lake below.   Moving
my position, I now see trees, tall, large and majestic,
and the light comes through their dense foliage.   They
shoot up very high before branching.   I can see trees
on the upland, but they are more scrubby.   Many
trees are lying in the water.

"1 go down the stream.   What quantities of drift-
wood!   The water is almost dammed by it.   What
monsters! — large, spotted lizards like crocodiles;
some in the water, and others crawling on the soft
mud.   The water and the swamp are full of them.
The spotted ones are too slender for crocodiles, and
their jaws too long.

" One I see with a short and broad mouth.   At the
connection of its legs with its body is a wing-like
extension of the skin.   It seems well suited for the
water, but is clumsy on land.

" I see many small animals that the large ones are
in pursuit of.   How rapidly they dart away!   One
dives right into the mud, as a fish would into the
water; its sharp snout being well fitted for the work.

" What monstrous reptiles!   Here is the struggle for
life.   I see many reptiles that look like newts, but
they are from three to four feet long.   The water here
is very different from that which I first saw."

Here the trees and the silicifying agencies seem to
have come up first, as most intimately related to the
history of the specimen; then its surroundings during
the Tertiary period, when it was drinking in the influences of the crawlers that abounded there.   If the examination had been continued longer, I have no doubt
that the images of the Tertiary quadrupeds would have

presented themselves, and perhaps those of the early human occupants of the country.

Here we have an evidence of the great deficiency of ordinary geological investigation, in revealing to us the various forms of life that have existed on the face of the globe. I think it probable that a thousand times as many animals existed, prior to the human period, as the paleontologist knows anything about. Take these Texan Tertiary deposits, and we find in them no bones, no footprints, nothing to tell of the myriads of animals that swarmed and rioted during countless generations, but the psychometric impressions, which seem to be the only means by which the gaps that at present exist in paleontology can be filled.

EXPERIMENT XLVI.

An experiment made with a Tertiary fossil, obtained near Calabazal, in Cuba, gave me a wider view of what this psychometric power is destined to do for science in the future than I ever possessed before.

Mrs. Denton.

" I see streams of water running down the side of a hill; the water is very much charged with foreign matter. There are rocks visible, that seem to have been formed by deposit from the water. There are fossils in the rock, but they differ from any I ever saw before.

" I go back in time, and see a volcano and a shower of fire. There is a long dark strip of rock from the low ground up to the volcano. The land seems very unstable; rocking, and heaving up, and sinking down; sometimes appearing above the water, and then vanishing beneath. I seem to be on an island. The eastern part is less stable than the western. All the western part is under water now. The island is longer from east to west than from north to south. It extends south of east, farther than directly east. I think it is south from here. The coast is very singular. I see what would probably be called a barrier reef along the coast, and so regular is a portion of it that it looks artificial.

" The climate is delightful. I seem to be on the north side of the island, west of the centre, and somewhat inland.

" I have a glimpse of a grove, with vines stretching from tree to tree, and naked boys climbing on them.

" Farther south and east there is a strip of land richer than here. This seems to have been washed by the sea. There is a kind of point here, and I see what looks like an artificial ditch."

At the time when this examination was made, I did not really know on what part of the island of Cuba the specimen was obtained; but on writing to Mr. McDonell, of Madison, Wis., of whom I received it, he informed me that " Calabazal is twelve miles south of the city of Havana, at a point where a railroad crosses a stream, half way between Havana and Santiago."

How wonderfully correct, then, were the statements of the psychometer. Cuba is seven hundred and fifty miles long from east to west, with an average breadth of about sixty miles ; consequently the island is " longer from east to west than from north to south." Its direction is E. S. E., hence " it extends south of east farther than directly east." The mountains increase in height from the west to the east end of the island, where they are diffused over nearly the entire surface, some of them being nearly 8,000 feet high; so that it is probable that the eastern part has been less stable than the western. The specimen was taken from "the north side of the island," "west of the centre," and twelve miles from the coast; and consequently, "somewhat inland." It came from a place "south from here," which has a "delightful climate;" and from a Tertiary bed, containing many fossils, differing from any that Mrs. D. had seen before. It was taken from a railway cutting, which may explain the ditch that was seen.

Let it be remembered that Mrs. D. did not see the specimen; that she had no conception whatever as to the character of it, or the place from which it was obtained; and that I did not know many of the facts stated during its examination, and its extraordinary character is most manifest.

What is to prevent the accurate exploration of the Arctic and Antarctic regions by a process incomparably easier and cheaper than the expeditions of Parry, Ross, and Kane?

EXPERIMENT XLVII.

Recently, the alligators that swarm in our southern rivers have been put to some useful account; oil being made from their bodies, and leather from their skins. A piece of this leather I had given to me by a friend, and in a few days had an opportunity of trying it psychometrically. In this, as in all other experiments recorded, where the contrary is not stated, the psychometer did not see the specimen, and had no idea of what it was previous to the experiment.

"I see an animal with a long neck and a long head. I see its skeleton. What a long neck! I believe I can count the bones; the processes are large and wide apart. It is an animal much larger than a horse. I get this indistinctly, as if it really did not belong to it, or only incidentally. The skeleton resembles that of the sea cow I saw the other day." (In the Academy of Sciences, Chicago.) "I see a large leg, bent as if in walking. It is an alligator's. A little old man passes before me, with his feet on a chair; he is bent over as if doing something.

"Now I am in another place altogether. Other scenery comes up, more tropical. I see plants and animals, such as live in warmer countries than this. One animal, I see, is an enormous bird. There are hundreds of reptiles, too; the water is alive with them. Two of them are eating the body of a dead animal. Some of them are alligators. There are many turtles of various kinds and sizes; fishes, large frogs, and other animals."

After informing her what it was, she said that she had come to the conclusion that it was an alligator's scale.

The first influence may have come from the oil with which the leather was curried; but the stronger influence eventually makes itself felt.

EXPERIMENT XLVIII.

Near La Salle, Illinois, on the Illinois River, there is a large high rock of white sandstone, known by the name of Starved Rock, from a legend, which states that the remnant of an Indian tribe was starved to death upon it, being surrounded by their enemies. On the top of the rock, and around it, are found, in great abundance, Indian arrow-points, arrow-heads, beads, and pieces of pottery. One of the latter was the subject of this experiment. Conditions as before.

Mrs. Denton.

"I see a round place, as large as the floor of this room; and on it a fire is burning. It looks like a fire around which Indians gather. There are woods nearly surrounding the fire. I seem to have a night view.

"There is a stream here, and I am hunted. A number of fellows are paddling across and yelling. I think they are after me; but I feel somewhat secure, though I know not why. Now they are across; I can see them, but they cannot see me. They go Indian file, and they look like Indians. How they shout and whoop! I am crossing over their track, and running into the woods on the other side. I have come to the conclusion that they were not after me. I seem to have too much calm, steady thought for an Indian."

Who was this fugitive, and how came this piece of pottery to record this incident in his life? The debris of the old Indian villages abounds with biographies of the old aboriginal warriors and their families, and if a man chose to devote himself to the work, he might write the histories of the Cæsars and Napoleons of the New World, whose names are all unknown.

EXPERIMENT XLIX.

The Autobiography of a Boulder. — At Jaynesville.

Wis., I obtained from a hill of gravel that had been cut through by the railroad, a boulder of dark trap, of somewhat peculiar appearance, and weighing probably four or five pounds. Breaking off a fragment, the following was obtained from it psychometrically, the psychometer knowing nothing of it, and the angular fragment conveying, of course, no idea of its character to the mere touch.

"Mercy! what a whirl things are in! I do not know what to make of it. I feel as if I were being belched out of a volcano; there is water and mud, and everything is in a perfect whirl. There are great pieces of rock beside me, some larger than I feel myself to be, though I am of great size.

"This is the strangest feeling I ever had. I am sent up whirling in a torrent of water, mud and rocks; not sent out, but it is puff, puff, whirl, whirl, all of us flying round together.

"Now I am lodged. I can hear that puff, puff, however, and with every puff, the water rushes out, so that it seems as though the volcano were vomiting. Now, a torrent of water rushing back sweeps me from my resting-place, and I am rolling in again. What fury there is down there! I did not go far down. Another gush, and I am washed a long way off. I can see it boil over now, but do not feel it. I see no fire about it, though there is steam, and, I think, gas.

"I am now away down the side of a mountain, and feel quite benumbed. I can just hear that belching sound and feel the heaving of the ground. Here I lie for a long time.

"At last I fall into a cavity, a deep one, very rough

and uneven. It is dark. I perceive the influence of water in my neighborhood. How shall we ever get out of here? I am surrounded on all sides.

"The water has burst in with great power, and it is spinning me round and round. I am being moved onward by little and little during a long time. (I must hurry along, for it is a vast period.) I am now in a kind of notch, where the rushing water keeps me in a constant whirl.

"At last I see the daylight. There is a long shelf that slants down into the water; I am washed right up on it, and the water has left me. It is a long body of water, larger and wider than a river; it looks like a lake, and has waves of considerable size.

"The water rises again; it washes around me, and I am carried back into it. All is dark now. I am washed on into a deep and wide hole. I am far under ground and under water. There is a strong current, and I am being rushed along by it. A strange feeling of passiveness possesses me, a disposition to go as it comes. It seems so strange to me. I feel as if a great deal larger then than now. I keep moving slowly along, slide a little, roll a little, stop a little, and knock against the side now and then — one side, however, more than the other; I do not know why that should be.

"I am out once more. I lie in a basin, in a large open place. I am not at the bottom of the basin, however, for other rocks are below me. (How cold the water is!) The basin is gradually filling up, by rocks rolling in. It is in a terribly cold latitude. I am all in a chill." (She fairly shook with cold.)

"I feel now as if there were something over me besides water. I don't know what it is, though." (The room was very warm, yet she drew her chair close up to the stove.) "It is strange that I see so little — I just feel and act. The basin in which I lie is shallow from me up. That which lies over me must be ice, for I can see light through it. I am fast in it too. My connection with this ice seems to give me a connection with all the country round, so that now I can see for many miles. There is a great depth of ice; I look up through it; it is a long way to the top, and seems unbroken for a great distance.

"How strange! The ice has broken loose, and I am in motion now, travelling southwest. It goes very heavily, hitching now and then. There is a kind of pitching forward of the upper part that surprises me; ice certainly could not do that; the under part seems to go slower than the upper; it cannot be possible, and yet it seems so. How intensely cold it is! The noise the ice makes in moving is awful to me, though I do not suppose it could be heard far; and yet here, it is a terrible grinding noise, with a ring to it.

"It seems as if I had come a long way; but it is strange how slow it moves. I do not understand how a solid body could move in this way, for a part of it moves faster than another part; and yet it seems all solid; it is incomprehensible. It is a flat, thick mass of ice, several miles broad. How insignificant a tree or a house would be in its pathway!

"It seems as if we had a hard time of it, scraping, scratching, and grinding along. It meets with obstacles and checks, more than would be produced by mere unevenness of the ground. I am so far back, that I do not feel all that the front has to contend with.

"It seems to be growing warmer now. I do not feel as cold as I did. It is a great deal warmer, and the heat seems to come from beneath too. The ice is melting, dripping, and running. It seems to melt away from under; I do not understand that. It does not seem as if we had come far enough south to make all this difference in climate.

"The ice is leaving me, I believe. Yes, it is. The length of the ice surprises me; it seems like a long coast of ice; great cliffs rising up like walls. It melts and melts, and keeps sliding on, faster since it melted so rapidly. I have dropped out of the place where I was, on to the ground, and I am only moved occasionally now. The front of the ice is miles ahead of me, and overhead the great mass still goes on. I am still moved on a little occasionally, but the ice is fast leaving. I am nearly out from under, but the front is still a long way ahead."

She was too much fatigued to continue the experiment any longer, or doubtless it would have revealed much more. What it did reveal is significant.

North of the fortieth degree of north latitude, on this continent, we find, covering the face of the country, beds of sand, gravel, or clay, and, sometimes mixed with these, or lying above them, boulders, or, as they are sometimes termed, erratic blocks and lost rocks. These rocks frequently differ in their mineral composition from the rocks in the neighborhood of which they are found; and the rocks with which they are identical in composition are generally found north of their present localities, sometimes, indeed, many hundreds of miles. Beneath these beds, which are known to the geologist in the aggregate, as the drift or glacial form-ation, we find upon the solid rock scratches or furrows, that have evidently been made by the passage of some body over them; that body, from the appearance of these furrows, having moved in a general direction from north to south. These beds and appearances excited the attention of thinking observers for a long time, before any theory was formed of their origin, ade-quate to account for the facts observed in connection with them. At the present time it is universally con-ceded that ice has been the principal agent concerned in their production; but with regard to its operation there is considerable difference of opinion. One party supposes that during the drift period, the time when these beds and appearances were formed, this northern country, over which the drift extends, was under water; and icebergs, laden with fragments of rock and detritus, swept by glaciers from some northern re-gion, came floating down, as they now do from the west coast of Greenland into the Atlantic Ocean, and stranded upon the shore; but, impelled by a south-ward-flowing current, they slid over the floor of the ocean, and their imbedded pebbles made the furrows or scratches; and, on melting, the material with which they were laden was left upon the floor of the ocean, forming, when that became dry land, the beds of drift to which I have referred. Another party supposes that, owing to some cause as yet unexplained, this northern country had, during the drift period, an intensely cold climate, so much so that snow falling could not melt, but became condensed by its weight into a grand sheet of ice of vast thickness, which covered the face of the country; and that this sheet of ice, moving in the only direction in which it could melt, namely, toward the south, passed over the country, grinding down the rocks in its march, and leaving upon them those plain indications of its progress, which the glacial furrows and beds present.

There are many difficulties in the way of accepting the glacial theory, as it is termed, but the psychometric experiments that we have made upon scratched rocks, point unvaryingly to the existence of glacial action at the localities from which the specimens were derived; and at the same time the action of icebergs is indicated as one of the auxiliaries in producing the varied phenomena belonging to the drift.

It is a remarkable fact, a fact with which Mrs. D. was unacquainted at the time that the above examination was made, that ice, moving in the form of a glacier, travels with unequal velocity. Thus, in an article on glaciers and glacial theories, in the Westminster Review, the writer says: — "The rate of movement of all parts of a glacier is by no means the same. Sometimes the commencement and the end appear to move somewhat faster than the middle, sometimes the lower end moves more swiftly than the upper, — differences which doubtless proceed from changes in the form of the valley, and consequent variations in the amount of resistance at different points. But there is a constant and most important discrepancy between the rate of motion of the central part of the glacier and that of the sides; the former being invariably found to be mov-

ing onward much more quickly than the latter.   The
same relation appears to hold good between the super-
ficial and the deeper portions, so that the motion of a
glacier resembles that of a flowing body.   It matters
not whether we choose ⌐ limpid fluid like water, or a
viscus fluid like tar, if we allow either to flow, and
then measure the velocity of its different parts, we
shall discern that the lateral and inferior portions are
retarded by friction against the walls of the channel,
and hence that *the top flows faster than the bottom*, the
middle than the sides."

On seeing this psychometrically, Mrs. D.'s astonishment was very great, and she could scarcely credit
the possibility of her vision being correct in this particular; yet, the scientific accuracy of it, the well-in-
formed reader will see at a glance.

There is one portion of the psychometric description that deserves particular notice; it is that in which
the heat is spoken of as coming up from the earth into
the ice and melting it.   The spot where the boulder
was obtained is on the edge of that singular region of
No Drift, which is nearly coincident with the lead region of Illinois, Wisconsin, and Iowa; extending all
around for a few miles beyond the district in which
lead is found.   On every side of this district drift is
abundantly distributed, especially to the north of it;
but within that charmed circle you cannot find even a
drift pebble.   What can be the reason of this?   Some
have suggested, that, during the drift period, this portion of the country was an island, so far elevated
above the waves that drifting icebergs never reached
it, and consequently deposited no drift.   But this ex-

planation takes for granted that all drift phenomena were produced by floating icebergs, which is far from being proved. How does it happen that the region of the No Drift is coincident with the lead region, and that there is no other portion of this continent, north of the fortieth parallel, in which drift is thus absent?

I have long been of the opinion that the lead in the region referred to, has come from below, in the state of vapor, through the underlying porous sandstone into the magnesian limestones in which it is found; the deposits having been formed by sublimation, at a time when the rocks were heated to a certain degree, even to the surface; indications of which are plain and abundant. This may have occurred during the drift period, and, as the glaciers came down from the nortn and northeast, they melted as they came near this heated district, leaving their detritus on the spot, and thus formed those immense accumulations of drift that are found in Wisconsin, north of the lead region. I had no thought of this theory at the time that we made the examination, but our examinations favor it very strongly; for, if so, the circumstances described in the ast experiment, must have taken place at or near the very place from which the boulder was obtained.

EXPERIMENT L.

Some glimpses of the ancient world that we have occasionally had, seem to indicate that the earth was once surrounded by a ring, or rings, like those surrounding the planet Saturn, which having become broken from time to time, have dropped to the earth in fragments. Some of them yet remaining in space, and

occasionally drawn within the sphere of the earth's attraction, may constitute a portion of those bodies
known as shooting stars and aerolites; while others
still remaining may produce the appearance known as
the zodiacal light. I have not had an opportunity of
verifying this by the statements of other psychometers, but hope to do so at some time. This experiment
gave us the first presentation of this appearance:—

Soapstone from the bed of a creek near Painesville.
Devonian formation.

Mrs. Denton.

"Did you get this from a stream? for I seem to be
in the bed of a creek. There are two trees on one
side and an open space on the other." (This is correct.) "I see a tropical region, and plants and animals in great abundance. I see the sun setting, but
the atmosphere does not look clear as now. It looks
much as it does when very foggy. There is a long
circular belt or arch of light in the water, that looks
as if reflected from something above. The sun is still
above the horizon, but I see the light of this body
notwithstanding, for the dark atmosphere seems to
prevent the sun's light from obscuring it.

"Now I see it in the sky; it is a segment of an arch;
but there seems to be more of it than I can see. It extends from the eastern horizon upward for about seventy degrees, at least that is as far as I can see it. It
looks about as broad as the full moon, yet has a faint
appearance of being broader."

A few days afterward, from the same specimen, the
belt was seen in the heavens again, but much broader
than before; apparently, three times as broad. The

sun's place in the heavens was about twenty degrees south of the belt. It did not appear this time nearly as bright as before; it looked as if covered with a veil, hiding its brightness, though through it the shape was distinctly revealed.

The next three experiments were made for the purpose of discovering the condition of the earth, and of its fauna and flora, during the Carboniferous period, and their revelations are of great interest to the paleontologist. In no case was the specimen known.

Small specimen from a bone bed in the Coal Measures, near Youngstown, Mahoning County, Ohio. There are impressions of plants in the shale below.

Mrs. Denton.

"I see plants as tall as a man; two-thirds of the way up the stalk, is a bright, yellowish red bud; I call it a bud for want of a more appropriate name; out of it the upper stalk appears to grow. It is really on one side of the main stem, but grows with it for some distance. There is just one bud on each plant. At the end of the stalk is something that looks like a corn tassel. The plants are quite succulent, and cover the ground completely, as close together as they can grow.

"I see ribs, naked ribs, and now the skeleton of a long animal. I see another skeleton, longer than the first, but the ribs are not as large. Now I see the animal; it resembles a lizard, and has a fringe of long spines along the back.

"I see another animal, with a scalloped shell upon

its back. It has somewhat the appearance of a turtle with a scalloped shell all round.

"I see a fish, with spines from the head to the end of the tail. All I see looks odd, strange."

Sub-carboniferous sandstone, Western Reserve, Ohio. Mrs. Denton.

"I see something that looks like a plant, but it differs from anything I ever saw before. It has several stalks that go up to a certain height, and a round body encloses the whole; then they go up again smaller, and are enclosed in a similar manner; then again; and then at the top it branches into heads, making it, altogether, about three feet in height. That which encloses the stalks looks something like a receptaculite.*

"The stalks that support the little heads, of which there are some five or six, seem to be furnished with cilia in constant motion; and from the heads proceed tentacles, also having a constant, wavy motion. They must be some low kind of animal, instead of plant; probably, belonging to the radiates. The heads, as I call them, move somewhat as I have seen crinoids. The bodies encircling the stems are of a brown color, the stems somewhat lighter. They are really beautiful.

"The water is very dark, and seems quite thick; it has much the color of smoked glass. It is not caused by mud, however, but it is chemically impure. There is a long, low, flat piece of ground with plants growing

---

* A coral-like fossil found in the Silurian formation.

on it, that look like high weeds. The water rises so as to cover it occasionally. The atmosphere is dark and heavy."

A piece of anthracite coal from Pennsylvania.

Mrs. Denton.

" I see a shallow stream of water that looks like a kind of bayou. A dense vapor hangs over it, that it is difficult to penetrate. I seem to be in a boggy place, where there is a great deal of vegetable matter beneath me, not floating on the water, but the water is all through it, so that it is soft and spongy. I should think there are two or three hundred feet of vegetable matter beneath my feet; and it seems as if I could shake acres of it all round.

" I see an island of higher ground in this swamp, with a dead tree twenty or thirty feet high upon it. I had a glimpse just then of an enormous lizard-like animal."

Such examinations have given me a more vivid, and, at the same time, what seems to be a more correct idea of the Carboniferous era than I ever had, before investigating the subject psychometrically.

Many may object to the apparent abundance of reptilian forms that were presented in these examinations; but the number of fossil reptiles, known to geologists, in the Carboniferous formation, is constantly increasing.

According to Lyell, previous to the year 1844, no remains of air-breathing animals were known as low as the Coal Measures. In ten years from this time, that is, in 1854, the skeletons, or portions of the skeletons, of no less than seven Carboniferous reptiles, referred to five different genera, were brought to light, besides numerous reptilian footprints, made by animals larger than those whose bones were discovered.

From the great number of genera compared with the number of species, we may safely infer that the number of species of reptiles, existing during the Carboniferous period, was very much greater than that discovered; and that we have made the acquaintance of but a few of a very numerous family, whose portraits Nature has carefully preserved in her rocky galleries. And although, at present, but one reptilian form is known to the geologist in the Devonian formation, yet, I am well satisfied, that, during the deposition of the Chemung group, one of the higher groups of the Devonian formation in the State of New York, reptilian forms abounded in the waters, although not a bone or track of them has yet been found. At some future time we may refer to these early reptiles again.

EXPERIMENT LIV.

A peculiar globular fossil, about an inch in diameter, found near Evansville, Wisconsin, in the Upper Magnesian or Galena Limestone. It is, probably, a fossil radiate of some kind.

Mrs. Denton. Specimen seen.

" A remarkably beautiful view is presented. I see a shell more than a foot long. Near it are several singular bodies, having roots like plants and stems five or six feet long; on the top is a green translucent body, with a soft gelatinous covering, fully half

an inch thick. The interior reflects through the translucent green, giving a mixture of orange, purple, and
a tinge of pink. Among them is a large star-fish, or
an animal of that kind; it is covered with spines. I
perceive branches spreading from the top of that
green animal. (This water is poisonous, I believe; it
seems as if it would poison me now.)

"I see a long body, a foot in diameter, which looks
like a green feathery brush, collected around some
small body.

"Two eyes come before me, and disappear in an instant. I see that shell again, and another one, curved
and thicker in proportion to its length. The animal of
the first is retreating into its shell. There is something at the end of the head, of the same shape as the
orifice of the shell. The animal seems slimy. Some
of them look double, as if there were two bodies in
one shell, or two heads united in one body. I see
one go right into the shell, and the cover, I saw, comes
tight down and closes it. It does not seem to do it
often, only when it is alarmed. As snails thrust out
horns, so this thrusts out two bodies that resemble
them. There are bodies at the end of them that look
strange; they are brick-colored, and I believe are
eyes; the animal itself is dark-colored."

These forms are in harmony with what we know of
life, during the period of the deposition of the limestone in which the fossil was found. The Galena lime
stone belongs to the Lower Silurian formation, and at
the time of its deposition, mollusks, articulates, and
radiates abounded; and we do not know that any
higher animals than these existed. Many beautiful

radiates, with plant-like stems and flower-like bodies, must have flourished in the heated waters of those early oceans.

Having obtained a specimen of Potsdam sandstone, when in Wisconsin, I subjected it to psychometric examination.

Mrs. Denton.

" I see shells; multitudes of them, swimming and floating on the water. Everything is so small and delicate here ! There are many small bivalves. A delicate fan-like leaf comes floating along; it is lightish green, and looks as if it grew in the water.

" I see a shell much larger than the bivalves; it seems a univalve, but it is still small. Everything is very diminutive. There are many species of minute organic forms, but they are too small almost for notice.

" The large shell, of which I spoke, has the mouth covered with a flexible membrane, through which the animal sucks. This membrane it sometimes presses out, so as to make it convex at the mouth of the shell."

The organic forms existing during the period of the deposition of the Potsdam sandstone, were generally small, if we may judge from the fossils whose remains have been discovered in it. This was not, however, invariable ; for the tracks found on slabs belonging to this period, in various parts of Canada, show that crustaceans, larger than our ordinary crabs, crawled along the sandy shores at this time. Life probably existed in much higher forms in some parts of the earth than others, during the same geologic period, notwithstanding the general similarity of organic forms in contemporaneous formations.

EXPERIMENT LVI.

The Potsdam sandstone, which lies at the base of the Silurian formation in North America, was long supposed to be the lowest fossiliferous rock on the continent; and its fossils, of which but few were known, were regarded as the earliest representatives of life that existed in the ocean, at that period, covering nearly the whole land.

To Dr. Emmons must be attributed the discovery of fossiliferous beds, on this continent, lower than the Potsdam sandstone. But it is hardly presumable that the Taconic formation, the name which he gives to the fossiliferous beds below the Potsdam, contains the remains of the earliest organic beings. As we have one formation, the Silurian, that contains no remains of reptiles, others still higher, the Devonian and Carboniferous, that contain no remains of birds, there may be a formation, yet to be discovered, in which no fish remains exist; another, lower, in which articulate fossils shall be absent; and another, still lower, in which even the mollusks shall disappear, and the radiata be the only representatives of animal existence on the globe. The Huronian rocks, largely developed in Canada, on the borders of Lakes Huron and Superior, are known to be older than the Potsdam sandstone, for that sandstone is found resting upon them; but the Laurentian group is still older, for the Huronian rocks are found resting unconformably upon it, showing that the rocks composing it were deposited, consolidated, and upheaved before the Huronian beds were laid down. How much older than the Potsdam sandstone then are these beds! These metamorphic beds of gneiss, crystallized limestone, &c., have been examined over a large area; but, as might be supposed, in such highly metamorphosed rocks, no recognizable fossil has yet been found, though bodies have been discovered that bear some resemblance to the coral *Stromatapora rugosa*, but no paleontologist, that I am aware, accepts these as actual fossils, though several have suspected their organic origin. Had not the limestones of the Laurentian group been metamorphosed, I have no doubt they would have yielded fossils in great abundance. As it is, their forms have vanished; but the heat that could destroy their forms, could not dissipate their influence, and hence the psychometer finds them instinct with life.

I gave to Mrs. Denton a piece of crystallized limestone, from the Laurentian rocks at Perth, Canada West, she being unaware of its nature.

"I see an object that consists of three leaf-shaped divisions, that expand and contract; when expanded, it is more than an inch across; but when contracted, it seems to sink into cells, somewhat like the coral polyps. There is a stalk about six inches long, on which this portion rests, which has cells all round it.

"I see many objects now that it is difficult to describe. One, about two inches long and one inch in diameter in the widest part, is round, grows on a stalk, and expands about two-thirds of the way to the top, and then diminishes more rapidly to an end that is not as small as the other.   It has some appearance of a crinoid, but differs from any that I have ever seen. The upper part branches out like foliage ; it has a pinkish tinge.   There are open places on the sides, through which tentacles are protruded and drawn in again.   I see those on the top contract and expand, but not as much so, I think, as the other.   I see many corals too, with larger cells than I ever saw before.   I can see the polyps very clearly.   There are many different forms here."

The Laurentian rocks, styled by the government geologists of Canada the oldest rocks of the globe, may possibly prove to belong to the Radiate era, the dawn of the morning of life on our planet.

EXPERIMENT LVII.

I placed in a box the following specimens, each wrapped separately in a piece of paper, so that no one by ordinary sight could be distinguished from another: Fragments of the Porcelain Tower, China ; Mastodon's tooth ; Bone of fossil fish ; Brick from ancient Rome ; Limestone from Mount Lebanon ; Temple of Minerva, Baii ; Obsidian, Mexico ; Sandstone from Connecticut Valley ; Limestone from Mackinaw ; Hornstone, Mount of Olives ; Fossil wood from Kansas ; Lava, Mount Vesuvius ; Antimony, Borneo ; Lead ore, Platteville, Wisconsin ; Boulder, Jaynesville, Wisconsin ; Silver ore, Mexico ; Aerolite ; White marble, Anti-Libanus ; Lava, Kilauea ; Conglomerate, Lake Superior ; Gold-bearing quartz, Australia ; Glacial-scratched rock, Wisconsin ; and Basalt, Fingal's Cave, Staffa.

Mrs. Denton took out one of these, no one knowing

which it was, and described what she saw and felt as
follows : —

"I can hardly tell whether I am on the surface or
under ground. I seem to be in a kind of cave, but I
do not have that chilly feeling that belongs to caves.
If a cave, it is a large one. It *is* a cave of some
kind, and yet cave is hardly a proper name for it. It
is open to daylight, with a wide entrance. I do not
know how I got in here. I do not seem to stand on
the ground at all, or on rock. It seems as if there
were water in there. How did they explore it ?
Parts of the rocks are drenched with water. The
cave is open to a great body of water that comes in.
On each side there are — what shall I call them ? —
pillars of rock.

"It looks dark farther in. I feel as if in water, and
not a great way from other land. I have glimpses
of land at a comparatively short distance. It feels
like the sea where I am. At the opening of the cave
there are shorter pillars that do not reach to the roof;
I see them on the left-hand side in going in. How
delightful to sail in there ! There is a grandeur and
novelty about it that few other places possess. How
high the entrance is ! The floor seems to be water ; I
can see no other floor. These are regular columns ;
they are not rough and uneven, as rock generally is. I
am reminded of Fingal's Cave ; it looks like the picture of it which I have seen.

"There is a sensation of sailing in there, or more as
if a vessel went dashing by me. I caught a glimpse
of rigging just then ; it vanished in an instant. I can
hear the sea roaring and dashing, both. There is

something terrific about it." (Mrs. D. had never seen the sea at this time.) "It has such a feeling of unceasing, never-ending motion about it.

"I see a large bird, and hear several screaming. What can they find on such a rock as that? I see no vegetation. They alight on some of those columns. How they delight in daring the dashing waves and the storm. I see a great many now; they inspire me. I see fishes in the water, but not distinctly; I just catch a glimpse of them now and then.

"The sensation of the whole is almost overwhelming; standing here all alone with the wide expanse, the roaring waves, the screaming birds, where human beings seldom come — how grand! There is a majestic loneliness about it that attracts me; I want to dare the elements with those birds.

"I think that roof has extended farther out at some time. Yes, a great deal farther out. I seem to hear it fall into the water with a terrible crash and splash. I think it bent round to the right and joined some other land at a vastly distant period. What a magnificent place this was once! How much we have lost of the beauty of the past! It has been more than as long again at one time; what remains is but the end of it. There are columns still remaining out in the water, at a distance from the shore.

"The land has been all around here for a long way at some time. There was once an extensive tract, which has sunk under water. The sensation I have, is more of its having sunk than of its being washed away, though that has been done to some extent. The land seems to have vibrated for some time before it became stationary. I see it rise and sink, rise and sink, over a considerable extent. I do not see how it could have been, but that is what I perceive.

"There is quite a number of islands around here. The main body of the land seems to have sunk and left them. I wonder if some of them are not the tops of mountains."

Half the examination was made, before she knew that I had a specimen from Fingal's Cave in my possession; yet, had she visited it in person, a more accurate description of the cave and its surroundings, according to the statements of many visitors, could hardly have been given.

Staffa, the island on which Fingal's Cave is situated, is one of the Hebrides, or Western Isles, of which there are one hundred and sixty. Sir J. Banks gives the following measurements of the cave: — Length from the rock without, 371 ft. 6 in.; breadth of the mouth, 53 ft. 7 in.; and height of the arch at the mouth, 117 ft. 6 in. There are pillars from thirty to fifty feet in height, and the sides are columnar throughout. "As the sea never ebbs entirely out, the only floor of this beautiful cave is the fine green water."

Some months afterward I accidentally met with a description of the island of Staffa, by J. MacCulloch, M. D., F. L. S., in the Monthly Magazine for 1815, in which are statements that corroborate some of the ideas advanced during the previous examination. He says, "I took notice of a fact of considerable importance in the natural history of this island, which had before escaped the remarks of visitors. This is the occurrence of a bed of alluvial matter on some parts of the surface, containing fragments of the older rocks. It is most easily seen at that side of the island which faces Iona, and on the summit of the cliffs of a semicircular bay opening in that direction. The bed is here broken at the edge of the cliff, so as to expose its thickness for a considerable extent. But the same appearance may also be observed immediately above the ordinary landing place, where the bed has also been broken. The stones which it contains are all rounded, and of various, often considerable, dimensions, and they exhibit specimens of granite, gneiss, micaceous schists, quartz, and red sandstone. Together with these are some rolled pieces of basalt.

" Here then is a circumstance in the mineral history of Staffa, adventitious it is true, but involving difficulties of no small importance. If we cast our eyes on the map, we shall perceive that it is embayed in a large sinuosity formed in the island of Mull, and nearly enclosed on the opposite side by Iona and the Treshanish islands. Beyond the latter a second line is drawn by Tiney and Coll; while to the north, but at a greater distance, are placed the islands of Muck, Rum, Egg, Canna and Sky." After thus examining the whole ground, he says that he has arrived at the conclusion that " Staffa has formed part of one continuous land with the islands of Coll, Tiny, and Mull." He is of the opinion, however, that the separation was caused by the sea wearing away the missing land, and leaving the islands as we now find them.

EXPERIMENT LVIII.

Mother-of-pearl opal, southwest of Lake Yajoa. Nicaragua.

Mrs. Denton. Specimen unseen and unknown.

" I see the action of electricity on fine particles of matter. A flat, circular surface appears, composed of fine particles of matter, segregated from the sur· rounding rock by electrical forces.

" I see a number of persons that seem quite busy; they are in a row, and are bent over doing something. This is a mountainous district, but the mountains do not seem to be in one continuous chain; the peaks are scattered. Between the mountains are broad lands that are to some extent inhabited. I see a village off at a distance; I think it stands on high table-land; I have to look between mountain peaks to see it. I see this like a panoramic view; I do not seem to be there.

" Near me is a deep chasm, very deep; yet there is land above me, — heights on either side. The country has quite a peculiar appearance, unlike any country I have ever been in before. There is a kind of dark shade to everything; it may be some peculiarity of the foliage, but I do not know.

" There is a human influence about this that is foreign; it is the influence of a people I am not familiar with. Their influence is singular; I cannot see them, but I feel their spirit. They might be called civilized, but they do not take the interest in art, science, or intellectual investigations that enlightened people do. They seem very well satisfied with things as they are.

" They are religious, but their religion does not seem to affect their conduct much; it does not enter into the soul. They may be very tenacious of their faith, and observe the ceremonies of the church with great precision, but their standard of morals is low; they lack strength of intellect and power of thought.

"One character comes before me every few minutes, — a team-driver. He carries a long whip, and shouts and sings by himself; shouts to his mules, and jumps on one and rides, instead of getting into his cart. Occasionally he sits on one side, like a woman. It seems as if he had no purpose in life beyond the enjoyment of the present. He comes up before me, among those hills and mountains, with his team. I think he comes from that village I saw. He wears a short kind of frock overcoat, loose pants, that look odd, and has a slouched hat.

"It seems to me I could spend months in wandering among these mountains, ravines, and deep cañons, — some of them so deep I cannot see the bottom of them. I cannot tell how the people manage to travel in this country, and yet they seem to do so, for I see roads here and there.

"This seems to me to be a district where either precious stones or precious metals are obtained, and I think those people, that were stooping, must have been engaged in getting something valuable, either out of the stream or out of the rock. There is very pure water in streams here, but it does not remain in sight for a great distance, they wind among the hills so. A beginning has hardly been made in developing the mineral wealth of this country; it seems so quiet, so utterly undisturbed. Why has there not been a different class of people here?

"At one place, underground, is an opening, deep and narrow, a kind of chasm, in which there are treasures. What a pure feeling there is about them; they must be precious stones, for I do not feel the metallic influence which gold gives. There is the common rock of the country, and these loose fragments of fine material. This place in which I now am, seems like an underground cañon the rushing waters have been wearing for ages; there is some water there now. At the bottom are precious stones in wonderful abundance. The feeling of purity connected with them is delightful. Some have been gathered from the surface, but underground, is wealth they never dreamed of."

It is unnecessary for me to dwell upon this examination; the description given of the country and its inhabitants will be acknowledged, by those who are acquainted with them, to be correct; while the psychometer plucks out the heart of the secret of the specimen under examination.

EXPERIMENT LIX.

One evening in December, 1862, when trying a crystal of amethystine quartz from St. Catherine's Bay, on the Saguenay, a tributary of the St. Lawrence, Mrs. Denton seemed to obtain, very readily, comprehensive views of the country to the north of there, and eventually appeared to pass into the polar regions, though nothing of the kind was anticipated when the experiment commenced.

" The Hudson's Bay region is a great deal warmer than I supposed. I see lakes and streams over such a wide surface that they seem like pictures. I had no idea that these extreme northern regions had as temperate a climate as they seem to me now to possess. I see a large river, much larger than I expected to find in this region. I see vast mountains of ice and snow. I do not know where I am, but I seem beyond the limit of the land, on the ice.

"In the distance are mountains that look as if they were land. Some are very high, and one I think is a volcano; if so, it is in a state of eruption now. There is a bluish, purplish, soft haze around it, and a kind of mellow light over all. It really seems warmer than it does here.* It is so strange, it appears like another world. It seems a long way beyond the boundary of this continent. I fancy that must be the very pole itself. There is water between me and it. It does not seem as cold as I should have expected to find it, and I see neither snow nor ice. The heat seems to come from the interior, and yet I cannot think it possible. There seem to be boiling springs there.

"Now I see mountains of ice and snow again; I think I must be returning."

SECOND EXAMINATION.

"How different from countries that I have previously explored! In the far north there are not those continuous forests to shut out the view, and hence the eye takes a wide sweep. The cold of that country, after all, is not as terrible as I had supposed. It is its continuity that makes it so dreadful. How those snow-peaks shine, as the sun glances on them! There are great plateaus all covered with snow, and beyond that the open sea, where it is much warmer."

* We were then in Quebec.

THIRD EXAMINATION.

"I go under the surface through the rock, for that is the easier, to the north of Hudson's Bay, on the western side of it. (I cannot control my movements when travelling over the surface, but diverge here and there; which is not as much the case underground.) After I get up there I go over the snow.

"I do not know where I am now, but I am drenched with water, as if a flood had rolled over me." (She looked at the map of North America.) "I do not think they have mapped that accurately. I see a great chasm,— very large; a little beyond that, and to the right, a rock towers up perpendicularly to a great height. I see round snow huts, and men riding in sledges drawn by dogs of some kind.

"I am among those icebergs, — stationary ones, however,— and mountains of snow again. Those mountains of ice are magnificent. I see now a long break in them. They stand up on both sides like two walls; and there is a long, straight opening through which I see for a great distance. The sides are so even that it looks like a way cut through. There is water at the bottom. It widens as I go along. It is now a broad channel, and I can see the water move in it. As I go up, it moves down. How water can run there I do not see; for there are mountains of ice on each side. There is a slope back from the water; then the ice rises in peaks. Now I come to a broad sheet of water; I cannot see how broad. I am much farther west than I was before. I have come by a different route. It is difficult to go farther north. I see the same hazy appearance that I did before; the same looking hills;

so far away that I can but just distinguish them. I have great difficulty in getting there. I keep coming back, and it requires great effort to go forward. There are hot springs in the sea, or inland near the sea. I see steam that rises from them. What a peculiar, yellowish, hazy light that is."

FOURTH EXAMINATION.

"I seem to be right there. There is the same singular light; the same hills and mountains. I am nearer than I was before. I see a volcano. I can imagine that to be the very pole itself, it looks so central. The rocks are more naked than I at first thought. I see spires of bare rocks, and nothing anywhere but hills and rocks. This side of it is a body of water, bounded on the south by mountains of ice and snow. It looks different, now that I am so much nearer. There is the same mellow, warm-looking light. Occasionally it seems colder than at other times. Sometimes it seems warm as summer. I see one or more streams of water. One of them is as wide as the Ohio River at Cincinnati, but not nearly as deep. It runs over and through naked rocks; not in a channel like our rivers; but spreads as they slope back, washing the whole surface of the bare rock. I see several orifices, out of which smoke is issuing."

The question of an open polar sea is one that has been frequently discussed, and many facts have been given in favor of it, especially by Dr. Kane. I was surprised on reading his Arctic Explorations, subsequently to the previous experiment, to find how much

the account given by Mr. Morton resembles the description given by Mrs. Denton, though she had never
seen it.   When an unbroken sheet of ice covered the
sea to the east, west, and south, Mr. Morton com
menced his journey due north, over snow-drifts, and
among icebergs, some of them more than a mile long.
After travelling four days, they discovered a channel
of open water, widening as they continued northward,
the water of which was several degrees above the
freezing point.   Still continuing their journey northward, the ice on the side of the channel became rotten,
and the snow wet and pulpy, until eventually they
found the waves beating upon the naked rock, the
channel having expanded into an iceless sea, which
they viewed from a cliff of considerable height, and
over which the wind blew from the north for thirty-six
hours, and yet failed to bring down any ice; indicating,
most plainly an extensive open sea beyond.   Supposing
this to be true, we have yet to learn the cause of this
remarkable condition of things.

EXPERIMENT LX.

The value of psychometry to the archeologist may be
seen from the five following experiments, which were
made as usual; the specimen being unseen, and no
knowledge of it given.

A small piece of mosaic pavement, dug up at Cicero's villa, at Tusculum, on a hill near Frascabi, fifteen
miles from Rome, and taken to England, October 15,
1760.

If we can obtain the influence of fishes, birds, and
beasts that existed millions of years ago, why not the

influence of men who lived during the last few thou
sand years, and thus glean facts of which the historian
is profoundly ignorant? Possibly, said I to myself,
this little fragment was pressed by the foot of the
great Roman orator; and if not, it may have seen him,
and treasured his likeness in its heart. I gave it to
my sister Anne, not a word being said with regard to
its character.

"I see a dense forest. The trees are very high.
Under them I see a mastodon, or something of that
kind. I see its head more distinctly than I ever did
before." (Come down to more modern times, I said.)
"I see nothing now but what I might call a milk house,
or more properly, perhaps, a grotto. There is a spring
near it, and trees around it. I see a hill, and an old
man walking round, who wears knee-breeches. A dog
is with him that looks like a carriage-dog. There is a
house near,— a large one. The place is evidently in
the country. There is a large porch in front of the
house, and gravel walks around it. The windows look
large." (Describe the man.) "The man is not tall.
He wears a dark blue, swallow-tailed coat, with brass
buttons. His hair is long, and he looks as if he wore
a wig or a cue. There are ruffles on his shirt, and he
has a very ancient look. He has a prominent nose, is
quick to perceive; has large locality, and is benevolent. He is not proud, but has confidence enough in
himself to be manly without being pompous. Consci-
entiousness and caution are well developed, and he has
great force and energy. His activity is connected in
some way with benevolence. He sits down upon a
seat under the trees, and a tall lady stands near, talk·

ing to him. She is dressed in very ancient style; short waist, long skirts, and no hoops; and has a large collar on her neck. A girl about ten years of age stands near her.

"Now there is a man walking up the steps in front of the mansion. He is dressed in modern style, with light vest, high hat, and long pants."

These were scenes in this specimen's picture-gallery that I had not anticipated, and did not feel very much interest in.

EXPERIMENT LXI.

A few days afterward I gave the specimen to Mrs. Denton, she knowing nothing of its history, or of my sister's examination of it.

"I feel Anne's influence very strong. I see her holding this up to her forehead as I am doing. She must have examined it."

She then desired to know what kind of impressions I wished from it. I answered, "Surface impressions."

"At some distance from me I see a gravelly bank with trees near, and at a greater distance there are gentle swells. At the foot of the bank there is a stream. Now I see a cascade, not very high, but rather broad. (There is human influence about this.) I see the inside of a house, and several rooms. In one room is a bed, with a person lying on it. The person seems to be fifteen or sixteen years of age, and sick. The bed looks like a broad couch; and the head of the person is elevated, owing to the bed being raised at one end, so as to give it a gradual slope. The place makes me feel gloomy. There seem to be many differ ent influences in this."

SECOND EXAMINATION.

Something occurred that prevented any further examination at that time, and the specimen was laid away for two or three days, when the examination was continued.

" I see a large building with stone steps going up,— six or eight of them; there are high pillars in front of it. It looks like a public building, but differs from any I ever saw. A little way from it, I see another building; there is something very magnificent about them.

" I am now inside of some building. At one side of a room, in which I find myself, I see something high and round, covered with crimson velvet. Everything looks strange. I do not know how to describe what I see. The style of the building is entirely different from anything I ever saw, and so is the furniture, if furniture it may be called. I neither know what to call it, nor what use it is put to. I see carved work on the walls, but not very clearly, for the light is not sufficient to enable me. The windows are very high, and are either heavily curtained or stained, for the light does not appear to come through freely.

" Now I see two pillars about eight feet high; they stand near each other, and are adorned with beautiful carved work at the top and bottom; they seem made for ornament. I can hear some one in another part of the building. There are many persons here, but it is difficult for me to see them. I had a glimpse just then of a woman, or a man with a long robe on. Now I see a man who looks like a servant; he has a dress that comes to his knees; his pants are loose, and he has a kind of cloak on his shoulders. I could not see him distinctly enough to describe him.

"Strange! I see long lines of people standing side by side, but they vanish in an instant. They look like soldiers; are all dressed alike, have on their heads a covering, high and pointed, and something in their hands.

"I am now in the house again." (Try to find the owner.) "I see a tolerably fleshy man, with a broad face and blue eyes. At times he appears merry. He wears a dress that looks easy, something like a gown, but not as long as a gown. He is a man of a great deal of spirit; seems very resolute. What can he be? He is majestic, yet has a good deal of geniality about him, too. He regards himself as superior, and withdraws from others, though he does not seek to manifest it. It seems to me that he has something to do with those troops I saw, though that does not appear to be his life-work. He has a powerful brain."

Was this the eloquent old Roman? Probably not, for Cicero is said to have been tall and slender; yet, a portion of the description is in harmony with what we know of him. His military talents, evinced when he was proconsul of Cilicia, would explain the appearance of the soldiers, and the feeling of superiority, spoken of, is in strict accordance with the character of the great Roman orator, whose vanity seems to have been his greatest failing. At all events, we have a description in harmony with the time and people of the days of Cicero.

Long after writing the above, I discovered, in the course f my reading, that Cicero's house in Tusculum had belonged, previous to his occupancy of it, to Cornelius Sulla Felix, or, as he is generally called, Sulla, the Dictator. The description given agrees better with what is recorded of him, than it does with what is recorded of Cicero. It is said of him that " he possessed in the highest degree the art of winning the affection of his soldiers," that " his love of pleasure was greater than his love of power," and that " women, actors, mimes, and buffoons were his favorite companions to the last years of his life."

Where specimens have taken in so many varied influences, it is necessarily difficult to obtain any special one of which we may be in quest. A year's examination would be none too much for a specimen of this kind.

EXPERIMENT LXII.

A small piece of marble, about the size of a pea, from the ancient Christian church of Smyrna.

Mrs. Denton. She also examined the specimens in the next eighteen experiments.

" A large stream of water is in sight. There is nothing around but wild scenery. (When I allow my mind to be diverted from the subject, everything is thrown into the greatest confusion.)

" I am in a building, and at one side is a high platform, extending across it, I judge, and above it, a high window. The platform is not as wide as some I have seen, and it is higher up than platforms generally are. At one end of it there is a beautifully finished railing, with steps down.

" There is an audience of some kind in the room One person I see with something in his hand, that ex

tends above his head. It may be a musical instrument; it is hollow, and bell-shaped at one end. The
congregation seems earnest, as if they had something
important on hand. All seem to have something to do.
It is not like a common meeting; they listen attentively, and look enthusiastic; their heads are bent forward. Some of those who sit evidently intend to say
something. I cannot see the speaker. One man, who
sits in front, is writing. There is good taste in the arrangement of the room, and much fine, beautiful work.
It must have cost a great deal. It is large and spacious, and its general style is quite different from anything that I am familiar with. Off at one side are curtains, but I cannot tell how they are arranged.

"Now I see a mass of moving people. What can
that be they have on their heads? They are dressed
differently from those I saw sitting, and differently
from us. How much there is that I cannot describe!
It passes before me with great rapidity, like a flying
panorama."

SECOND EXAMINATION.

Eight days afterward the examination was continued.

"I see a large body of people; there must be thousands of them. They stand in an oval form, their
backs toward the interior, and their faces fronting me;
they are partially bent over. They have high, light
caps on their heads, that are quite peculiar. In their
hands are long spears with square shafts. Now, I see
another body at a distance that come and join them.
Each company has a banner; they put them together
and cross them.

" I can see outlines of towers and buildings. One building of stone I notice in particular; there is a door at the side of it. It does not look like a house; it is heavy. There are trees off in one direction, and a pretty country.

" I am now looking through an open door into a room, but cannot see far. There is a deep window, with a shade of some kind before it."

What an interesting picture of the primitive Christians this fragment of marble contains! What questions psychometry may be expected to answer in the future, about which theologians have been wrangling for centuries !

EXPERIMENT LXIII.

Small fragment of a flower in relief on the border of a garment, on a limestone slab, from Nineveh.

" I see a square block of stone, and another on it placed there by artificial means. The edges are hewn off, and the stone has been cut for some special purpose,— prepared for something ornamental.

" A great deal passes before me like lightning. I see several slabs lying in rows, but I cannot see them distinctly. I see another large slab, but I cannot see any of them connected with any particular structure.

" Two or three times I have had a glimpse of a pillar on those limestone slabs that I first saw. Now I see a slender pillar; on one side are open places, like side-doors, but I cannot describe them properly. Past and present are greatly mixed in this specimen. I see fences and houses of the present, though a moment ago I seemed ages back.

" I am in a building that seems to have been used

as a temple. It is deserted, part of it broken down and gone; and it seems like the ruins of some temple or place of worship. Trees seem to have grown all around, and even in it, they come up so before me. There seems to have been a great deal of labor expended upon the building. At one door there is an opening, with two short pillars that seem to have been erected as ornaments to the entrance. There is a kind of railing that comes around to the door. It is a very large building, with apartments divided off by pillars and arches, where curtains probably hung."

These descriptions are of course very fragmentary. We could have done much better if we could have had more favorable conditions. Many of these experiments were made at hotels, in the evening, after my lectures were over, and we were both much fatigued by the labors of the day. I present them merely as evidences of what may be accomplished by persons of means and leisure, and who have cultivated these wonderful powers from their youth. The imagination cannot overleap the eventual realization.

EXPERIMENT LXIV.

A small piece of the porcelain tower of China.

"I am in a room. A little way from here there is a mound or elevation, very regular in shape, with a tree in the centre. I am in the room again. There is something peculiar in its style. It is massive, with dark-colored walls, adorned with carved work, that I cannot see very distinctly. It seems to be divided by curtains, and in connection with them there is beautiful carved and ornamental work. The room has raised seats, or narrow platforms, the whole length and on both sides. It seems to me to be in a different climate from this; it must be farther south, for it is ↑ armer, and the vegetation is more luxuriant.

"I get the idea of a place used as a temple — a gorgeous, magnificent place. I *feel* that influence about it, irrespective of anything I have seen as yet. I go back into the room; it is difficult to keep out. The sides are more clearly visible to me now; they are gorgeously festooned with gilt leaves and flowers arranged in clusters, with vines running from one to the other. What wealth it must have required to make such a temple as this !

"I obtain the influence of a people whose politics and religion are united; both seem blended in this room. What crowds of people ! too many for me to individualize any of them. Now I see two or three more definitely. Their head covering strikes my attention; it is neither a hat nor a cap; I cannot describe it. It is crimson, I believe, and edged with gold leaf. I see other persons with caps on.

"I see a place now where there are many dishes of silver and gold on a table. How rich this place is ! This is near the place where the religious ceremonies are performed by priests or leaders. There is a small room or recess where they go in; it is adorned with most elaborate carved work, and looks, altogether, much like a Catholic place of worship. I see some shining object extend from the ceiling to the floor. Broad steps lead to a place higher than my head; behind that is a platform, and behind that is another room with figures in relief upon the wall. Every lit tle while I see fire. On that platform I see two large urns. I see people again with something in their hands like flags. There is a pole eighteen or twenty feet high, with a turtle on the top, made of some kind of metal.

"I am outside now, where there is a grove. I can see the whole building; it goes up, then there is an open place with pillars, and a bell-shaped roof extending over it; and so it goes up several stories, one above another, to a spire."

At the time this examination was made I knew little more about the Porcelain Tower than the fact that a tower called by that name existed somewhere in China. But on reading an account of it in the Iconographic Encyclopedia, I found many of the previous statements remarkably verified.

The walls appeared massive, and well they might; for they are "twelve feet in thickness below, gradually reduced to eight feet at the top." It seemed to be "used as a temple," and it is a part of the Temple of Gratitude, near the City of Pekin, and was doubtless visited by multitudes of devotees, who left their influence, as well as their offerings, behind them.

The rooms were seen adorned with carving, gilding, and ornamental work; and it is stated that the walls of the room in this tower "are covered with fantastic painting, and bas-reliefs, and gilded throughout."

All intelligent readers will perceive much in the above psychometric description in harmony with what we know of the Chinese and of this Tower; and from the accuracy of this description we may see what may be done when the ruins of Copan and Uxmal, of

Thebes and Karnak, and of cities and temples yet to be exhumed, shall be fully examined and their story faithfully translated and recorded.

Old coin, probably Grecian. Specimen unseen by the psychometer, though its shape might possibly have given some idea of its character.

"I seem to be looking through a stereoscope. Fig· ures look smaller than their real size. There are two houses that look like boxes or play-houses. There is one with a spire to it that is quite small also. I do not understand this appearance. The one with a spire looks larger now. One house has a round roof. It seems to be solid below and tent-like above, the roof made apparently of some soft material. I am up where I see the tops of things.

"I am in a room now that seems strange. There is a box in it, having a trough proceeding from one cor- ner, and on the other side a double wheel. I see another singular object, a small trough, with a wheel at one end, as if made to go by a current of water. The trough is inclined. Here is something hanging against the wall that has round figures stamped all over it. Some larger than this." (The coin was a copper one, about half an inch in diameter.) "This is one of the smaller ones. There is a plate of metal lying down that has the coins raised above its surface. There are four or five sheets of metal standing near each other; they seem to have been hammered rather than rolled. They lean against a frame on the side of the room.

"There is a large roundish vessel made of metal, with bands or ridges around it. It seems to be for melting metal. It stands in a metallic scalloped basin. There are holes all around the vessel, and grooves, that correspond with these, in the vessel in which it is set.

"I see a solid body, with a bar attached to the centre, that covers three impressions at one time. Just then I had a glimpse of some person."

After the examination was over, she remarked that these impressions were not obtained from the surface of the coin, but from its heart.

There is one great difficulty in these archæological investigations; and that is, in describing what is presented to the vision. Much is presented that differs so widely from what the pyschometer is familiar with, that language is needed by which to describe the objects seen to those who cannot behold them. Special education of psychometers for particular branches of investigation will, in time, remedy this defect.

EXPERIMENT LXVI.

Small piece of hornstone from the Mount of Olives, near Jerusalem. It was taken out of a box containing more than twenty specimens from various localities; and during the early part of the examination I did not know what the specimen was, nor did Mrs. Denton know till the close of the experiment.

"I see what looks like a projection of a partly demolished breastwork. Near it is a rather tall and very solid-looking building, which seems to be square. From it a wall extends a long way, with buildings here and there for persons to go into; they do not look large, but are very strong. Some of them are round, and I think they were built for strongholds in connection with the wall.

" I seem to be north-west of some large city. I am above it, a little to one side of the central portion, and I can look down upon the tops of buildings which are below me. There are some very fine buildings. I notice one particularly, that I judge to be a temple or some public building, which is near me. It has a round tower, but that is below me. The city seems in great commotion, a tide of people flowing through it. Its size is great; for the influence as it comes up to me is very extensive.

" The whole influence that I receive from this is entirely different from that of this country. The climate is warmer. I can feel the influence of the sea, but it is at some distance; yet not so far but I can feel its soft breath. I consider the climate and country superior to ours, but the people are inferior.

" I see a tent-shaped building of three stories, with pillars and spaces between, filled with lattice-work all round; each story diminishes in size to the top. The building is large and round, but what it is used for I cannot tell.

" I see the entrance of a place that looks like a culvert, large enough for a person to walk into. It appears to go underground for a considerable distance, but is carried on the surface so far that it can be seen a long way off.

" I feel the influence of a stream of water, though I do not see it; it seems somewhat large, and runs I think to the south, with a pure stream over a clean bed.

"I saw a grand ruin, but it vanished in an instant. Large blocks hung as if ready to fall. The very ruin was magnificent.

"I see now a naked-looking mountain, that seems connected with a range ; there are green hills, too, on which are scattering trees.

"I am in a building that seems like a city under cover. In one place is a high dome. In a room I see a long table, and upon it what seems to be a crown made of gold, and decked with precious stones ; and near it is a silver bowl. This room is beautifully ornamented with carved figures of various kinds.

"The people live a good deal out of doors, for I see some kind of tables and seats outside of the houses, such as we nowhere see in this country. These people are not as well developed intellectually as we, though they are as well developed religiously, and are very ceremonious. The whole country seems permeated with the sentiment of worship. I have such a feeling as is described by the poet in the lines, —

' The cedars of Lebanon bow at his feet,
And the air is perfumed with his breath.'

I should think the Bible might have been written here. What an excellent place for a ceremonious religion ! I cannot tell how I get this, but it breathes over me ; the atmosphere of the place seems full of this feeling. It produces a joyous, worshipful sentiment, about which there is nothing sad or gloomy. It recognizes joy in everything. One of the Psalms seems to give this feeling : ' The mountains skipped like rams, and the little hills like lambs.'

"Now, I have a sense of destruction and desolation, that contrasts most strangely with the other. It seems like another age and another place, the feeling is so different." (I said, "Go as far back in time as you can within the human period.")

"I obtain the influence of a people whose principal business seems to be looking after their flocks that feed on the hills. They seem to have no idea beyond the present life. The country is wild, and the people live in groups of relatives; this must be the patriarchal time. They are not energetic, but fully occupied with their employments.

"My opinion is that this is from the neighborhood of some city on the Asiatic continent, between the twentieth and fortieth parallels of N. latitude."

Jerusalem, the capital of Palestine, is about thirty-three miles from the Mediterranean, and half that distance from the Dead Sea. The Mount of Olives, on which the specimen of hornstone was found, is a mountain or ridge lying to the east of Jerusalem, from which it is separated by the valley of Jehoshaphat. The elevation of the central peak of the Mount of Olives is stated by Schubert at 2,556 Paris feet, or 416 Paris feet above the valley of Jehoshaphat; and hence it appears to be 175 Paris feet above the highest part of Mount Zion.

The summit of the Mount of Olives is about half a mile east from the city, which it completely overlooks, every considerable edifice and almost every house being visible. Hence the feeling that she was "above the city," and could "look down upon the tops of the buildings."

The wall surrounding the city, and the towers upon the wall, seem to have been the first objects presented, and very naturally so. For many centuries they must have been one of the most striking features on looking at the city from the Mount of Olives. The tall, square, and very solid-looking building was, probably, the tower of Hippicus, which, Josephus says, was a quadrangular structure, twenty-five cubits, or about forty feet, on each side, and built up entirely solid to the height of thirty cubits. The altitude of the whole tower was eighty cubits, or about 128 feet. At the present time it is styled the tower of David, and is near the centre of the west side of the city. This tower, and the towers of Phasælus and Mariamne, were left standing by Titus when Jerusalem was taken and destroyed by the Romans. The buildings that she saw upon the walls were doubtless towers or turrets, of which Josephus says there were on the outer wall ninety, on the middle wall forty, and on the inner wall sixty; though the number is very much smaller now.*

The tent-shaped building, and the building that seemed like a city under cover, refer, I think, to the Armenian Convent, which is one of the largest, if not the largest establishment in the city. It occupies several acres, and is capable of entertaining 8,000 pilgrims.

Those acquainted with the situation of the Mount of Olives will see that a mistake was made with regard to its situation, which is stated to be north-west of the city, instead of north-east. What part of the Mount of

---

* Kitto's Biblical Cyclopedia, articles Mount of Olives and Jerusalem.

Olives the specimen was brought from, I have been unable to learn.

How strange that a flint pebble, on a hill outside of the city, could become imbued with the worshipful spirit of the people who lived in it! How much more must houses and churches be imbued with the spirit of the people who live and worship in them.

EXPERIMENT LXVII.

Piece of red damask that hung over the speaker's chair in the House of Representatives, Washington, when that city was taken by the British in 1814. It was taken to England, and then a piece of it brought back to the United Sates.

Specimen seen, but nothing known of its history.

"I see a long hall. I seem to be at one end of it. Straight before me is an opening like an aisle; it is wider, however, than I should suppose an aisle to be. It seems to be an open space where I am, and, I think, semicircular. I feel higher up than the objects around me. I see a short curtain above a raised place or platform, and, if such a thing would be allowed, I could fancy this had been cut from that curtain.

" There is activity of some kind here; something is being done. There seems to be more than one operating in some way. Persons move in and out, but I cannot yet understand what their business is. They become visible, and then seem to go behind an open place on the platform at the end where I am.

" There is a table, or something like it, and persons come to it and do something and then retire. There is a curtained recess at each end of the platform.

The persons officiating on the platform seem to have something to do distinct from the others.

"The hall is large, and all about is on a large scale. There is an air of general magnificence about it. The influence of this place is very different from what I perceive in churches; there is not that solemnity about it, but an air of cheerfulness, and, at times, even of merriment.

"Something is placed in front of me that shuts out my sight of the hall. It has representations on it of figures with different colors; it seems like a painting on canvas.

"One person comes from the right-hand side to the table, raises up what looks like a spread, and puts something under it. I see a door open."

SECOND EXAMINATION.

A second examination was made about a week after the first, nothing more being known by the psychometer regarding the specimen than the previous examination had developed.

"I think I know what this place is now; I see objects more clearly than before. It is a council chamber or hall. The person who comes out lays a paper on the table; he lifts up something and puts it under. These seem like people that I am acquainted with. It seems almost or quite like our own times. There is a great deal of earnestness of feeling here.

"I see seats with something up before them in front of each person; what they can be for I cannot imagine. I now see they are for papers and writing. I have seen pictures of places like this.

"They have something up for discussion now that is very amusing; awhile ago they were quite grave. They seem as changeable as an April sky. There are some who profess to feel very much, but I can see their earnestness is mere sham. They talk very glibly, but it is mere talk. It is sickening to contemplate them.

"There seems to be a gallery here; and those in the gallery take no active part in what goes on below; but they listen with attention, and some are amused, while others look on with admiration.

"Now there is a great concourse of people outside. It must be some political gathering, celebration, or something of that kind. I see several marshals. There is a platform, and speakers on it, and a large flag at one side of it; there are red and white stripes on it, I see. I see some long, broad steps, but cannot tell where they are." (What place do you think it is?) "I think it is the capitol of some state, or else of the nation."

Little thought the members of that house that the damask hanging over the speaker's chair was such an attentive observer of their doings; that it was reporting their proceedings with greater accuracy than the clerk, and looking into their hearts like an all-seeing eye. Little supposed that smirking hypocrite that, though he was deceiving his fellows, and receiving the plaudits of the crowd for his mercenary eloquence, the curtain waving before him was reading his inmost soul, and preparing to transmit to the future a faithful statement of his true condition. What a cloud of witnesses surround us on every side at all times! There is no darkness so dense but their keen eyes can pierce; there is no sound so feeble but they catch and hold it forever. No bribes can suborn, no eloquence can move them from their purpose; no lawyer can break them down. The brick can reveal the character of the occupants of the house, and tell tales that may make the haughty cower and tremble. Bury it in the ocean, and it still carries along, and will keep for ages, what has been committed to its trust. Break it to pieces, and you have but multiplied it; for every fragment, equally with the whole, can tell the tale.

EXPERIMENT LXVIII.

Piece of Sandstone from the walls of Melrose Abbey, Scotland. Specimen unseen, and nothing known regarding it.

"I stand within a very large building, in which there are several persons. On one side a gentleman is just going through an arched doorway; he seems a long way off, the building is so large. I see a semicircular place, but cannot imagine what it is for. This building is on a magnificent scale, very lofty and spacious. The windows are deep. (I obtain glimpse after glimpse, which vanish in an instant.) In another part of the building is a large aisle, and at the end of it a very high place, richly ornamented, which is separated from the rest of the aisle by a curtain. It seems intended for persons to go upon. Architecture and sculpture have lavished their resources upon it. There is some stone about it, but whether it is all stone or not I cannot tell. How massive it is, and how elaborately worked! no place is plain. There is some design or other wherever it is possible. The very railings are carved, and everything is beautifully figured.

" I see what looks like the corner of a building on the outside, with the sun shining upon it; it looks as natural as if here before me.

" Now I see Gothic windows; one that looks like three united together. There seem to be hills near here.

" I can only see detached parts of this building; it is impossible for me to get the connected whole."

SECOND EXAMINATION.

A second examination was made nearly three months afterward. There was nothing known regarding the specimen, nor was Mrs. Denton aware that she had ever examined it before.

" I am inside of a building, and can see a corner of it on the outside. It is of stone, and singularly notched and uneven. I see three arches side by side; but this seems to be a night scene, and things are very indistinct. I see in this way two domes, and a high pillar standing by itself on a pedestal that appears to consist of slabs, the broadest at the base.

" Inside of the building I see a great heap of rubbish, as if it had been cleared from one place and deposited in another. Where it has been cleared away I see what looks like the support to a floor. The building seems filled up to a great extent with rubbish. It must be a ruin. I see objects occasionally, and when I look again they are gone.

" I am in a place now where the beams overhead

are placed so as to make figures. I think this is a place of worship. (I can feel much better than see.) I have a sense of enthusiasm in connection with the worshippers that reminds me of the early Christian times. These people are ignorant and bigoted, but very zealous. There seems to be a contention going on between them and others. When they meet here their zeal is enkindled and their spirits renewed, so that they feel strong to resist the opposition they meet with, which is greater than religious people meet with at present, in our country at least. The religious strife between them and some other party is great. Here they feel at home to speak and plan. They have confidence in each other.

"I seem to be present at one of their conferences. One says, in substance, 'We must wage this warfare to the bitter end;' another, 'We must meet them on their own ground.' One quite sedate old man says, 'I am prepared for anything in this matter.' There is another party, less bitter in their opposition, who are inclined to take things more moderately. I cannot learn what the subject is they refer to."

From the Parliamentary Gazetteer, of Scotland, we learn that Melrose Abbey, at the foot of the Eildon Hills, in Scotland, and the most beautiful of all the ecclesiastical edifices ever reared in that country, was founded by David I. in 1136. It was destroyed by fire, and rebuilt and decorated during the two centuries extending from 1326 to the Reformation. "The vast magnificence of the abbey, with its innumerable adjuncts and sculptured adornings, seems to have been the result of a constant, untiring and ambitious effort of the resident monks, powerful in their skill, their numbers, their leisure, and their enthusiasm."

"At the junction of the south and west members of the cross, a hexagon tower rises, terminating in a pinnacle roofed with stone, highly ornamented; from thence the aisle is extended so as to receive three large windows, whose arches are pointed, each divided by three upright bars or mullions, the tracery various and light."

What a beautiful description of this structure we have in Scott's "Lay of the Last Minstrel:"—

> "The moon on the east oriel shone,
> Through slender shafts of shapely stone,
>   By foliaged tracery combined;
> Thou wouldst have thought some fairy hand
> 'Twixt poplars straight the osier wand
>   In many a freakish knot had twined,
> Then framed a spell when the work was done,
> And changed the willow wreath to stone."

The description given by Mr. Hutchinson of the interior of the building, which is quoted by the Parliamentary Gazetteer, agrees very well with that given by Mrs. Denton. He says, "The floor is nothing but the damp earth; nastiness and irregularity possess the whole scene."

Are there any facts connected with the history of Melrose Abbey that would account for the strife that was felt in connection with its occupants? I think there are, for we learn from the same authority that "In 1269, John, of Edenham, the abbot, and many of his conventual brethren, for the crime of violating the peace of Wedale, attacking some houses of the bishop of St. Andrews, and slaying one ecclesiastic and wounding many others, were excommunicated by a provincial council that sat in Perth; and as Melrose stood near the hostile border, it was usually involved in the rancorous events of border feud and international war. In 1285 the Yorkshire barons, who had confederated against King John, swore fealty to Alexander II. in Melrose chapter house.

"In 1322, at the burning and desolating of the abbey by Edward II., William de Peebles, the abbot, and several of the monks were slain. During the reigns of Henry VIII., Edward VI., and Elizabeth, it suffered collisions and dilapidations, chiefly from the English."

So that what was seen and felt may be readily explained by what must have taken place in the history of this remarkable structure and its possessors, during these troublesome times.

EXPERIMENT LXIX.

Piece of stalagmitic limestone from the Rock of Gibraltar.

Specimen unseen, and nothing known regarding it. It was not known that I possessed any specimen from the locality.

"I see down, down; three apartments, one below another, but not all in a direct line. In the second I see three men, who seem to be considering the place and talking of its history, which they regard as worthy of note in some way. I think it has been a place of great interest. What interest it possesses now, seems more in consequence of what it has been than of what it is."

SECOND EXAMINATION.

Conditions as before.

" I am looking from a small opening out upon the landscape, which has quite a stereoscopic appearance ; there are hills, and water beyond. I see a very high hill, with a large notch in the face of it, about half-way up ; it is very wild, and yet very beautiful. This country is both hilly and rocky. I see cliffs everywhere. I am surprised that any one should live here, it is so rocky, uneven, and naked.

" I am now at the foot of a great hill of rock. What a strange-looking place ! It is very rugged in places, and in others smooth. A steep, rough road leads up the hill on one side. I cannot conceive how people get down without sliding.

" I feel the influence of a body of water, which seems to come in here and form a kind of bay, and then at a distance communicates with a larger body of water.

" On the top of the rock is a round, castellated structure, which is, I think, on the highest point. It is too extensive a building for a light-house. It has a somewhat ancient look."

THIRD EXAMINATION.

" This place sustains a relation in some way to other distant places, but what that relation is I cannot tell. I cannot see any physical connection, yet I sense influences passing from here, and coming from some distant place to this. I see what looks like a long, winding road, that extends to a large town ; it is crowded with people.

"I see the same castellated structure that I saw before. This is a picturesque country. I seem to feel the influence of the sea, though I do not know the distance to it. On one side it seems to come very near. There is a large town near here; indeed, it surrounds me, I think; but more of it on one side of me than on the other. There are winding ways all round, that give it quite a romantic appearance.

"There is something remarkable about the people of this country; they are intellectually strong, and yet they cling tenaciously to the old. There is great independence and daring, yet great veneration for ancient forms. They possess a warlike spirit. There does not seem to be any war in the country now, but they have the disposition to resist encroachment by the sword, if need be. There is nothing cringing about them; what they do is done because they will, and not because they must. I have seen in the English character something like it.

"I can partly see and partly feel chains of mountains, back in the country; they are not long, but there seem to be several of them. I feel the influence of the sea extending on both sides almost round the country. It may go all round, but I do not see it.

"I obtain the influence of very heavy structures. I thought at first that they were walls, but they are not. I think they are massive structures of some kind; they might be called fortifications; they are intended to protect the place from the attacks of enemies. They extend for a considerable distance. I seem to be more connected with these fortifications than I am with the city. It seems as if the approach of the enemy was by water; I can hear the report of cannon booming over it. The people are so resolute, determined, and strong that a powerful force would be necessary to overcome them; I should not like to be one of the attacking party.

"I am in a building now in which there are many apartments. (I seem to be in the past.) In one of them many persons of high rank are assembled, and on a large raised place sits a lady, who, from her appearance, must be a queen. Those persons are presenting something for her consideration; it is evidently something important. They are all richly dressed, and she is gorgeously arrayed. I do not know that this is the same place as before, but it seems connected with it in some way. Now, all have vanished.

" There has been much suffering in this vicinity, especially mental suffering; the people have been cursed by tyrants.

"This is not Switzerland, though it is rough and mountainous. It does not seem far enough south for Italy; it is not far enough inland for Germany; it is too mountainous for England, and it is not an island. It seems like Scotland in many respects, but I cannot really tell what country it is. It seems longer than wide, though there is a part stretching to the east and southeast that I cannot see. It is in Europe somewhere."

On turning to the map of the world, after some consideration, she covered, with the head of a pin, the spot where Gibraltar was marked. "That," said she, " seems to be about the place where I was."

The following description, taken principally from

the Encyclopedia Britannica, will show the accuracy of many of the previous statements. Gibraltar, a British town and fortress, in the most southerly province of Spain, stands on the extremity of a small peninsula, washed on the east side by the Mediterranean, and west by the Bay of Gibraltar. The top of Europa Point, the southern extremity of the rock, is surmounted by a fine light-house.

This may have been the tower seen, or O'Hara's Tower, which was built upon a portion of the rock 1480 feet above the level of the sea. Originally it was intended for a signal station and light-house, but being struck by lightning, is now a ruin. On the western side of the rock the hill slopes gradually to the sea. On this slope stands the town of Gibraltar, containing about 15,000 inhabitants. The town is connected with the isthmus by a narrow causeway, in the defence of which science has exhausted its resources. The most remarkable of the defences of Gibraltar are the galleries, excavations cut out of solid rock, with great difficulty and immense expense; they are two or three miles long, and broad enough to allow carriages to pass.

Gibraltar has been in the possession of the Saracens, Spaniards, and English; being taken and retaken many times. During the years 1779–1783 it was besieged by the combined land and sea forces of France and Spain. On the side of the sea they brought to bear against it forty-four sail of the line, and a countless fleet of gun and mortar boats, and numerous floating batteries, but in vain; though the besieged suffered for years the horrors of disease and famine.

It is unnecessary for me to point out all the points of agreement between what was seen, and what is known of Gibraltar and its history. Those who wish to examine this subject thoroughly, would do well to read and judge for themselves. Many of the statements made were entirely new to me, and it was only after considerable research that I was able to verify some of them.

I know of no time in the past when a connection existed between Gibraltar and the court of Spain, likely to lead to the vision recorded of a queen and persons of high rank. I give it, because it came up spontaneously, and future research may shed light upon this also.

EXPERIMENT LXX.

A square of mosaic from the baths of Caracalla, near Rome. Specimen unseen and unknown.

"I am in a very large building. Directly in front of me is a large circular structure, built as if there were a fountain in there, or a bath for water. It is quite high and round. To come in here I went up some steps on the other side, and down some steps on this. The two rooms are separated by what looks like a half partition wall. The room with the vat in it is, I think, a little lower than the other.

"Now that I am lower and nearer to it, I see the structure which contains the water is either square or nearly so; and has a circular basin in the centre, with a beautifully ornamented rim. The base of the square structure has two broad steps passing all round; and on one corner of the base I see an immense pitcher, which rises higher than the top of the basin. On an-

other corner is a large urn, standing on a massive
base. The handles are richly ornamented. On another corner is the figure of a beautiful naked boy.
It looks like a Cupid. All these figures seem to be
chiselled out of stone, and rise to about an equal
height. On the rim of the basin is a bird that looks as
if stooping to drink; and the whole rim is ornamented,
except where there are steps that rise from the base
up to it, apparently for persons to walk up and go into
the water. It must be a bath. What skilful artists
they must have been to cut stone in this manner!

"In one part of the room I see a large pillar richly
ornamented. Above the base the pedestal has figures
upon it in relief; the shaft is fluted, and the capital
is richly adorned. An arch passes over from it to a
similar pillar.

"I see something now that is difficult to describe.
It is about three feet long, two feet wide, and three
feet high. It stands upon a block about a foot thick,
and is rounded the whole length, bulging out in the
middle. It is hollow, and has over the top a dish with
a rim about three inches wide. It is made of stone,
and looks quite symmetrical.

"The influence of this room is that of great gayety
and voluptuousness. This influence is very strong,
and I feel as if it must have been frequented by men
and women, who, at certain times, laying aside all restraint, abandoned themselves to the intoxication of
pleasure and sensual enjoyment.

"I go outside of the building, and see a very large
and high pillar, or tower, with something like bands
around it. It is some distance off. The streets seem

narrow and the buildings high; but I do not see them clearly.

"I am in the room again, and see the upper part of one corner, which is richly ornamented. On the sides of the wall are varying appearances, but I cannot distinguish them. I see also a stand, apparently made of stone, ornamented also; there are lamps upon it."

This must have been, I think, one of the private bath-rooms, of which there were several, in the magnificent Thermæ of Caracalla.

Sixteen hundred years have passed, probably, since these pictures were impressed on the mosaics of the bath-room; sixteen hundred years since the influences of the voluptuous Romans that frequented it were communicated to them, yet how distinctly they remain, and probably would for as many thousands or millions of years; and thus are we recording our histories, impressing our mental and moral conditions on our surroundings, to be read by the coming ages.

EXPERIMENT LXXI.

Out of nearly two hundred specimens of various kinds, from different parts of the world, wrapped up in paper, Mrs. Denton took one, no one knowing which it was. She said:—

"1 seem to oscillate between the city and a country which is rough and rocky. The buildings in the city are high, and the streets being narrow, they look dark. There is a good deal of grandeur about it. The people seem to be busy, and move about as if they had great interest in what is going on. It is not merely an interest in physical matters, either. There seem to be two or three influences in this, son.ewhat different from our own time.

" Now, I seem to be in a long room of a large building. At one end the ceiling comes down lower, and is supported by pillars or columns, some of which have broad capitals that are ornamented with deeply-cut figures.

" I see a large temple.   I am standing, I think, in front of it.   The entrance is at some distance, under a grand archway ; there are stone steps in front going up for some distance.   This end of the building seems much higher than the other.   After passing through the door, I see a part of a very rich building.   It seems to be a place of a great deal of ceremony.   I feel the influence of persons about, but they are not as much here as in other parts.   The impression I receive from this place comes nearer to my idea of a Jewish synagogue than any other building.   I feel the influence of priests with long robes on.   What a great deal of ceremony there is ; but I do not obtain a very strong sense of devotion.   They seem to have lost the true devotion in the form of it.

" On one side is a place that, I judge, is for the priests.   All the work about it seems plain, but grand. There are no *little* ornaments ; but all is substantial. A great effect seems to be produced here by different colors ; but it does not seem like paint.   I cannot tell what it is.   It seems to be inherent in the material itself.   In one place I see gold color ; seems pure enough to be gold itself.   There are either precious stones, or something resembling them.   If artificial, there is a great deal of purity about them.

"I see three places that seem made for persons to stand in. They are near each other, yet separated. Persons seem to stand in them and talk to some one on the other side. I believe this is a Catholic place of worship, after all. I feel that influence now. Yes, that is it. There is a place connected with this that is very little ornamented, and seems gloomy. It is very massive and prison-like. I see a great many people outside. From this I obtain an idea of what may be done in architecture with sufficient means."

On examining the paper in which the specimen had been wrapped, I found it marked "Modern Mosaic, Rome." From what part of the Eternal City it came, I am sorry to say, I do not know.

EXPERIMENT LXXII.

Marble from temple of Serapis. Specimen unseen and unknown.

"I see the ruins of a building which must have been very extensive, or there was more than one. It was a magnificent structure. I can feel the influence of persons who have visited it. There is a feeling of reverence associated with it, which seems to have been felt by the visitors. There are long, large pillars prostrated, and what look to me like beams. I see stone-work about a foot high enclosing a paved space that seems to have been a yard at the back of one part of the building. It forms an arc of a circle. There is a great pillar standing; the only one that I can see erect. I obtain the shadowy form of the original building; there are many parts to it. The country seems low. I see water at a distance; I think it must be a sea of some kind; it hardly seems the ocean, for I feel the influence of land on the other side of it, though it is broad. I think there is a river near here too.

" Now I see ruins again. There seem to be huts here, or low, poor buildings; they look very mean by the side of this. I see animals that seem very intimate with the people. (This view seems recent.) The people are singular, and considerably removed from us. They seem quite out of place here. If they are of the same race as the builders of this structure, they have sadly degenerated.

" The surface here seems changeable; at one time level, and then hilly and uneven. Wandering tribes of half-civilized people have passed over here occasionally. The ruins look as if they were buried part of the time ; being covered and uncovered alternately."

The ruins of this celebrated temple are near Puzzuoli, in Italy, on a low terrace near the Mediterranean Sea. It has been much visited, and has excited great geological interest from the fact, that three of its pillars now standing, only one of which was seen, bear evidence to the sinking and uprising of the coast on which they stand. It was below the level of the sea, then elevated ; and, as Lyell says, " Showers of volcanic ashes, and materials washed in during storms, covered up the pillars to the height, in some places, of thirty-five feet above the pavement." It sank again below the level of the sea, and was again elevated ; but is said to be sinking now. Alaric and his Goths sacked Puzzuoli in 456, and Genseric in 545. These may be what are referred to as the "wandering tribes of half-civilized people," that passed over there.

A fragment of fresco painting from "Cicero's House," Pompeii. Examined under the same conditions as in the last experiment.

"I obtain a mixture of objects. I see a deep window in a thick partition wall, but there is no glass in it. I notice small statues and colored images of deities upon the walls, that are very numerous and varied. On a level with that window are pilasters with square capitals. (The place I am in seems to be low.) On one side of the apartment in which I am, is a balustrade, which divides off a portion of it; that may be for a couch or bed. Through an arched opening I see the shadowy form of a man, and now another one with something peculiar on his head. Both sit on something quite high, compared with the height of the place. They sit with their feet up in some way. The first I saw is beckoning to some one. The men's dresses are full; not tight, as men's are now. I see a head occasionally that does not seem real. (There are hills at one side of this place.) What I see is more elaborate than I can describe; there is too much for me to individualize.

"Now I am in a darker room, that is very beautifully adorned. In the centre of it is a structure built up and ornamented; there are steps to it. I obtain the influence of a place where they worshipped idols. The walls seem full of that influence.

"I have passed to a large room where there are pillars; the work about them seems heavy. The walls are all decorated with those figures; they are well done for their style, which I do not much admire. These people care much more about art than worship.

"I see a great concourse of people; but they are shadowy. They seem to be in columns. There is a chariot with one man in the centre of a multitude. They go into a large hall, and then out again. They preserve a regular order and are united to each other in some way. They seem to be drawing something. Some carry lances in their hands, and some have sharp-pointed head-pieces. I think they must be a fighting people; but there is a great love of merriment in their nature. It shows itself in these processions. In an engagement with the enemy, even, I should expect them to manifest it to some extent. There is considerable solidity about them too. They are fond of music. They think a great deal of woman, but do not treat her as an equal. Among the masses the women seem coarse. They are out of doors a good deal, and ·doing what we should consider man's business. This seems to be a war time, and the women seem to feel a great deal of interest in it, and would do the meanest kind of services to assist the men in carrying on the war. They seem to feel that there is much at stake, and they must help. I think they are preparing for battle, and the men I saw must have been soldiers.

" The street from here goes straight for some distance, and then becomes very crooked; farther on it seems to have been made for the convenience of the scattered houses, and goes from one to the other."

I was disappointed in the previous examination; twice before I had tried specimens from Pompeii, but without anything being said of the terrible catastrophe that overwhelmed this beautiful city, which I supposed would have been presented at once. I had in my possession a portion of volcanic tufa obtained from the excavations at Pompeii, and this I thought would be more likely to give the particulars of its destruction. It was not larger than a small bean, but quite large enough to contain a psychometric volume, as will be seen. All knowledge was carefully concealed from the psychometer, who was also still unaware of the locality from which the previous specimens had been obtained.

"I see colored figures on a wall.

"Now, I see a yard, but it differs from all I ever saw before. It is diamond-shaped, with the corner in front of me. I feel the influence of something back of me; it seems like a building. It is a very heavy structure. I do not see it, but I feel its influence behind and on each side of me. This comes from some old country; the influence is ancient. It reminds me of Dickens' song of the Ivy Green,

'That creepeth o'er ruins old.'

One side of this building looks out on the water; it may be the sea, for I feel the influence of some large body of water. The side of the building next to the water, and I think another side, have square towers rising up. I hear the rustling of long, heavy curtains in the building.

"In front of me, and to my left hand, the view is all shut out, and I have been trying for some time to find out the cause. It seems as if there was a great mountain, so high that I have to elevate my head to see the top of it. The abrupt rise of the ground here seems to have caused that yard to be made in the peculiar shape it is. That mountain looks volcanic, and there are smoke, and stones, and cinders, and dust, all issuing from it in a dense body. They are thrown up with such force that, for a great distance, they form a perpendicular column, resembling somewhat a tall chimney, and then spread out on all sides. The mountain seems a hollow shell to a vast depth, the crater at the top being merely an orifice of small dimensions compared with the great cavern in the interior. The mountain has two peaks, the lower one much smaller than the other, but much sharper. I have been standing in the space between them, and I now go up a little higher. I hear the mountain bellow. What a depth that comes from! The influences that produce this eruption seem different from any I ever felt before. How strange it seems that I did not see this at first; for now everything seems so insignificant compared with it. The amount vomited out is immense. It is not like lava, but spreads out in a great black cloud, that rolls over and over and covers the country like a flood. I can hardly believe that what I see is correct. It looks as if it would bury everything all around it. What a sight! There it goes, pouring, spreading, foaming, as it rolls down the mountain-side in great black waves. It seems to me there is water too, running down the side of the mountain. At first all seemed dry; but now the mountain belches out water that sweeps everything before it. It is washing away the cinders and ashes that it previously threw out. I see the water rush through the cleft between the lower and upper peaks, and sweep a vast amount of material down. What a desolation it spreads over the land! It is not a dash and then over, but it continues to pour out for a long time. The lower part of the mountain seems entirely buried. It appears to extend for several miles, and makes it seem like night, it is so dense and dark. There are occasional flashes that look like lightning, and others that are not as evanescent, seen through that dense cloud. They seem to be caused by irregular bodies of fiery matter shot up from the crater. I can think of nothing but electricity that could produce the tremendous force necessary to eject this material to such a height that it falls miles away." (Go below and see how it affects the country.) "There is utter ruin to everything below. I do not see any place at the bottom. It is a great barren field; or rather an immense desert of cinders and dust everywhere. (I do not feel the heat that I expected.) I cannot recognize any place. There is nothing visible that was there before. Even the water for a long way looks converted into land, being covered with a deep, dark scum of this same material.

" I feel the influence of human terror that I cannot describe; it is awful. I see no one; but the feeling is almost overpowering. I feel like screaming. There are many different sensations commingled; but there is a horror more overpowering than all. This is either Herculaneum or Pompeii. There is no fancy about this; it is too terribly real. Some seem to regard it as a judgment of the gods. There is wild agony, prayer, and blind dread. Now I see them. Some wring their hands; others throw out their arms wildly. I see no one injured; that is, I receive no impression to that effect.

"I feel the influence of some persons at a distance from here. Now, I see a very large crowd of persons, some hurrying along, and occasionally looking back; others seem to feel as if they could never leave, but are compelled to go to save their lives. The scene is agonizing in the extreme. I see one woman dart from the rest, and rush back, as if she had left a helpless parent or child to perish, that she was now determined to save; but she is compelled to give it up in despair, for there is a fresh burst from the mountain, and she sees there is no hope. A darkness almost as great as night is now around them. How wild they seem! Many know not what to do, nor where to go. They act as if they thought there was hardly any place left in the wide world for them. There is a town at no great distance, to which many of them seem to be fleeing. I feel the influence dividing off in different directions; but I think many who escaped afterwards perished. Such is the impression I receive.

"Those flashes from the mountain have a slight tinge of purple.

"I am in the city now, and, under the material, I can see something of its previous condition. I am surprised at their structures, now that I see them more clearly. Their architecture is not of that massive kind that I have supposed it to be. The place resembles a modern town much more than I ever imagined. There is a good deal of taste manifested in the ar· rangement of the town and buildings, and much time and means have been employed in making it beautiful and cheerful. I see a large open space that looks like what we call a square. In the distance I see a long dwelling; but with this specimen it is very difficult to obtain conditions as they were before the eruption."

EXPERIMENT LXXV.

I told her that I had another specimen from the same place, and that from it, I supposed, she could obtain previous conditions readily. This specimen she did not recognize, though it was the specimen of fresco painting, from "Cicero's House," that she had previously examined.

"All is in a perfect whirl." (Pause.) "Now it is more calm. There are multitudes in the streets on business. Many of them are collected in one place. It seems the early part of the day. Some never went home from here, they started off in such haste. They must have had some idea of danger for several days before this. There is a feeling of fear and insecurity among them, but the great catastrophe came so suddenly, at last, that they never returned to their houses again.

"Now I am farther back in time. I see a great many persons in the streets. What most singular-looking vehicles they have! they are straight up and down behind, and generally very narrow, as if intended only for one person. I can see a head sticking up here and there, above the odd-looking backs. The front part has a curve from the top, and looks better than the back. There seems to have been much labor and art bestowed upon them, but they are clumsy affairs.

"In one place I see a long bar or railing along the street, and over it there are long poles bent into arches, each end being in the ground. Business seems to be done there, for I see many going up and down. At times, I think, coarse cloth is spread over those arches to keep off rain or sunshine, or both. It seems to be a kind of market-place, and this is where, I think, many people were on that dreadful morning. I see a large building that must have cost a great deal of labor; it has a circular appearance, and is very different from any building I ever saw before. The lower part of it is larger than the central, and has arched openings all round it that seem like rooms. The second story has openings all round farther in. People seem to be going there.

"I am in the building now, in which there is a great number of people. They do not seem to take any part, but merely look on. I feel no solemnity about it, as in a church. In it I see an oval space. The people seem to be seated very singularly; I cannot account for it, unless the seats rise as they extend back. It is built in the fashion of an amphitheatre, so that those farthest back can see over the others' heads. There is some mirthfulness in their feelings, but I cannot see what is going on down there.

"Now, I see persons singularly dressed; some of them are on animals that look like horses, but they seem smaller than ours. Some of them are women;

one of them on horseback. There is an entrance, where they come in, beautifully decorated with flowers. I see one young lady, with small features, of straight and rather slender figure, standing on horseback near there ; she seems to have just ridden round. She looks beautiful. There is nothing on her head but a wreath of flowers. She has a light-colored dress, which is in good taste, and rides on a light-colored horse. The men have dresses on, that give them the appearance of possessing wings, as they fly round, standing on their horses. I can fancy some of them to be fixed up to resemble birds. Some of them are dressed in black. The lady on the pony is gay, merry and nimble ; the men do not seem so light-hearted. What a rider she is ! It is fearful to see her ; I can scarcely credit that any one could ride like that. I sometimes think, some of the men are dressed to represent dark angels, and she a bright one. This is a very large place, and is strongly built.

"I see a street now, in what seems twilight. There is an archway, and under it, at one end, is a statue ; and figures in *alto relievo* on the sides. I thought at first that it was connected with the market, but I now think, it is the entrance to that amphitheatre. On each side of the statue, which seems to represent a woman, is an animal couched.

"My attention is turned to the eruption again. The first thing that I notice, is that hollow sound from the mountain ; then a rumbling. I hear a kind of sharp, hissing noise occasionally. All die away, and the people seem to recover from their fright. This appears to have been some days before the destruction."

(Were any persons in the amphitheatre when it commenced?) "I think there were. Those near the entrance heard the screams in the streets, and then the intelligence seems to have been slowly communicated through the whole mass.

"I see and feel the rushing water now; that *was* water. There was a pause after the first outgush. Every eye is turned toward the mountain. A great many moved before the worst came. All the light seems to be colored; it takes its color from the cloud through which it passes. A purple twilight is thus produced, — a rather dark twilight. What a scene for a painter! In-doors it is absolutely dark, and the people are rushing into the streets in every direction. I see them carry off their valuables. They load them into their vehicles and drive off; others take loads of people and drive off furiously. I am now up where I can see them nearly all over the city hurrying in every direction. They carried off the more helpless, the old, and the feeble and sick, while the strong ones walked. I can see some of those with vehicles, ahead of that crowd I saw with the other specimen; they are driving with all speed, apparently to return again. I see some covered vehicles among them, but they look strange."

Pompeii was a city in Italy, situated on the river Sarnus, near the Bay of Naples, and, unfortunately for its inhabitants, within a short distance of Vesuvius. All the neighboring heights were crowned with villas, and the loveliness of the whole region, favored by nature and adorned by art, was unsurpassed.

In A. D. 63, an earthquake threw down part of the

city. From time to time, smaller shocks occurred, un
til, on the 23d of August, A. D. 79, Vesuvius awoke
from the slumber of ages, and poured out rocks, ashes
and dust, that buried the city and surrounding country. The contrast between its previous and subsequent condition is thus given us by Martial: —

> " Here verdant vines o'erspread Vesuvius' sides;
> The generous grape here poured her purple tides.
> This Bacchus loved beyond his native scene;
> Here dancing satyrs joyed to trip the green.
> Far more than Sparta this in Venus' grace;
> And great Alcides once renowned the place:
> Now flaming embers spread dire waste around,
> And gods regret that gods can thus confound."

The younger Pliny, who was an eye-witness of the
eruption that destroyed the city, gives us a very interesting narrative of it, many portions of which corroborate the statements made during the preceding examination. He tells us that a cloud was seen to ascend
from Mount Vesuvius, of very unusual size and shape.
" I cannot give a more exact description of its figure,
than by resembling it to that of a pine tree, for it shot
up a great height in the form of a trunk, which extended itself at the top into a sort of branches; occa-
sioned, I imagine, either by a sudden gust of air that
impelled it, the force of which decreased as it advanced upwards, or the cloud itself, being pressed
back again by its own weight, expanded in this manner. It appeared sometimes bright and sometimes
dark and spotted, as it was more or less impregnated
with earth and cinders."

For many days previous to the eruption there had

been earthquake shocks, but on that night they were particularly violent. The next morning, which ushered in no daylight, the cloud seemed to descend and cover the whole ocean. Pliny and his mother fled for their lives, and he says: —

. . .   " The ashes now began to fall upon us, though in no great quantity. I turned my head, and observed behind us a thick smoke, which came rolling after us like a torrent. I proposed, while we had yet any light, to turn out of the high road, lest we should be pressed to death in the dark by the crowd that followed us. We had scarce stepped out of the path, when darkness overspread us, not like that of a cloudy night, or when there is no moon, but of a room when it is shut up, and all the lights extinct. Nothing then was to be heard but the shrieks of women, the screams of children, and the cries of men; some calling for their children, others for their parents, others for their husbands, and only distinguishing each other by their voices; one lamenting his own fate, another that of his family; some wishing to die from the very fear of dying; some lifting their hands to the gods; but the greater part imagining that the last and eternal night was come, which was to destroy the gods and the world together."

Mrs. Denton, it may be proper to say, had never read this account of Pliny's, nor in fact any description of the event she so truthfully describes.

There is one statement made by the psychometer that is contrary to the generally received opinion respecting the phenomena attending the destruction of Pompeii. It is generally supposed that ashes, falling as

the snow falls, in process of time enveloped the city;
but, according to the preceding examination, water
vomited from Vesuvius, and sweeping the loose ashes
along with its current, must have contributed materially to the catastrophe.   There are many facts, which
have been brought to light by the excavations at Pompeii, which are in harmony with this idea.

Various skeletons that have been discovered were
found enclosed in hardened tuff, which appears to
have flowed around them, for in some cases perfect
casts of bodies have been found; as in the case of a
woman found in a cellar, with an infant in her arms.
Casts have been recently discovered, so perfect, that in
pouring into them plaster-of-Paris, there were formed
statues of the ancient Romans, true to the life.   Lyell
informs us that a mask imbedded in tuff has left a cast,
the sharpness of which has been compared to those in
plaster-of-Paris; the mask was not in the least degree
scorched, as if it had been imbedded in heated matter.
The cellars and vaults of Pompeii are filled with matter that seems to have flowed in, which can hardly be
accounted for, except by streams of mud resulting
from a flow of water from the mountain; for no quantity of rain upon the dry ashes and cinders could have
caused such a flow.

It is generally considered that the Roman amphithe-
atres were devoted exclusively to gladiatorial shows.
What was seen in the experiment, however, more
nearly resembles our modern circus performances.   I
have no historical evidence to offer in favor of what
was thus seen, except the fact, which some may think
of but little importance in this connection, that when

the amphitheatre at Pompeii was first opened, paintings in fresco were found, representing gladiators, min-
strels, musicians, and *winged genii.* These latter may
have been what were seen represented.

EXPERIMENT LXXVI.

A piece of charcoal from a beam in Herculaneum.
Conditions as in previous experiment.

"I see low buildings on a low piece of land, that
looks to me like an island; but that is perhaps a mistake. The buildings are so far away that they may
look lower than they really are. I am on high ground,
and look down upon them; and from where I am they
have quite a hut-like look. South and southeast of the
land there is water; the northern part seems higher."
(Long pause.) "There are many and conflicting influences in this.

"I obtain the influence of a city, of a palace, and
again, of a garden and water. The palace, as I call it,
is a large building and highly decorated, and has a pa-
latial appearance, at all events. There is an extensive
garden attached to it. (There seems to be a mixture
of present and past that I do not understand.) This
seems to be near the sea; I feel the influence of it,
and see ships that stop at a point near here; I should
think within the limits of the city. There is a curious
mingling of modern sensations with ancient appearances, and I cannot imagine the cause of it. Either I
obtain two different ages mixed together, or there is a
very distinct difference between one part of the inhabitants and another part. Yes, I obtain the influence
of the city; one part of the inhabitants seems refined,

in many respects, and the other, coarse, uncultivated.
The difference between them is very marked; but I
do not exactly give it. In this palace there is great
refinement and cultivation, but it is different from
ours; it seems occupied by a different people. I feel
that their customs would appear very singular to us.
They must recognize caste in a very different way
from what we do. There seem to be two distinct
castes, that do not mingle; the distinction between
them does not arise from intellect in any way, but
from wealth; there may be an intermediate class.
There is a great deal here that is rich and magnificent.

"There seem to be hills beyond where I am. I do
not think that was an island that I saw, but a low place
extending into the water. In some places I see women doing out-of-door work, but there are some too
much refined for that. There is a great deal that is
romantic in the appearance of this city. On the city
heights is a great gorge, with something built over it
like a bridge. There must be a good many inhabitants in that upper part of the city. The people are
much engaged in fruit-growing, I think. I see extensive grounds covered with vegetation. It may consist
of vines; but there seem to be fruits, that are not
grown in this country. Many people are engaged in
attending to them. I judge it is a warmer climate
than this. Some of the women appear quite mascu-
line in their habits; they attend to the fruits and
grounds, and drive teams. They have no long skirts,
their dresses are quite scant; I cannot tell what they
are made of.

"I now obtain the influence of the country around. I see very high cliffs, and, at some distance, there is a range of country that has a volcanic appearance; at all events, I obtain that sensation from it. I should not be surprised if they felt earthquake shocks here; they certainly feel, occasionally, interior disturbances of some kind, and they are quite strong at times. I am on the Eastern Continent somewhere, for there is an oriental appearance about the people and country. This is from some country facing the south or southward, and the sea lies toward the south. I see several spires in different parts of the city. I am part of the way up the heights now, and I cannot readily go down into the city. I overlook part of it. I see shining appearances here and there, that I do not understand; they are caused, I think, by something bright reflecting the light. I see steps that go up to the higher parts of the city. In some places they go up very steep to great heights, where teams cannot go, unless by very circuitous roads.

"The religion of these people does not enter into everything as with the Egyptians. There is a good deal of show about it, but little devotion; they seem a perfect contrast to the Egyptians in this respect. The forms of the Egyptians were the offspring of the inward principle; but among these people, the form calls up the feeling."

SECOND EXAMINATION.

Continued next day.

"I stand in a very different position in reference to the city from what I did before. It is now in front of me, with the hills in the background. I see piles, or heaps, that are smoking — several of them — in the city; they are some distance from me.

"I am now in an immense building; it looks very singular; it is open, to a great extent, and very roomy. I do not yet see the whole; either I do not see the dividing walls, or they are not there. There is a long circular stairway, on which I see crowds of people. What an extensive place it is! it is used for great public gatherings. A great many people are in it now. It looks like an immense amphitheatre (what I see, comes up in fragments); the lower part open to some extent, and the people above. It reminds me in some respects of the amphitheatre of Pompeii, but the influence seems more modern, and the people more modern; yet, they are not of the present time. Now, I see more fully the arrangement of the place. It *is* a large amphitheatre, and full of people; but I cannot see what is going on in the arena. There is an unclean influence down there; it seems like a stable, though I cannot conceive of its being tolerated in such a place. It does not proceed from the arena so much as from its surroundings, though I cannot tell why; I see nothing to indicate it. I should think this would be a disagreeable place for refined people to visit. There are places in connection with this where animals are kept. I cannot see anything in that pit.

"I get the idea of its being consumed; fire and smoke come in and crowd out other views."

She took an atlas, turned over to the map of Europe, and after a short pause put her finger near the Bay of Naples, covering the very spot where Herculaneum lies buried.

This from a piece of charcoal, no larger than a hazel-nut. The chemist looks at it, and says, — "A fine piece of carbon, of the same chemical composition as the diamond; by no means, at my command, distinguishable from a piece made by the charcoal-burner last week." The artist looks at it, and says, — "This would form outlines of figures very readily, and I see no other use to which it could be put in my line." But the psychometer takes it, and what a revelation of sights, sounds and feelings! Who can tell the infinite number of pictures that it contains; the knowledge that might be gained from it in reference to subjects on which all history is silent, and yet subjects in which we are deeply interested? I believe that a true history of the lava-buried city, more full and more accurate than historian ever wrote of any city, might be obtained from that fragment of a charred Herculaneum beam. The eruption that overwhelmed the city, would have been seen, no doubt, if the experiment had been continued for a sufficient length of time.

I have been unable to verify many of the statements here made with regard to Herculaneum, from the great paucity of definite information, in all books that I have been able to obtain, bearing upon the subject. I have no doubt, however, that a searching investigation would result, as it does almost invariably, in establishing the correctness of the psychometric vision, even to the minutest particular.

EXPERIMENT LXXVII.

Piece of limestone picked up on the surface, near a limestone quarry, about two miles west of Chicago. Conditions as before.

"City scenes come before me.

"Now I see another town, made of huts, with a hill or mound back of it. There are many men and women, who look something like Indians, but smaller and different from any that I have seen before. In the town is a large, heavy, dark building, with a raised platform at the end of it, and an image upon it, something like a human being. The platform takes up the whole breadth of the building, and there are six or eight steps up to it. There are props supporting the roof, consisting of pieces of wood one above another." (Interrupted, and after a little time tried it again.)

"Similar scenes all come over again in the same order. I have,

"1. Glimpses of present conditions;

"2. Forest, all wild;

"3. Indian town, with trees in the distance. They have been taking out rock to a great depth here; at one place there is quite an excavation."

Who were these people that looked like Indians, but were smaller in size, and more advanced in the arts; who built temples, and carved rude images? Have they disappeared, like the mastodon that once rambled over the wide land, or were they driven south by the Indian Goths and Vandals who poured in upon them from the North and West? The soil we tread, the rocks we carelessly trample under our feet, abound with the records of the primitive inhabitants of the land; and we leave our traces, in like manner, to be read by those that shall come after.

I know of no traces of an Indian town in the neighborhood where the specimen was obtained, though such might possibly be found on examining the spot, for the situation is one well suited for an Indian village, as it must have been, at one time, the first ground in the vicinity of Chicago, west of Lake Michigan, that was not overflowed every spring.

EXPERIMENT LXXVIII.

A piece of stalagmitic limestone from one of the Tombs of the Kings near Thebes.

Specimen seen, but nothing known regarding it.

"What I see has the appearance of being reflected, as if near a river and reflected by its water. It looks like the side of a room, though, in some respects, it differs considerably from that. It has a natural feeling, but an artificial look. It looks to me like an opening in a bank; it has quite an artificial appearance, and yet seems so natural. I think it has been used by human beings. I cannot tell, though I have been trying for some time, what makes this union of the natural and artificial. There seem to be many influences mixed up with this.

"The human influences are of a very peculiar kind. I see a long train of persons going to and coming from this place; they are carrying something. Some have animals, which they lead, walking by the side of them; the animals look strange; I cannot tell what they are. These persons differ from all with which I am familiar. Two rows of them stand facing each other.

"I cannot imagine what this means. I see several faces that seem to be looking out of holes in a wall-like surface; they are human faces.

"Now, a great company, connected together in some

way, are moving something high over the ground, and again, I see others quite independent.

"I see some that look as if they were building; hundreds are moving, hurrying in every direction; but what I see is not distinct enough for accurate description.

"Now, they are all collected in a great crowd before a place where there is a large door. As far as I can see, there are rows of persons carrying something. Now, they have their arms raised up. Above and around that door the hill is cut away, so as to form three truncated pyramids, one above another, becoming smaller to the top, the door being in the centre of the lower one. All over this, crowds are standing, wherever there is room; some looking down at the spectacle below. All seem to have some common object. There is a sensation of gloom here, though the appearance of the people seems to contradict it; but that may be in accordance with the custom of the country. I think this must be a burial place; and they have either carried a body in there, or go and see a body, and then make wild demonstrations of extravagant, showy mourning, that we should regard as quite indecorous; there is nothing quiet or subdued about it.

"I see a portion of a high building, with three statues of human beings standing on the top of it. I see another building, with smaller figures on each end. There are many buildings in the distance. I seem to be in a city, or something like it. They are a busy people here,—like ants, moving continually in a hurry from one thing to another. They work together in large numbers; so differently from our people. They take great pleasure in their labor.

"I see a building now, that has four or five terraces all round it, smaller and smaller toward the top. The ceiling has a very substantial look.

"It fatigues me to follow the motions of these people. Every man in the city seems to work with every other man. Whatever is done, is done by the multitude. There is another long procession, just going round the corner. Some kind of animals — I think they must be camels — take part in the procession, not as beasts of burden, but as if they were esteemed.

"I see a square kind of opening, apparently an entrance to a building. If a building, it is a curious one. It is ornamented with sculpture, and reminds me of the cave temples of India, though I do not know that this is the same. The people have a darkish look; much more so than Europeans."

The Tombs of the Kings are chambers, hewn out of the solid limestone, on the side of a mountain, seven or eight miles from the river Nile, and near the ancient city of Thebes. That mixture of the natural and artificial, which the psychometer could not understand, may be referred to the artificial excavations thus made in the natural rock.

From the city of Thebes, through whose streets, at the time of her visit, the tide of life was flowing, and the tide of death ebbing, she sees the processions as they march with the embalmed bodies of the deceased to their resting-place. It was the custom to draw the bodies to the tombs on sledges, accompanied with long processions; on which occasions that extravagant

mourning was indulged in, which so excited her attention. Wilkinson thus refers to the Egyptian customs
on occasions of death and burial : —

"When any one died, all the females of his family,
covering their heads and faces with mud, and leaving
the body in the house, ran through the streets with
their bosoms exposed, striking themselves, and uttering loud lamentations. Their friends and relations
joined them as they went, uniting in the same demonstrations of grief; and when the deceased was a person of consideration, many strangers accompanied
them, out of respect to his memory. Hired mourners
were also employed to add, by their feigned demonstrations of grief, to the real lamentations of the family,
and to heighten the show of respect paid to the deceased." *

The present funeral customs in Egypt throw light
upon their ancient practices. As soon as a person is
known to be dying, "the females of the family raise
the cry of lamentation, one generally commencing in a
low tone, and exclaiming, 'Oh, my misfortune!' which
is immediately taken up by another with increased
vehemence; and all join in similar exclamations, united
with piercing cries. They call on the deceased according to their degree of relationship, as, 'Oh, my
father! Oh, my mother! Oh, my sister! Oh, my
brother! Oh, my aunt!' or according to the friendship
and connection existing between them, as, 'Oh, my
master! Oh, lord of the house! Oh, my friend! Oh,
my dear, my soul, my eyes!' and many of the neigh-
bors, as well as the friends of the family, join in the

---

* Wilkinson's Ancient Egyptians, Vol. II. p. 402.

lamentations. Hired mourning women are also engaged, who utter cries of grief, and praise the virtues of the deceased, while the females of the house rend their clothes, beat themselves, and make other violent demonstrations of sorrow." *

The great similarity between this and what Mrs. D. saw, must be apparent to all; but, to give an explauation of all that was presented during this experiment, would require a knowledge of Egyptology to which I can make no pretension.

From a gentleman in Quebec I obtained a small mummied crocodile, taken by him from a crocodile pit at Maabdeh, Egypt. Some time afterward I took a small portion of the cloth in which it was wrapped, and pulled it into fine tow; then wrapped it in three thicknesses of writing paper, and presented it to Mrs. Denton, who did not see it, and had no idea of its nature.

"I see a great mound or hill, with a place cut into it on one side.

"I am looking over the heads of a great many people, who are busily engaged in doing something, I cannot yet see what. I see a long, deep place, that goes away under the hill. I do not know what to call it. Near it is an extensive wall; but it does not seem to be connected with any building.

"The people here, are, I think, Egyptians; they look like it. There is an honesty about them that I

---

* Wilkinson's Ancient Egyptians, Vol. II. p. 403. Quoted from Lane's Modern Egyptians.

like. They are destitute of that hypocrisy which I have so frequently noticed, when examining psychometrically. They seem to carry their religion into almost everything they do. In all their work they seem to give expression to their religious ideas. The universality of this expression is truly wonderful. It does not seem to be confined to any particular place. They seem to regard everything as a partial embodiment of the Divinity, or an embodiment of some part of the Divinity. They are exceedingly religious in their way; the religious people of this day cannot compare with them in the habitual exercise of devotion.

"I see shadowy appearances of very large forms, some of which resemble human beings, but they are stationary. All the buildings have a solid and substantial appearance. The architecture is all heavy.

"There seems to be a dark passage to that place, that I said looked like an excavation. It seems closed up. The entrance looks very singular; I know not how to describe it. Light and ethereal forms are moving in the air in that entrance, some human, some animal. I could fancy them to be the spirits of those that are buried in there, for I think it must be a burial place. They seem as much more refined than common psychometric objects, as these are more refined than ordinary objects. One seems like a turtle; another looks like a rabbit, but the ears are not as large. There is a great deal about this that I cannot give, for I am unable to describe it.

"I see great numbers of crocodiles, some large and others small.

"I see hills, all of dust, that look as if they might be changed from one place to another; or, as if the wind might blow them away.

"I seem to oscillate between the far past and a more recent period; which makes accurate description difficult. I think those hills must be sand; they have too bright a look for dust.

"(There comes up occasionally a being of the human form, having a wild appearance, very different from the people I have been seeing.) These people do a great deal of work in stone, cutting it into many different forms. (I feel the influence occasionally of high rocks.) They are as industrious as ants in building, excavating and cutting. They work together. They have many projects, but are by no means idle dreamers, for they execute, too. I see objects that tower up in the air to points; they are distinct from the buildings, and seem three-sided; they must be obelisks. I see several of them. Now, I see a live crocodile, a large one, that seems to be in the street."

That the ancient Egyptians were a very religious people, there can be no doubt. "The Egyptians," says Herodotus, "are very religious, surpassing all men in the honors they pay to the gods."[*] A similar testimony is borne by others. "The Egyptian priests," says Porphyry, "profiting by their diligent study of philosophy, and their intimate acquaintance with the nature of the gods, have learnt that the Divinity permeates other beings as well as man, that he is not the only creature on earth possessed of a soul; and that nearly the same spiritual essence pervades all the

---

[*] Herodotus, II. 37.

tribes of living creatures. On this account, in fashioning images of the gods, they have adopted the forms of *all* animals, sometimes joining the human figure with those of beasts; at others, combining the shapes of men and of birds." [*]

How exceedingly refined must that influence be, which, passing from a small piece of linen tow, permeates three thicknesses of writing paper, and then gives to the psychometer the sensations recorded!

EXPERIMENT LXXX.

I had long desired to investigate psychometrically some of the human relics discovered in the drift deposits of England, France, and Germany; and after many fruitless inquiries for specimens, in museums and geological collections, chance threw in my way the opportunity I had so long desired. While in Montreal, in December of last year, I observed at the bottom of McGill Street several heaps of flint shingle, laid there previous to being used for macadamizing the street. This flint shingle surprised me, for I had seen nothing of the kind in America; and, of course, Canada was the last place in America to look for it. On inquiry, I learned that it had been brought from England as ballast. Though I was unable to discover from what part of England these particular heaps were brought, it was evident that they came from a cretaceous neighborhood, and I thought, likely, from the southeastern portion of the island. Among the flints I found two fine specimens of the echinus, and several smaller fossils, nor dreamed of higher game; but just

* Wilkinson's Ancient Egyptians, II. 109.

as I was about to give up my search, in the twilight
of a cold December evening, I found a fragment of
bone, hard frozen into the heap, which, on splintering,
proved to be fossilized; and on the next morning, in a
neighboring heap, I discovered some twenty or thirty
black or dark brown splintered fragments of fossil
bone. Some appeared like portions of the skeletons
of bovine quadrupeds, others of deer; one, the bone
of a bird; and a few smaller pieces, from the size of
the bone cells, I considered as probably portions of the
mammoth, or *elephas primigenius*. From portions of
clay attached to them, they had evidently been buried
in a bed of blue clay originally; they adhered strongly
to the tongue, and one that I fractured showed a
bright metallic lustre. Probably, said I to myself,
these were washed out of a drift bed, or more recent
alluvial deposit, by the waves, and thus became mingled with the shingle of the beach, from which the
sailors loaded them into the vessel; and, possibly,
from them I may obtain some knowledge of those human beings who inhabited Great Britain at an early
period. I accordingly took one of these bones, which
had apparently been cut with some sharp instrument,
to extract the marrow, and gave it to Mrs. Denton for
examination. She knew something of my ideas on
the subject, but had no faith in them.

"I see a head; the lower part of the forehead is
very prominent, so that the eyes seem deeply set.
The forehead is very low, and round and receding.
The face has an awful look; it is dark, and feathers
are stuck round the head. (It was merely a glimpse.)

"Now I see the chest and arms. It seems hardly

human; yet it is not savage and wild, for I have no such sensation in connection with it, as I have felt before in connection with early men. There seems a good deal of fun, frolic and good-nature here. The mouth is crescent-shaped, the face short, and the front head slopes on each side, forming quite an angle. I see an older and larger one, that shows its teeth, which are large. It is coarser and uglier, and seems very bad-tempered.

"I see one sitting on a log, his long legs hanging down, crossed at the ankles, and his hands between his knees. He is looking off. In front of him is a cave. It is sad to see such a pitiful object in the shape of a human being. I question whether he can stand perfectly upright; his hip-joints appear to be so formed that he cannot, though he sits comfortably. Whether this is natural to him, or is a condition produced by disease, I cannot say. Now I see him perfectly. I can hardly credit that he is human, yet there is a human expression in the face. His body is very hairy; it appears as if the natural hair answered the purpose of clothing. A part of the face is destitute of hair, but it is dark-colored. That is not a log that he sits on, I see, but a rock. He must have gone there frequently to sit. He seems to be in a kind of study; there is evidently some power of thought.

"I have a glimpse of another one, smaller, more slender, and less hairy. One hand is raised. (My excitement prevents my seeing.) Occasionally, I see part of the body of one of those beings that looks comparatively smooth. I can see the skin, which is lighter-colored. I do not know whether it belongs to the same period or not.

"It is rather dark in that cave; I can only see a little way. There is something in the back part of it, but I cannot see what it is.

"In the soft floor, at the bottom of the cave, are curious markings. It looks as if some one, for pastime or for play, had made a number of shallow holes. There must be quite a number of these beings around here, for I see others occasionally. I see one more slender than the first, and another larger, heavier, and yet smoother and more delicate. I think this is a female. She is fuller and more rounded, and her limbs are shorter; but her face is far from being that 'human face divine,' of which the poets speak, though I only obtain its general appearance. I see another female, smaller than the first. They are more erect than those hairy ones I saw, who are males, I suppose ; but it is strange there should be such a difference between them.

"I see an animal, in a kind of enclosure, that seems partly tamed. It is a large, herbivorous animal, and I fancy now that the first man I saw was watching it, till some one else came ; two or three of them taking turns.

"There must be a number here, from the influence I feel, — more than one family. All that I have seen hitherto, have been perfectly nude; but I see the back of one now, that seems to have some kind of covering on; I think it is a skin. The wearer is one of the fairer, erect kind, as most of them are that I see now. They seem much more human than the others.

"In that cave I see objects that I cannot tell the use of; they seem made of stone. Some are five or six feet long; but they must be made of wood, with a sharp point of stone at the end; they have a round end where they are handled, and I think now are used as spears for killing animals. I see smaller ones hanging on the side of the cave. There seems to be a belt of skin, several feet long, fastened against the wall, and through it different implements are placed. Some are seven or eight inches long, and others but two or three. Some are bulky, and look like hammers, while others are slim and sharp." (Are they made of flint?) " They look hard, and some seem to have been chipped, but I am not near enough to distinguish the precise material of which they are composed.

" I feel a great many of these beings about, going in and out, but I cannot see many. That cave is quite a large place. There are some implements hanging on the wall that are quite sharp; they seem to be flint. They use them to cut up their meat with. (I feel this.) They did not eat their flesh raw; I have the impression of its being cooked.

" I see green trees; the vegetation seems like that of a warmer country than this. I see grape vines. There is much more intelligence among these beings than those I saw with that specimen from Mount Ararat. (Experiment 83.)

" These dark ones do not seem as savage as I should expect. There is something mild and submissive about them. At a distance the face seems flat; the lower part of it is heavy; they have what, I suppose, would be called prognathous jaws. The frontal region of the head is low, and the lower portion of it is very prominent, forming a rounded ridge across the forehead, immediately above the eye-brows. The hair bushes up full in front and seems inclined to curl. I think there is hair on the chin and sides of the face.

"I see something peculiar at the edge of a wood. Between the rocks and the wood is an open space; and near the wood is something built that seems intended to shed rain. There are vines growing over it.

"I see an animal now, much larger than the largest ox; with large, long horns, three times as large as any I ever saw, that curve over on each side and almost meet under the head."

EXPERIMENT LXXXI.

A few days afterward, other and different specimens having been tried in the interim, I broke off a small fragment from the same bone and gave it to Mrs. Denton for examination. She might have supposed it to be bone from its feeling, but she certainly had no idea of its being a portion of the one previously examined.

"I see a rude bucket hanging on a cross-bar supported by two forked sticks. It is long for its width, and seems to have been dug out of solid wood. There is something around it near the top, probably to fasten something to, to carry it by. It is rough on the outside.

"I see a very low place, that looks as if made to live in; it goes up to a sharp peak. (There is some animal influence about this specimen, from the feeling I have.) That house is made by poles put in the ground and poles on the top connecting; then it is banked up with earth, and skins are put over it — so it seems. I see the poles have forked tops, and the top poles are placed in the forks. I see another, that is round on top; and in the distance are three or four little ones. I see shadows of people moving around; I cannot see any one distinctly. I now see the facial bones of a human being; the teeth are very prominent, the jaws large, and the front part of the face very prominent and large.

"I feel now as if I were in one of those places in the rock that I saw the other night. I do not see that long row of implements, but I am in a place like that. I see some great branching horns in there, but no animal. The horns are much longer than any I ever saw. There are two main branches on each side and a number of smaller ones. Between the two, short points stick up, that give it a singular appearance. It seems to be on a kind of seat above the ground.

"I see an animal lying down, that has a tapering face and nose, more so than a sheep; though it looks more like a sheep than any other animal I have seen. Its eyes are large. It has short horns, and is herbivorous; but what is most remarkable about it, and what I cannot understand, is that it has four horns. I see many things, but not distinctly enough to describe. Many that I see seem quite incongruous and must have been brought here; for instance, I see a singular-looking spiny fish lying on the ground. I have seen several times the head of an animal resembling an ox, but with a thin and short under jaw, compared with the upper, which is heavier than in our cattle. It has a curly front. The whole head looks very heavy.

"Now I see a face that looks like that of a human being, though there is a monkey-like appearance about it. I also see several persons trying to roll a large angular stone. One I can see quite plain; he looks like that one I saw sitting the other night. All these seem of that kind having long arms and hairy bodies. The face of one is toward me and the backs of the others. None of them are clothed. One looks like a female, with some kind of ornament bound around her head. I cannot tell what it is made of. I seem to be in about the same place and period that I was the other night with that bone, but I do not see any of the smooth people, as I did then.

"In rolling that stone, one of them seems to act as overseer; he seems to be the same tall, ugly one — the second I saw the other night.

"I see a very low entrance to a cave, in which it looks quite dark. The front of it, over the top, has an artificial appearance, as if something had been put up to make the entrance smaller. The climate is not warm all the time; sometimes, it seems chilly, cold and damp.

"I see now a point of land stretching into a large body of water that seems to be the ocean. On this side of it are many people down by the water. I wonder if that long weapon I saw the other day was not for spearing fish? I see one of these people holding up something in his hand, as if for some one at a distance to see. Another one is bent over. They seem to have a monstrous fish on the land which requires several of them to manage. Its mouth is open, and seems full of sharp, white teeth.

"Toward that point of land are more persons than here. Some of them have dresses on that reach from the shoulders to the knee, and are fastened at the waist; some are shorter, and others are unfastened at the waist. I think they are the skins of animals. They seem to be fishing, and are not very particular about what they catch. These are the smooth-skinned people, and the others are, I believe, either their prisoners or slaves that work for them. There is more intellect and craft among these, and they have a greater range of ideas. There is more calculation and cunning about them. The others seem inefficient compared with them; they may become terribly enraged, but they lack ability to accomplish much. These are shorter and stouter people; they have round faces, low foreheads, but not with that protruding ridge I saw in the others; they have flat heads, and nothing like beard or whiskers. The fairest of them have a dark, tawny look. I do not like them, they are so designing and selfish. They are largely in the majority here I find, and *they are the same people I saw the other night.*

"I had a glimpse of an awful-looking creature just then, with his hair hanging all around his face. He has an ugly-looking face, and his hair is terribly tangled.

"I see more animals penned up that look somewhat like oxen, but with thicker skins and less hair; they are of monstrous size.

"I see faces of some animals that resemble our dogs, yet they differ from them considerably; but they are more like dogs than any other animals with which I am acquainted."

Another bone from the same locality, gnawed by some small rodent; the bone seen, and the circumstances of its discovery known.

"The first thing I see is one of those hairy men sitting with his back against a tree. The same things come up that I saw with the other specimens, or nearly so; but I see the animals more distinctly. A great many are visible. One kind that I see resemble oxen, and have very large and long horns; they are larger than my arm, curve upward on each side of the head, and have two or three twists in them. I see one about as high as an ox, but smaller. It looks young, has no horns, and seems like a calf; it has the look of a yearling. So many objects crowd upon me, I am unable to describe them. One animal, that I suppose to be an ox, has frowzy hair, and thick horns, heavier than the others I have seen, but not as long.

"This must be a horse that I see now. Yes, I see two of those men on the back of one; they are going with great speed. They seem to have something to guide it with; but I do not know what.

"I see a long string of skulls of different animals; they are hanging against the face of the rock; the first looks like a human skull.

"Several of those hairy ones are here; first at work, and then at play. Now, I see them climbing up a rock as if pursued by something. (The pictures come up in such abundance, I cannot disentangle them. In whatever direction I look, figures are darting to and fro, singly or in groups; but so rapidly that I cannot describe them.)"

I advised her to lay the specimen down and try if she could see them without.

" Now, they seem less than the natural size, and just as if they were pictures. That is strange! it seems to me as if they were painted on the outside of my forehead, and I were just looking at them so. I almost turned round to ask you to look at them, they are so plain. Now, they appear more natural, and move more slowly than before, though I do not see them as distinctly." (She now put the specimen on her forehead again, and said she would tell me all she saw as rapidly as she could.)

"A man lying down.

"An ox-head.

"A place marked off, and the ground tracked round.

" Enclosure, with an animal in it.

"Another animal, large, unenclosed, and that looks tame.

" The sun shining on the water.

"A cave, with an arch-like entrance.

" Now I see a man with a club, and it seems as if some kind of fighting were going on. I see one of the smooth ones with a club in his uplifted hand.

" The influences I receive now seem more recent. There is more skill manifest; all artistic work seems superior, and more genius is apparent.

" There is a wide and deep river running into the sea not far from here. I see a place with artificial steps like wooden blocks.

" Now, I see some of the hairy fellows working in stone. One of them is doing something with a very large one. Now he sits on it, and puts his hands behind him, and leans back on another to rest. I see two in the water wading, with a pole bet veen them. Now there are a number wading out. That is a pleasant stream, but large and wide."

As we travel into the night of the past, in search of facts regarding the condition of our race at an early period of its existence, we find history burning with a dim and uncertain light, before we have advanced three thousand years; and if we had history alone to guide us, beyond this, in midnight, we should grope our uncertain way. But when history can no longer be depended upon, archeology comes to our assistance, and we continue our journey with light sufficient to behold the salient features of the landscape lying be· fore us.

We have learned from archeology that, prior to the historic period, men knew the use of iron, and fashioned it into tools for ordinary use, and weapons of war, and this for a long time before history gives any record of their doings. We also learn that previous to the iron age, there was a bronze age, in which men knew not the use of iron, probably, because they had not learned to produce heat sufficient to melt it from its intractable ores. This bronze age, archeologists have discovered, existed for a long time. Lyell says, " The number and variety of objects belonging to the age of bronze indicate its long duration, as does the progress in the arts implied by the rudeness of the earlier tools." *

Immeasurably back in the far past, the use of metals was unknown; and men fashioned their tools and

* Lyell's Antiquity of Man, p. 11.

weapons principally of stone. This was the stone age. Already the existence of this stone age has been demonstrated in Great Britain, France, Denmark, Germany, and Switzerland. During the early part of this age, gigantic elephants, nearly twice as large as existing ones, roamed in herds through the forests of Great Britain, France, and Germany. Oxen, of several species now extinct, and some of them of immense size, fed in the natural meadows, while tigers, bears, and hyenas prowled through the woods in pursuit of their prey, or hid from the hot rays of the sun in the dark recesses of the rocks. In the rivers, extinct species of the rhinoceros and hippopotamus sported, their tough hides impervious to the rude weapons of the rude men that occupied the land.

The scenes described in the three preceding experiments, belong, I think, to this stone age, and give a lifelike representation of the people, their condition, and pursuits.

Probably, during the early human period, man had attained the highest point of comparative civilization in Central Asia; and from that, as a centre, wave after wave rolled westward over Europe, as the desire for change, or need of wider territory, or love of conquest, or the persecution of a dominant race, compelled them. Finding a people inferior to themselves in form, color, and intellectual ability, they enslaved them, after taking possession of their lands by the right of the strongest; themselves to be supplanted at some future time by another wave of humanity, as much in advance of them as they were of their predecessors. Just as in the present day the Arabs have overrun Northern Africa, enslaving the negroes; and the French, in their turn, are driving them out and occupying their domain. The conquest of Great Britian by the Romans, the first of which authentic history speaks, was probably but one of a number that had preceded it, during what may be termed the pre-historic period.

EXPERIMENT LXXXIII.

Small fragment of obsidian, from Mount Ararat.

Mrs. Denton saw it, but thought it was coal.

" I am near a soft, wet place; below me it is marshy. On one side is a steep ridge, and on the side of that, a square hole, lined with poles or sticks; they do not seem to have been hewn. There are different animals around, which seem to be much afraid. One, with slender body and legs, looks like a deer, but is taller. Some are larger still, and more clumsy-looking. One is as large as a hog, but is in shape like a mole. Another has a broad face, curved horns, and peculiar curled hair; it looks frowzy and quite fierce.

" The strangest sight of all comes up. It is a man-like animal; it is pursuing the other animals, and that is the reason they run, and are so afraid. This animal built that place I saw, I believe. I see one in the distance now; he has something on his head; and another with something in his hand or paw, — the left one, — which he swings. His head is very angular. I seem to see the dawn of thought, as he holds that out, and watches it swing. It is a wild animal, and he holds it by the entrails, I believe! His arms are long as legs, and covered with hair; but the face is nearly smooth, yet looks fuzzy. The color is dark, but has an olive tinge. This one has some mirthfulness about him. Oh, *oh*, what a yell! I never heard anything equal to it. It thrills me, and I fairly tremble. Yet it had a kind of silvery ring to it. The mouth of this animal is crescent-shaped. It has a very large nose, three or four times the size of a man's; it is rounded and very prominent, and seems in keeping with the face and head. The forehead goes up and back to a ridge, giving it a triangular shape."

If my thought were at all concerned in the production of these pictures, on this occasion the vision would certainly have differed most widely from the one presented. I was looking at the time for a volcanic eruption and its accompanying phenomena; and was very much surprised, as I have frequently been, at the difference between what was presented, and what was expected.

EXPERIMENT LXXXIV.

Small flint arrow-head, found near Chesterfield, Madison County, Indiana.

Mrs. Giles, of Randolph, Cattaraugus County, New York.

"I go south to the water's edge, but cannot cross it. I see grass of a yellow color, a few trees, and various small animals that I am not familiar with. I see pieces of rock in the earth that look something like glass.

"Now, I see a wilderness; there are no trees cut down, and in its depths are birds, snakes, and bears. I see a village also, and pass through it; it is built of bark and skins, and what looks like cloth. There are a good many men near it. I see no women. The men are poorly dressed, almost naked. The skins they wear look rough; some are worn with the hide out, and some with the fur. They have nothing on their heads, and their skins are dark-colored. Now I see more of them; they look lazy, dirty and shiftless. They really don't seem to know anything. Their foreheads are small, and their heads run up to the crown, sugar-loaf shape. They have large noses, large mouths, and thick lips." In reply to a question she said, " I should not call them Indians ; they are lighter-colored, and short and thickset. They look more like monkeys than any human beings I ever saw.

"I see a woman now; she has a loose skin in front of her breast, and another round her hips that is fast. There is a small hut; I have to stoop to enter it. In one corner I see grass and stuff, where I suppose they lie. Here is a larger hut; I will go in. I see square stones that seem intended for seats. There is a place made of stones for a fire, and I see one burning, and meat, with a pole stuck through it, cooking. The bed in this hut has skins on it. I see a woman with ornaments in her ears; she has nice furs on.

"A man is pounding against the side of a tree with a stone to loosen the bark. The stone is sharp at one end and thick at the other; he pounds with the large end, and cuts with the other. He has a rough kind of basket into which he piles the bark.

" There are spots as large as a house here and there, that seem to have been cleared for cultivation."

A very life-like picture of the aboriginal times. Mrs. Giles assured me that she did not know what the specimen was till the examination was over.

EXPERIMENT LXXXV.

Piece of encrinal limestone, obtained near the reservoir at the foot of Mount Royal, Montreal. Mrs. Denton knew it came from somewhere in the neighborhood of Montreal, but not what it was.

" I see a tremendous waterfall, of great breadth, wider than any river that I ever saw. Niagara, from what I have heard of it, must be a baby in comparison. There seems to be a good deal of what looks like steam. I see beams of light that shine through it; at the lowest part it is dark, but higher up the light is more diffused through it. Those shafts of light that dart through it remind me of lightning, they are so clear and well-defined.

" I am under the fall now; there is an arch of rock overhead, but I do not see the water. The archway is extensive; it is a great open place. The light in the water seems to vibrate.

" There is that fall again. What a tremendous fall it is ! it seems to hold me. A rock rises up in or near the centre of it, high and steep. It is water-worn all round, and is smaller at the bottom than higher up. The fall must have been miles wide. (It is difficult to shut out modern influences.)

" I wonder if this has not been exposed to heat. What can have made it so hot?

" I see animals resembling crinoids."

At the time this examination was made, I did not know that Mount Royal was composed, to a considerable extent, of trap, sent up from below in a heated condition, of course; but when I learned this, the heat that Mrs. Denton recognized was readily explained; the trap lying in place but a few rods from where I obtained the specimen.

EXPERIMENT LXXXVI.

A few days afterward, tried a piece of trap from the top of Mount Royal. Specimen seen, and its locality known.

"I can see the St. Lawrence plainer than when I was on the Mount, and parts of the city fully as plain. I cannot see the bridge distinctly; I merely see a dark line across the water. I should not have known what it was, if I had not seen it before.

"Now I am a little way back in time from the present occupation of the country. It looks very wild; the water rolls on, with no human being present. How lonely! There is no steeple in town nearly as high as the rock on that island; it was magnificent. It looks very craggy on top, as I go back in time.

"Now, I see a fall, — very wide; there are rocks in it higher than the general bed over which the water dashes. I can hear the rushing of that stream; the roar is terrible. There is a hollow sound, too, that I cannot account for, but I think it comes from there. It is the broadest sweep of water in the shape of a river that I ever saw, but I do not think it was as deep then as now."

EXPERIMENT LXXXVII.

When in Montreal, I broke from the first pier of the Victoria Bridge, on the north side of the river, and on the east side of the pier, a small fragment of lime-stone; this, about six weeks afterward, I gave to Mrs.

Denton, who did not see it, had no idea of the charac
ter of it, and knew not that I had any such specimen.

"I see a point extending into the water, and vessels
around it; and I see another point farther away that
has buildings upon it. Now I see high cliffs. There
seems to be a kind of archway here, but I cannot tell
yet what it belongs to. It looks, however, like a tunnel, and yet like a bridge. I do not know what to call
it. • I am looking through the arched entrance, and
that is the appearance presented. There are hills in
the distance. There is a city here.

"I see now what this is; it is a long bridge over a
stream. Down the stream I see that high pinnacle on
an island that I saw once when we were at Montreal.
This must be from the long bridge at Montreal."

If Mrs. Denton had been placed bodily on the spot
where I obtained the specimen, she could hardly have
described more accurately the principal features of the
view presented from it. There is a point of land on
the lower side of the bridge, which was either made or
enlarged during the building of the bridge, and used
as a wharf for vessels that were employed in conveying material for its construction. The bridge appeared long, of course, for it is the longest bridge in
the world. The iron tube, of which the body of the
bridge is composed, has very much the appearance of
a tunnel when looked into from the end. The high
pinnacle referred to is the same as that noticed by her
in the last experiment; and it is a little remarkable
that it was not the present appearances observed that
determined the locality of the specimen, but an appearance that has had no actual existence for ages:

for it was the observance of this remarkable pinnacle of rock that enabled her to determine that the specimen was from Montreal.

Since the discovery of petroleum, or rock oil, in such great abundance in Western Pennsylvania, Canada West, and other localities, much interest has been excited in reference to it, and many theories of its origin propounded. One supposes that it is the oleaginous matter from antediluvian whales, buried in the localities where the oil is discovered; another, that it is the drippings of coal-beds; subject to enormous pressure, they are supposed to yield oil, as a cake of linseed subjected to the power of a hydraulic press; and hence the occurrence of this oil in beds underlying coal. Others again believe that the oil was driven by heat from beds of coal into the neighboring rocks; the coal after parting with its oil assuming the form of anthracite. A wilder theory is, that the oil was driven out of coal by heat, in the condition of vapor, condensed in the upper, cold atmosphere, and rained down in greasy showers; and thus it is found in localities where there is no coal in the vicinity. Some, despairing of finding any philosophic solution of the question, tell us that God made it when it best pleased him, and we must receive it thankfully, asking no questions.

It will be seen that most of these theories assume that the coal-beds are the source of the oil. The reason may be, that an oil, somewhat resembling petroleum, can be obtained from coal by distillation: though that consideration should not be allowed to outweigh the stern facts that are in complete opposition to this favorite idea.

In the neighborhood of Titusville, Pennsylvania, where the oil was first discovered in the United States in large quantities, it is obtained by boring into shales belonging to the Chemung group of the Devonian formation; and in these shales, which are at least six or seven hundred feet below the Coal Measures, the oil is sometimes obtained at a depth of six hundred feet; and when obtained, frequently rushes to the surface with great violence; showing clearly that the fountain supplying it lies still deeper. There is no coal in the immediate vicinity, the nearest being more than twenty miles distant. The beds between the coal and the shales, in which the oil is found, consisting of sandstones and conglomerate principally, it is difficult to conceive of oil soaking through them and travelling twenty or thirty miles to the spot where it is now found.

In Canada West, about twenty miles east of Port Sarnia, petroleum is found in the greatest abundance. The whole country seems to rest on a lake of oil, which has burst through at some time and flooded the land; when, the volatile parts evaporating, the ground for acres has become covered with asphaltum, in places two feet thick. Here we should certainly expect coal, according to the common theories; but when we examine the limestone underlying the deep bed of drift clay, which covers that part of the country, we find in it the characteristic shells of the Devonian formation, and discover that it is one of the members of the Hamilton group of that formation. It lies, therefore, still lower geologically than the Pennsylvania oil; and as, on boring into the limestone, the oil is found in greater abundance and of better quality, it is evident that the source of its supply lies deeper still. There is no coal nearer than the Michigan coal basin, probably seventy miles distant; and there, the thickest coal seam is not more than four feet, which, under no circumstances, could yield oil enough to flow half a mile toward the Canadian petroleum region.

At Louisville this oil, so readily recognized by its peculiar smell, may be seen in the limestone rocks blasted out in forming the ship canal; rocks laid down ages before the Coal Measures were deposited. In Chicago, where I have observed it floating on the surface of water in a limestone quarry, and where the limestone is thoroughly saturated with it, we find it in the Lower Silurian; as we do near Hamilton, in Canada West, and many other localities.

It is most evident, then, that this oil does not proceed from coal. What does it proceed from? After visiting the Titusville oil wells, in Pennsylvania, on the breaking out of the oil excitement in that region, I sent a piece of the shale, obtained from one of the wells, to Mrs. Denton, requesting her to see what psychometry could do towards revealing the mystery of the origin of this remarkable product. The following I received by mail: —

"All is perfect darkness around me; I do not think I shall see anything to-night. In a twinkling the darkness is gone, and I find myself deep underground; how deep, I cannot tell, but I feel a great weight above me.

"In front of me, at my right, at my left, and apparently behind me, though I do not see that distinctly, is a gorgeous scene. I seem to stand in a perfect forest of — (what shall I term it?) I know of nothing that it resembles, in its general structure, but the coral forests I have seen, when examining fossil coral; and again, a portion of its structure resembles the honeycomb more nearly than anything else to which I can compare it. The cells are, however, different in form, having a hanging appearance, the lower portion of each cell being more extended, and somewhat smoother and rounder than the upper extremity. These cells, when entire, seem filled with a liquid; but many, great multitudes of them, in the part of the forest next me, have been crushed and broken, and the whole space, or nearly so, is filled with this expressed liquid.

"In many places this coralline forest seems to prop the roof, or stratum, above; and in every direction, through this grove, I see clusters and groups reflecting all the colors of the rainbow, and presenting most beautiful and singularly effective arrangements. The liquid is readily distinguishable from water by the appearance; but, aside from that, there is the taste and effect of being in communication with oil. I do not know what may be above or below this, but *here*, at least, *I see no appearance of coal, or the vegetation of which coal is formed*, though I have looked faithfully for it."

In several oil districts she has observed similar appearances, and on more than one occasion watched the coral polyps as they filled their cells with the oil secreted from the impure waters of the early oceans.

My own observations corroborate Mrs. Denton's psychometric views. I have found a reef of fossil coral
belonging to the genus *favosites*, with the oil dripping
out of it, within eight miles of Buffalo; and near Wil-
liamsville, in the centre of solid limestone blocks, are
multitudes of corals, the cells of which are filled with
this oil, *which is visible nowhere but in these cells.* In
the New York Geological Rooms, Albany, is a fine
specimen of oil-bearing coral, marked *Favosites Goth-
landica*, Erie County, from which the oil has dripped
to the bottom of the case. I saw several specimens
in the geological rooms at Montreal.

I have no doubt whatever that this oil owes its origin to the coral polyps, principally of the Silurian and
Devonian periods. They seem to have accomplished a
work analogous to that performed by the plants of the
Carboniferous period; they purified the water as the
plants did the air; and though no oil-bearing corals
may exist in the ocean at the present time, it may be
because the material from which the oil was obtained
is exhausted, and the family of oil-bearing corals has
become extinct. I know of no living corals whose
cells at all resemble those of the oil-secreters, where
was deposited this very valuable article, which by heat
and pressure has been driven out of its original recep-
tacles into crevices and reservoirs, where it is at present found. By long exposure many of the original oil-
containing corals have lost their oil, and hence their
cells are frequently found empty.

EXPERIMENT LXXXIX.

If caves can be examined psychometrically, and

their windings traced, why not mines and mineral veins? Many persons have existed who professed to have the ability of seeing objects deep buried in the earth, and I have no doubt that, in some cases, these professions were in accordance with the truth. In the Seeress of Prevorst, it is said, quoting from Del Rio, that in Spain there is a race of people called Zohuris, who can see things hidden under the earth, as water, veins of metal, and dead bodies. Gamasche, a Portuguese, who lived in the beginning of the eighteenth century, had the faculty of discovering water and metals at a considerable depth under ground.

Zschokke, the well-known German author, says: —

"In almost every canton of Switzerland are found persons endowed with the mysterious natural gift of discovering by a peculiar sensation the existence of subterranean waters, metals, or fossils. I have known many of them, and often put their marvellous talents to the proof. One of these was the Abbot of the Convent of St. Urban, in the canton of Lucerne, a man of learning and science; and another, a young woman, who excelled all I have ever known. I carried her and her companion with me through several districts entirely unknown to her, but with the geological formation of which, and with the position of its salt and sweet waters, I was quite familiar, and I never found her deceived. The results of the most careful obser-vation have compelled me at length to renounce the obstinate suspicion and incredulity I at first felt on this subject, and have presented me with a new phase of nature, although one still involved in enigmatical obscurity. To detail circumstantially every experiment

I made to satisfy myself on this point, would take up too much space at present; but I think it right to mention some of the cases which led me occasionally to vary from others in my views of nature and of God." *

Catherine Crowe says, in her Night Side of Nature, "Numerous cases are met with, in which metals or water are perceived beneath the surface of the earth. A man called Bléton, from Dauphiné, possessed the divining power in a remarkable degree, as did a Swiss girl, called Katherine Beutler. She was strong and healthy, and of a phlegmatic temperament, yet so susceptible of these influences that without the rod she pointed out and traced the course of water, veins of metal, coal-beds, salt mines, &c."

Our experiments confirm these statements remarkably, demonstrating as they do the possession of this wonderful and valuable power.

On visiting the Lake Superior copper region, some years ago, I brought from there a number of specimens, which I submitted to Mrs. Cridge and Mrs. Denton for examination; they, as before, having no previous knowledge of the specimen, which was carefully concealed from view when a sight of it could give any clue to its character.

A piece of conglomerate from the bed of Eagle River, and one mile from the Phœnix Copper Mine.

Mrs. Cridge.

"I feel the influence of copper, but very slight. The vapor of the metal must have passed into this. I should say this came from next to the copper. I can

* Life of Zschokke, p. 143.

see a vein of copper; it is not more than eighteen inches thick in the thickest place, and seems to extend a mile."

Whether there is copper beneath this conglomerate or not, I cannot say ; but from the fact that it is found so immediately in the vicinity, and that the psychometer had not the slightest idea of the locality whence the specimen was derived, I think it more than probable. The copper region of Lake Superior has not been one hundredth part explored yet.

EXPERIMENT XC

When at Copper Harbor, I picked up, from a gravel-bed near the burying-ground, about half a mile from the lake, a fine specimen of crystallized quartz, which was also examined by my sister.

"I feel the influence of copper. This came from near the lake, and near the surface, and beneath it is loose rock or gravel for twelve or fifteen feet. Beneath that is a brown stratum, quite thin, not more than a foot thick ; then trap-rock, very deep ; it must be sixty or seventy feet. I see something yellow in that trap ; it does not look like copper ; it is not in veins, but scattered around.

"A little from there, toward the west, the trap rises and comes to the surface. There is copper beneath the trap, but it is only a thin vein."

About two hundred yards from where I picked up the specimen the trap does come to the surface, and a large cliff of it overlooks the harbor. The yellow substance that she saw was probably the sulphuret of copper, which she had not previously seen, either psychometrically or otherwise. It is obtained at a mine about half a mile from the spot where the specimen was found.

I found near the mouth of Eagle River, on the Lake Superior shore, a small pebble of amygdaloidal trap, with a speck of copper in it about as large as a pin's head. The pebble is somewhat angular, however, and a person would hardly suppose that it had been rolled by water.

Mrs. Cridge.

"I seem to be standing on the shore of the lake, and before me the water spreads illimitably. Banks rise to the left, and behind me. The strata seem to have been cut away, so that all lies exposed. I see great masses of copper lying bare against the side of the cliff. This seems to have been broken from the cliff above the copper. Near there, is a copper vein dividing into three branches, and extending for half a mile. It is thickest near the cliff, and is pure copper."

I determined to try this specimen again, and discover what it would reveal to another psychometer, who was totally unacquainted with it, and equally so with the examination that had been made.

Mrs. Denton.

"I see water. Now I see, but it cannot be right, a vessel with sails.

"I seem to be standing some distance above the

shore, and either there is an island in the distance, or the land stretches out.

"I see a man in dark clothes, sitting on a rock, looking at the water; and now I see a steamboat.

"I am at the place where this was broken off. I see a vein filled with pure copper. It comes out in a cliff, and extends apparently for a mile, never running very far from the lake. The cliff, I should think, is one hundred and fifty feet high, and the copper is some distance from the foot of it. Pine trees grow all over the land, but they look small.

I see another vein larger than that, — thicker and deeper. It heads about on the same level as this, but to the west of it; both veins, as it appears to me, go to the southeast; the last more than the first. This vein has large rugged masses in it; but it is not as continuously rich as the first."

EXPERIMENT XCIII.

Six weeks after this, many specimens from various localities having been examined in the mean time, I tried the same specimen again.

"This seems to have been moved through the water with a wavy motion. It has been moved a considerable distance by the waves." (In what direction?)

"I cannot tell. I am surprised, for I see a boat on water, some distance from me, — a steamboat.

"I see shining metal that looks like gold, or copper with the sun shining upon it; and it is a good deal like a place that I have seen before. There is a long line of copper at my left. I seem to have a night view of it; but the copper is very bright. This must be a specimen that I tried once before."

I could not deny it, and thus the experiment terminated; but Mrs. D. said that on first trying it, she had not the most distant suspicion of what it was.

EXPERIMENT XCIV.

Nearly a year after this time, I broke the pebble, that it might not be recognized, and gave a small fragment of it to Mrs. Denton, for examination again.

Nothing seen or known.

" Many scenes pass before me like lightning. They are principally water scenes; they seem to carry me back to the Silurian period. I see rocks projecting into the water, the sea occasionally passing over them; and in the sea are myriads of living forms of an inferior grade of organization." (I do not wish the paleozoic impressions.) " I go to the land. It seems as if the earth was all open. To my left are rocks that seem two hundred feet high. I am away down in a crevice, and there is a narrow continuation of it for a long way below me. It seems as if the rocks all round me had been shivered into fragments; crevices and veins run in every direction. I am now at an immense depth. I see fire; no, not fire exactly, but liquid matter in motion; it is of a deeper color than flame. I must be a long way down. The molten matter pours up like a tremendous fiery spring. I follow it up, but it does not rise to the surface of the earth. There are long crevices, filled with this matter, off to my left. They seem to be to the south of me.

" I stand with my face to the west. The fluid matter in the crevices is now hard; it is metal of some kind; but whether gold or copper, I cannot tell. There is a gas arising from it that gives me the feeling of copper to some extent; but the metal has a pure look like gold, and I feel almost sure that it is; but what an enormous amount! These crevices that I am tracing are hundreds if not thousands of feet below the surface." (Turned the specimen over.)

"Now I see a vein of copper. This is higher up and near the surface. There is a great difference between this and the other. This I *know* to be copper; there are several veins. Some seem to come very near, if not quite, to the surface. Some of the veins are very large.

"I seem to stand and look through the earth for miles, as if it were transparent as water, only the metallic veins obstructing my vision. The veins look skeleton-like, all standing up and ramifying in every direction. What a singular sight! There is a good deal of dark trap beyond that, in which there is no metal for a long way."

The Potsdam sandstone may be seen at the outlet of Lake Superior, at Sault St. Marie, and also along the southern shore. It is the only fossiliferous rock that is known in that region. Back to the period when this was laid down flies the psychometer, views the tepid ocean swarming with animals of strange forms and inferior organization; then, turning to the land, dives into the heart of the earth, and sees the gurgling floods of molten gold come rushing through its veins. It is not unlikely that the massive copper deposits, for which Lake Superior is so justly famous, are underlaid by equal or still more remarkable deposits of gold. Free to arrange themselves according to their specific gravities, the heavier metals would as-sume the lowest place; and when the Lake Superior region shall have been mined as long as the tin and copper region of Cornwall, it may be more famous for gold than it is now for copper.

I have two small specimens of gold obtained from the diggings at Pike's Flat, California. I gave one to Mrs. Cridge, which she saw, but knew nothing of its history.

"I seem to be in a country that is level or flat, but there are hills all around at a distance. There is gold here, near or on the surface. I don't like the look of the country, it is so wild and broken; and there is no grass.

"I see men walking around with wheelbarrows. They are shovelling dirt into a trough. I see a shaft too, and men working at it. The gold does not lie in veins there, but is scattered all around in pieces. It is not in hard rock, but in soft stuff. In some places there are large quantities of gold that seem to have been poured into holes and crevices. The shaft is a curious one; I see a long kind of beam that goes up and down. The miners have blue smocks on."

From what I know of Pike's Flat, this is a pretty correct description of the place and of the mining operations going on there when the specimen was obtained. The gentleman from whom I obtained it said it was such a description as a person would be likely to give, who, having no previous knowledge of mining operations, should see the place.

But I had another specimen from the same place, taken out of the same shaft; and here was an oppornity for an excellent test. Would this lead her to the same spot, and would she recognize it? This second examination was made a month after the first.

"I can see a river, but it is not deep. The scenery around is hilly and broken and somewhat rocky. There is a great deal of gravel, and the rock that I see is not hard. In that water I can see gold, but in very small pieces; it looks as if it had been washed down from above. *I go to the same place as I did with that other specimen.* I can see the men at work, the wheelbarrows, shaft, and washer, as before. The washer is a long trough into which they put the sand and gravel. The men look rough and strong and young. Why I should see that old place again I cannot tell."

After the examination was over, she said she found she was at the same place, and tried her best to get away, assured that she was receiving incorrect impressions; but, though she travelled up the valley a short distance, she was compelled to return. She was much surprised when told that it came from the same place.

The same specimen was subsequently tried again by another psychometer, who did not see it and did not know what it was.

Mrs. Taylor.

"I am on board ship, going back. Now I am on land; it is a new country and hilly. I see a stream, and banks on each side, and off to the right is a village. I stand on the right-hand side of the stream. Now I see a hole that has been dug through the soil and gravel and dirt to the rock. All through the rock they have cut into are shining particles. I see men digging. How greedily they act! They look pleased; those shining particles must be gold. There are large quantities in that hill.

"I see the top of a mountain covered with large trees. One mountain goes up to a peak. I see huts dotting the country over, near where the men are digging. The stream goes off small up into the mountains."

EXPERIMENT XCVIII.

Sulphuret of copper from Canada West. I think it was obtained at the Bruce Mine, but I am not certain.

Mrs. Cridge. Had no conception of what it was.

"It seems as if I were in a tunnel, and I see the light at the other end. I am under ground, and yet I can see the light and water when I look out. I am quite a distance from the mouth. How chilly it is here! This must be a mine. I can see a little track laid down, and men about. There is a good deal of metal here. The mine is damp. I can see a vein of metal, and it differs from all that I have seen before. It has a greenish appearance, as I see it stretching along. They have cut out the thickest of it, and they will not find as much in the direction they are going. They have missed one large branch of the vein where the ore is quite thick. They are coming to where the vein separates into two branches, neither of them as wide as half the vein they have gone through. The metal is not copper, and I do not think it is iron. It causes a pain down my back. I see a gentleman and lady in the mine examining it."

Having in previous examinations seen copper only in the native or metallic condition, she did not recognize the greenish yellow ore as being copper.

EXPERIMENT XCIX.

Lead ore from near Galena.

Mrs. Denton. Specimen seen.

"I seem to be standing with my face to the west. Behind me is a large excavation, at one end of which I stand, as if the earth, for some distance and to a considerable depth, had been removed; I cannot tell how deep nor how far in extent behind me.

"Before me, and extending to my right and left, or rather N. N. East and S. S. West, for a long way, is a vein of metal resembling in all respects, as far as I can judge, this piece of lead. I should think large blocks as pure as this might be removed without difficulty. It does not, however, look as I expected to find it; for, instead of being in one continuous solid mass, it appears separated by dust, or something similar, into blocks of irregular shape, not thrown carelessly together, but closely packed, the interstices being filled with sand or dust. If the appearance indicates the amount, there must be thousands of tons as pure as this. But the most inconsistent feature seems to be its nearness to this excavation, and, at the same time, its undisturbed appearance. Not a grain of it seems to have been touched; it rests in perfect quiet."

At the time when this examination was made, nearly four years ago, Mrs. D. had never seen a mine of any description, nor had I visited any of the lead mines of this country; and I was not aware, until my visit to the lead region of the Northwest, of the remarkable agreement between her description and the actual appearance of the large lead deposits throughout that region. The galena is found in irregular blocks, not thrown carelessly together, but closely packed, the interstices being filled with clay or ochreous dust.

EXPERIMENT C.

If the psychometer can go down and describe the interior of the earth for thousands of feet below the surface, why not pass through the earth's crust and visit the great fiery ocean, whose waves no human eye has ever beheld? For this purpose a specimen from some deep mine would, I thought, be favorable, and accordingly a piece of copper ore from the Cliff Mine, Lake Superior, was chosen.

Mrs. Cridge.

"I am in the mine now, from which this came. It is a rich mine, containing much copper. There are several branches from the main one, but none that I see as large as it." (Go down as far as you can.) "It is not very pleasant going down, yet I can go a long way. I go down, and then return; and thus keep flitting back and forward." (Pause.)

"I went down an immense distance, passing rock after rock, till it seemed all light from the material around me. It was not light, however, but I was surrounded with rock as white as snow, and sparkling.

" Now I am below it; it is dark, dark again. I should think I am now three or four miles down. What metal I see ! yellow metal; it is bright as gold. It *is* gold. It seems very dense, and is many yards thick. It seems half a mile across, and looks to me as if it had once been a lake of gold. This lake is concave in the centre, so that it forms an immense golden amphitheatre. As the gold has cooled and sunk, it has left a considerable space between it and the roof, and in that space all is dark.

" I go down again in the centre of that amphitheatre. There must have been an opening here once, for I go by a circuitous route. I feel the heat; it seems to take my breath. Every now and then I obtain glimpses of flames, as if they came up thus at one time. All is dark, dark again; what an Egyptian night this is !

" I see a faint dawn, becoming every moment brighter and brighter.

" Now, I am standing on the shore of an ocean of still fire. The stillness that hangs over it seems never to have been broken.

" It does move, though; it ebbs and flows like the ocean. I feel much safer than I should have thought possible. There is a space, strange to say, between this ocean and the superincumbent mass, and in its heavings to and fro it is depositing rock all the time.

" It is not always calm here; there are storms at times, when it surges and dashes in fury. This is hell indeed ! nothing wanting but the devils."

That the earth was once a molten mass of matter, is now almost universally believed by those who have

made geology a matter of study. Its hot springs, volcanoes, and other phenomena, indicate that its interior is in a highly heated state at the present time ;
and there is no doubt that a condition of things exists
there very similar to that so graphically described by
my sister. I have tried to induce other psychometers
to make a similar journey. As far as they went, their
descriptions agreed with the one given; but their terror was too great to allow them to reach the goal.

EXPERIMENT CI.

Amethystine quartz.

Mrs. Denton.

" I see a mound, covered with tall grass and flowers;
there are three terraces on the sides. At a little distance there is a marsh, in which tall reeds and grasses
grow, that have a straggling appearance. At a distance, I see a few very pretty low trees, and a stream."
(See what is under the surface.) "I do not know
where I am, but I see metal; it seems loose, as if in
sand. It is yellow, and there is a good deal of it, but
it is in small pieces, like scattered drops; pretty close
together in some places, however. I think it is gold;
indeed, I feel sure of it. What a tremendous amount!
The sand containing it seems to lie in three streams,
and, at some distance south, I see another stream containing gold, but the pieces are more scaly, and lie
nearer the surface."

At the time when this examination was made, I was
not aware that gold had been found in the neighborhood ; but have since learned that it is obtained within
a few miles of the place where the specimen was

found, though in nothing like the abundance that this psychometric experiment indicates.

A few days afterward I gave the specimen to my sister for examination, she knowing nothing of it.

" I see mountains away off, but it is a plain where I am. I see a lot of trees, that look like palms. This must be a torrid region. I can see a road that seems to have been made.

" There are rocks below, though it looks sandy above. I see gold in great quantities, very near the surface, too. There is a good deal among the sand, that could be got at very easily."

It would be very strange if these independent observers, with no such idea in their minds, should see what had no existence.

About six months afterward I broke the specimen, and gave a small piece of it, from the centre, to Mrs. Denton; and though what was seen differed very widely from that of the previous examination, it does but confirm the truth of its most essential feature.

" I see a mass of softish material, about the color of flame; there are openings in it of various sizes, and at unequal distances. As the mass slowly moves, steam arises from these openings, or what seems like steam to me, and the openings change their shape with the motion of the mass, but do not close. The surface is occasionally a little disturbed, but there is a feeling of rest and quiet connected with it.

"Now I see it hard, and it alternates between a hard and soft condition several times. Some of the openings gradually fill up. I see a body of rock, with long rows of nodules of harder rock in it." (How were they produced?) "Very slowly. I can see how it was done but it is very difficult to describe.

"As I watch, there is a terrible convulsion or explosion, and the rocks are thrown, with most tremendous force, into great confusion. Huge caverns are formed deep underground. Again all is still, and I observe dark gray rocks behind me, and in front, beautiful rocks, that are almost transparent. Now, there is another grand convulsion. I stand where all is calm, but in front of me, miles of the massive rock are moved along. It looks as if there was rock enough to make a world of. Again all is calm.

"Now, I see metal ejected from below, a great deal of it. I think it is gold. There is little comes up, however, compared with the amount below. Much sent up, settles down again. One large rock drops miles into a profound cavern."

The interior of a specimen gives most readily its early history. On the exterior this is generally obscured by the impressions more recently received. In this case, she seems to have gone back to the time when the country was in a condition of intense igneous activity, and the precious metals were vomited to the surface from their grand reservoirs in the interior.

We obtain a glimpse of the way in which precious stones are formed; by openings in the rock slowly filled, probably by segregation from the surrounding rocks, till amethyst, agate, and the more precious ruby,

emerald, and diamond, are, during long ages, collected
into nodular or crystalline bodies.

Gold-bearing quartz from Columbian Reef, New En-
glewood, Victoria, Australia.

Mrs. Denton.   Specimen unseen, and nothing known
respecting it.

"I see a rock rising up to the northwest of me.   I
am in a road, where there are trees on one side, and
off at a little distance the ground seems to rise.   This
country has a pleasant atmosphere; I like its influence.   It seems very still.   There are hills west of
me, extending as far as I can see.   One chain of them
comes circling round to where I am.   The influence
of the country is inspiring.

"Shall I go under ground?"   (Yes.)   "I do not
think I can here, but I will try.   I obtain the influence
of some kind of metal, but I do not see it.   Now I
see a white rock, with yellow metal in it, in all manner
of shapes.   It looks as I have seen metal when melted
and thrown into the water.   I can see one large, uneven mass, that looks as if it had received two or three
twists when soft.   It looks like gold.   There is one
mass of rock with thin flakes all through it, and another
with the dust distributed through it; this extends a
long way.   There is more gold toward those hills.
The rock seems disturbed here; they have been digging, and have come near that large mass, if they have
not obtained it.

"The gold is not in a vein, at least I should not call
it that; but it leads along for many miles, though there

are several breaks in it, where it seems to have been cut off; and in these places there is no gold at all; so that a person might readily suppose that they were at the end of the profitable lead, when it was by no means the case. Many places around here have been disturbed. There is another lead off, farther to the south, that has a good deal of gold in it, but I cannot go to it.

"Toward the hills they would have to dig deeper; here, it seems to be quite near the surface.

"The atmosphere of this country is soft and balmy. There is a good deal of fine, warm, hazy, rich weather, and it is continuous.

"That part of the lead which they have disturbed seems quite small; it is nothing compared with the undisturbed portion of it. It is narrow where they have been working, but very much wider near the hills, though broken and cut off here and there. Quite near the hills it is one continuous lead, and seems very rich. In digging here, they have gone in the wrong direction for getting the greatest amount of gold, owing, I suppose, to a break or interruption near, which is quite wide. Beyond that, however, it continues on, but dips lower and lower the farther it goes."

I wrote to the gentleman from whom I received the specimen, and sent this description, requesting him to let me know whether it was correct as far as he knew. I have not heard from him, but have little doubt of its accuracy, from my general knowledge of the auriferous deposits of Australia. The specimens obtained at the Columbian Reef are the richest gold specimens I ever saw.

Silver ore from the Washoe mines, California.

Mrs. Denton. For a test I requested her to look for oil.

"I see coral. Has this been lying near coral? I think so, for the appearance of the coral is shadowy" (It had been in my pocket for several weeks along with a piece of oil-bearing coral; both, however, wrapped in paper.)

"I see eight or nine layers of rock, with the edges towards me; there is a thin, dark layer between every one. There is a curved, open place in them that seems to have been dug out.

"I am away off now. There is gas here. It seems as if it would suffocate me. The gas is thick, of a purple color, with an orange tint at the edges. It must be different from oil gas; there is some metal with it. I cannot see anything, for gas. Do you wish me to look for oil? There does not seem to be any oil about it?" (Told her what it was.) "There is a great deal of ore there, but I do not think they have found the richest place yet. Standing with my face to the southwest, to the left there is a vein of ore like this specimen; but to the right there is one with pure silver in it in masses."

I am not acquainted with the Washoe region, so cannot speak of the correctness of this, beyond its general accuracy, which all can see.

When travelling through the lead region of Wisconsin, Mrs. Denton indicated a spot as being very rich in lead ore, where a " sucker hole " had been dug for a few feet, in search of lead, and then abandoned. I brought from the place a piece of chert, resolved to test it at some future time.

Let it be remembered that the specimen was not seen by the psychometer, nor had she any knowledge of it whatever.

" There is an immense amount of lead ore here. I see a vein with tiff,* much lead, and a little ochre, in a compact rock. Higher up there is a good deal of lead, but in no crevice; it is in blocks, and looks so like ——'s place, on that hill by the timber, that I cannot trust myself to speak of it. This is a rich place, and does not seem to have been disturbed much, if any. The vein seems a good deal deeper than the other part. The lead extends over a large territory; I can see it in a great many places."

This description agreed precisely with that given by her when we were at the spot. Lead has been obtained in considerable abundance within a quarter of a mile.

EXPERIMENT CVII.

A month afterward I broke a small fragment from the same specimen, for a farther trial. As before, nothing was known of it.

" I seem to be in a mine, as near as I can tell. I cannot tell whether it has been worked where I am or not. There has been digging here. I can see lead, however, that does not seem to have been touched. They do not seem to have got to it. I feel positive

---

* A term used by the miners for carbonate of lime.

they have not got down to the lead; it is undisturbed and there is a great deal of it. It does not seem to be very far to it. They could not go very deep without finding it. It lies in large slabs or blocks.

"I know where I am, now that I am on the surface. I am at ——'s place." (Designating the same place as in her previous description.) "The whole lead region seems spread like a map before me. I view it for miles. The most lead lies north of where this came from. There is a perfect mountain of lead north; rising somewhere near the surface, and dipping toward the east. The lead in other places seems to be in drops compared with this. There is, however, a good deal where this came from, and I am sure it came from ——'s place."

EXPERIMENT CVIII.

When at Mineral Point, we examined a number of specimens connected with the lead mines of that region, nor did Mrs. Denton know that copper was found in that part of the country. Having obtained a specimen of rock entirely free from ore, from the copper mine, about two miles east of the town, I gave it to her for a trial, she supposing it to be connected with some lead mines in the vicinity.

"It does not look like lead here. I see rock with metal in it that looks like silver." (Some of the sulphurets obtained from the mine have that appearance.) "It is not disposed like lead; it is in small pieces a few inches long; not thick like lead. I see a crevice now. There is a good deal of ore, mixed with earthy matter, scattered through it; it is not pure like lead. The crevice seems to have a northwestern direction. I see a place where another crevice joins, and they both widen, making quite a large opening where there is a great deal of ore. One of the walls of the crevice is split into a number of columns, that are so even they have quite an artificial appearance. The interstices between them are filled with ore.

"There is something else here. I can taste it. It is copper. There is a vein of it mixed with other material a little way from the crevice, or else it is the same crevice a little farther on. It is not alone; there seems to be silver with it, though it may not be; it is white and bright. There are several small veins within a short distance of each other.

"Deep down I see a great cave that has a brilliant appearance; it glistens all over, for it is lined with crystals, some of them large. There is a purple vapor in it."

This mine has never paid for working, and probably never will. There is a fissure in the limestone, in some places nearly twenty feet wide, that has been traced for several hundred yards. In this, sulphuret and carbonate of copper are very sparingly distributed through clay and rock.

EXPERIMENT CIX.

Piece of quartz from a gold mine in the Pike's Peak mining region, obtained of Mr. Henry, Peru, Illinois. Mrs. Denton did not see the specimen, and had not the most distant conception of the locality from which it was obtained.

"This is unlike any place I ever saw before. I am

between rocks that are high up; it is a magnificent place. I can see a long way down a deep valley to a turning. I see metal. The specimen takes me away to some distant country. They have been excavating here for some purpose. I notice one place where the water has been made to run into an artificial channel.

"I wonder if that can be gold I see. It certainly looks like it. There is a good deal of it at that turning, farther in the rock however. There is a little where this was found, but not much; there is more in several places around. The gold is contained in seams in the rock generally, but in some places I see it without. The rocks are damp and cold where I am now. There is a place in the distance where the gold shines in the rock like stars. It is well calculated to disappoint the miners, it lies so scattering. There is very little continuity about it."

Those who are acquainted with the gold region of Pike's Peak will recognize the accuracy of some portions of this description at least.

EXPERIMENT CX.

When visiting McChesney's cabinet in Chicago, I obtained several pieces of silicified wood. Some time afterward I thought I should like to know the condition of our planet during the time of its petrifaction, and gave one of the smaller pieces to Mrs. Denton for examination, not remembering at the time where it was obtained. She said, —

"It affects my face and eyes. I am underground, in a place open here and there; it looks like a large open crevice. I see metal and most beautiful rock. I stand with my face to the northwest. Forward of me is an open space with rock scattered here and there. The beautiful rock extends a good way to the left, with metal distributed among it. It seems to be a kind of vein, to the left, rich in metal and continuous for some distance. I see now and then a bright yellow substance that seems like gold; if gold, it is in great quantities. There are several metals here however; there is lead in large masses by itself, and a good deal of sulphuret of iron. Off at my left, there is a massive piece of gold, and a good deal of gold dust distributed through the rock in the vein. Lead, however, would be a better name for it than vein, for it is wide and open almost like a cave."

I thought this strange; for of gold or metals connected with the specimen I had never dreamed; but on examining it I discovered a label marked, "near Gregory's Diggings, P. Peak." Here was the explanation then: gold, apparently possessing superior attractive force psychometrically, as it does normally, had drawn the psychometer to its sphere; and hence this description, probably, of some unexplored gold lead near Gregory's Diggings.

EXPERIMENT CXI.

Piece of ore from the copper mine at Acton, Canada East.

Mrs. Denton. Specimen unseen, and nothing known by her respecting it. No ores had been examined for several months.

"The first thing I see is a group of objects in water, not well defined. Shall I notice them?" (No.)

"I see something in spots that is very bright. Now I see a rock jutting out, and under it I see the same bright appearance. I see something artificial; it is heavy at the bottom, and runs up high; there seems to be a wheel there. I do not know but I am in a mine. I had a glimpse of a ladder. I am underground; I think I am in a mine. There is an artificial light, I think a candle. I cannot yet tell what kind of a mine it is. The material has not the purity of gold about it. There seem to be two kinds of metal here. I do not see both, but I see one and feel the influence of the other, though it may be at some distance.

"There is a bluish, purplish vapor that rises and produces a feeling of suffocation. I think this must be copper; but there is something else. The vapor seems poisonous; it is this which makes me think it is copper. This *is* a copper mine; but it is not like the copper mines of Lake Superior; it is differently arranged. There is a great deal of copper here, I think, but I am only where they have disturbed it. I could not be induced to work in such a mine, it seems so poisonous. (There seems to be gas with that vapor.) This mine must have yielded well; for, though the bodies of ore are not as large as I have seen them, they are thickly distributed. There seems to be a pit dug at one place. They do not seem to have taken out all the ore, even where it is open. There are some large bodies, mixed with yellow sulphuret, that have not been touched yet. I see a mass as long as this room is high. It is very jagged, and has an average thickness of five or six feet. It seems to lie to the northeast of the part that has been worked. Some of the ore is blue, some purplish, and some has a green tinge. I do not seem to be far underground anywhere. The excavation here seems large. Ore is all scattered through the rock, and it seems much easier to obtain than in the Lake Superior region."

I read this description to two mining engineers who were familiar with the Acton mines, and they both agreed that it was a very accurate description. One of them excepted the statement about the ladder that was seen, and the other, the rising vapors. Ladders have doubtless been used in the vicinity; and in reference to the vapors, Mrs. D. did not mean to indicate that they were rising at the present time; she merely received the impression of the long past, when from the interior came the dense vapors whose sublimation probably gave rise to these immense cupriferous deposits.

Since writing the above, I have visited the Acton mine; and one of the first things I saw was a large ladder against the wall of rock, and a miner upon it drilling for a blast. I consider the description given a very correct one; and when it is remembered that Mrs. D. did not know that the specimen she tried was an ore at all, much less a copper ore, it must be regarded as truly wonderful. I present the facts as they occurred; certainly none the less worthy of consideration because they are remarkable.

How far psychometry can be practically employed in developing mines, remains yet to be tested. The greatest difficulty seems to be, in precisely determining the depth at which deposits lie. A hundred feet more or less are but a trifle to the psychometer, whereas to the miner, who has to drive through them, they involve considerable time and expense. In time all difficulty in this direction will be outgrown, I have no doubt, and the world be greatly advanced by the discovery of its rich mineral deposits.

CHAPTER V.

FROM a consideration of the statements made in this volume, it is but reasonable to suppose that phenomena springing from the accidental application of the psychometric faculty must have been frequently manifested in the history of the world. If, by placing specimens of various kinds in the hands or on the foreheads of sensitive individuals, they can behold pictures connected with the history of those specimens and perceive sensations that have been treasured up in them, we may naturally suppose, among the many sensitive persons in the world, that some must have had such pictures presented to them and such sensations produced, though they may have been altogether unconscious of the source from which they emanated. This supposition is borne out by many facts that I have met with in reading, since we commenced the investigation of this subject.

Under the head of "Spectral Illusions," Dr. Abercrombie gives the following : — " A gentleman of high mental endowments, now upwards of eighty years of age, of a spare habit, and enjoying uninterrupted health, has been for eleven years liable to almost daily visitations from spectral figures. They in general present human countenances; the head and the body are distinctly defined; the lower parts are, for the most part, lost in a kind of cloud. The figures are various, but he recognizes the same countenances repeated from time to time, particularly of late years, that of an elderly woman, with a peculiarly arch and playful expression, and a dazzling brilliancy of eye, who seems just ready to speak to him. They appear also in various dresses, such as that of the age of Louis XIV.; the costume of ancient Rome; that of the modern Turks and Greeks; but more frequently, of late, as in the case of this female now mentioned, in an old-fashioned Scottish plaid of Tartan, drawn up and brought forward over the head, and then crossed below the chin, as the plaid was worn by aged women in his younger days. He can seldom recognize among the spectres any figure or countenance which he remembers to have seen; but his own face has been presented to him, gradually undergoing the change from youth to manhood, and from manhood to old age." *

I recognize this case at once as one in which psychometric influences, probably proceeding from articles in the house in which the gentleman lived, operating upon a sensitive organization, made sensitive by age, as others are by sickness, caused him to see the images of the persons from whom the influences originally proceeded; in the same manner as psychometers see the animals whose influence is contained in the fossils with which they come in contact. It is very common for psychometers to see a portion of a body only, the rest being "lost in a kind of cloud," as in the case of this gentleman's apparitions. The individ-

* Abercrombie's Intellectual Powers, p. 255.

uals appearing to him wore the dresses of the time
when they existed; the pictures of dresses being impressed on objects as readily as those of persons, and
just as capable of psychometric vision. The elderly
woman, so frequently seen, may have been a former occupant of the house in which the gentleman resided,
and its very walls may have been saturated with her
influence. Dr. Abercrombie, practising in Edinburgh,
his patient must have lived there; and this former
occupant, supposing this to be the true explanation,
must have been a *Scotch* lady; and hence the probability of her wearing the "old-fashioned Scottish plaid
of Tartan, drawn up and brought forward over the
head, and then crossed below the chin, as the plaid
was worn by aged women in his younger days."   He
did not recognize among the spectres the countenances of those that he had seen, because these pictures
did not proceed from his own brain originally, but
from the objects surrounding him; and hence those
objects having taken in his influence during his lifetime, he saw himself in the various appearances that
he presented "from youth to manhood, and from manhood to old age."

These anomalous facts, that seem to forbid all explanation, and set at defiance all law, will be found,
like the cometary wanderers in space, to have their
orbit, too; and every waver in their track will be
shown to be produced by the operation of some law,
though its discovery may remain to reward future explorers in this great ocean, where the dim outline of
grand continents may be faintly seen on the distant
horizon.

"Monsieur Andral, in his youth, saw in La Pitié the putrid body of a child, covered with larvæ, and during the next morning the spectre of this corpse, lying on his table, was as perfect as reality."* In a statement of this, that I have met with in some other work, it is said that this was visible to him for a quarter of an hour. He saw nothing of it until he came to the table on which the child had lain, and then its image was at once presented to him; its influence proceeding from that table bringing up the image before him; for if it had been the image of the child impressed upon the retina of the eye or the brain, he would doubtless have seen it at a distance from the spot as readily as when there.

Dr. Damon, of Coaticook, Canada East, informed me that when a young man, attending medical college, he had a fit of illness; and, when confined in his chamber, he saw the lecture-room and all the students, and heard every word of lectures that he had previously heard, though an hour long. He also saw books that he had read, and was able to read page after page, the words on which were so plainly visible, that he noticed even the typographical errors. This condition continued for about two weeks.

Thousands of such experiences might have been recorded, if a feeling of shame had not prevented parties to whom they occurred from making them public. Many persons who have made public statements of what they have thus seen, have been rewarded for their candor by being charitably supposed insane, or uncharitably suspected of being drunk.

---

* Philosophy of Mystery, by Dendy, p. 64.

" The late Lieutenant-General Robertson, of Lawers, who served during the whole of the American war, brought home with him, at its termination, a negro who went by the name of Black Tom, and who continued in his service. The room appropriated to the use of this man in the General's town residence (I speak of Edinburgh) was on the ground floor; and he was heard frequently to complain that he could not rest in it, for that every night the figure of a headless lady, with a child in her arms, rose out of the hearth and frightened him dreadfully. Of course nobody believed this story, and it was supposed to be the dream of intoxication, as Tom was not remarkable for sobriety; but, strange to say, when the old mansion was pulled down to build Gillespie's hospital, which stands on its site, there was found under the hearthstone, in that apartment, a box containing the body of a female, from which the head had been severed; and beneath her lay the remains of an infant, wrapped in a pillow-case trimmed with lace. She appeared, poor lady, to have been cut off in the ' blossom of her sins,' for she was dressed, and her scissors were yet hanging by a ribbon to her side, and her thimble was also in the box, having apparently fallen from her shrivelled finger." *

Through the hearthstone came the influence of mother and baby, and their images appeared to the terrified Tom, who appears to have been the natural possessor of considerable psychometric power.

The case of Nicolai, the bookseller and author, of Berlin, has excited more attention perhaps than any other of this kind; and, though there are some difficul-

* Mrs. Crowe's Night Side of Nature, p. 411.

ties in it, is I think explicable on the same principles.
His narrative was read before the Academy of Science, at Berlin, in 1799, and its substance is thus
given by Mayo: — "Nicolai had met with some family
troubles that much disturbed him.   Then, on the first
of January, 1791, there stood before him, at the distance of ten paces, the ghost of his eldest son.   He
pointed at it, directing his wife to look.   She saw it
not, and tried to convince Nicolai that it was an illusion.   In a quarter of an hour it vanished.   In the af-
ternoon, at four o'clock, it came again.   Nicolai was
alone.   He went to his wife's room, the ghost followed
him.   About six other apparitions joined the first, and
they walked about among each other.   After some
days, the apparition of his son stayed away; but its
place was filled with the figures of a number of persons, some known, some unknown to Nicolai, — some
of dead, others of living persons.   The known ones
represented distant acquaintances only.   The figures
of none of Nicolai's habitual friends were there.   The
appearances were almost always human; occasionally
a man on horseback, and birds and dogs would present themselves.   The apparitions came mostly after
dinner, at the commencement of digestion; they were
just like real persons, the coloring a thought fainter.
The apparitions were equally distinct whether Nicolai
was at home or in society, in the dark as by day; in
his own house, or those of others; but in the latter case they were less frequent, and they very seldom made their appearance in the streets.   During
the first eight days they seemed to take very little notice of one another, but walked about like people at a

fair, only here and there communing with each other. They took no notice of Nicolai, or of the remarks he ad-dressed regarding them to his wife and physician. No effort of his would dismiss them, or bring an absent one back. When he shut his eyes they sometimes dis-appeared, sometimes remained; when he opened his eyes they were there as before. After a week they became more numerous, and began to converse. They conversed with one another first, and then addressed him. Their remarks were short and unconnected, but sensible and civil. His acquaintances inquired after his health, and expressed sympathy with him, and spoke in terms comforting him. The apparitions were most conversible when he was alone; nevertheless, they mingled in the conversation when others were by, and their voices had the same sound as those of real persons. The illusion went on thus from the 24th of February to the 20th of April; so that Nicolai, who was now in good bodily health, had time to become tran-quillized about the nature of his visitors, and observe them at his ease." The doctors now prescribed leech-es; and the figures became fainter and fainter, as he lost blood, until at length they became invisible, and Nicolai saw them no more.[*]

I have no hesitation whatever in referring the vis-ions and sounds perceived by Nicolai to the operation of the very same power by which, from archeological specimens and fossil remains, the psychometer sees the apparitions of beings, and hears sounds apparently made by them. At first, the psychometric power in him does not seem to have been so fully developed as

[*] Mayo's Popular Superstitions, p. 53.

it subsequently became, and he only sees the appearance of his deceased eldest son, toward whom his
thoughts during this period of trouble were doubtless
frequently directed, and whose image was so vividly
impressed upon his brain. As this power increases,
his vision is no longer confined to objects previously
impressed upon his brain, but the influences proceeding from surrounding objects call up the images of persons known and unknown, dead and alive, that fill the
place. Nicolai was at this time sensitive enough to
see the great picture gallery, or a portion of it at least,
where hangs the likeness of all that light ever beheld;
and he at length becomes sufficiently sensitive to hear,
issuing from the great store-house of sounds, the con-
doling words which his friends had uttered, as faithfully registered and repeated to his interior ear.

That this is the true explanation of this remarkable
phenomena, is strengthened by the fact that, thirteen
years previous to this, visions had presented themselves
to his gaze such as psychometers are well conversant
with. Thus he writes: — "In the year 1778, I was
afflicted with a bilious fever, which at times, though
seldom, grew so high as to produce delirium. Every
day, toward evening, the fever came on, and, if I happened to shut my eyes at that time, I could perceive
the cold fit of the fever was beginning, even before
the sensation of cold was observable. This I knew
by the distinct appearance of colored pictures, of less
than half their natural size, which looked as in frames.
They were a set of landscapes, composed of rocks,
trees, and other objects. If I kept my eyes shut, every minute produced some change in the representa-

tion; some figures vanished, and some appeared; but if I opened my eyes all was gone; if I shut them I had a different landscape. In the cold fit of the fever I sometimes opened and shut my eyes every second, for the purpose of observation, and every time a different picture appeared, replete with various objects, and which had not the slightest resemblance to those that appeared before. These pictures presented themselves, without interruption, as long as the cold fit of the fever lasted. They became fainter as soon as I began to grow warm; and when I was perfectly so, all were gone. When the cold fit of the fever was entirely past, no more pictures appeared; but if, on the next day, I could again see pictures when my eyes were shut, it was a certain sign that the cold fit was coming on." *

Nicolai's clothing, or articles contained in his pockets, or objects in his room, may have furnished the pictures; the fever producing the condition in him necessary to the observance of them.

"Then we have the case of Professor Hitchcock, detailed by himself in the ' New Englander,' and which is one of the most striking on record. He had," during a fit of sickness, "day after day, visions of strange landscapes spread out before him, — mountain and lake and forest, — vast rocks, strata upon strata, piled to the clouds, — the panorama of a world shattered and upheaved, disclosing the grim secrets of creation, the unshapely and monstrous rudiments of organic being." †

* Natural History of Creation, T. Lindley Kemp, M. D., p. 43.
† Dream Land and Ghost Land, by E. P. Hood.

If sufficiently sensitive, this was no wonder, when he was handling from day to day the rocks that contained these landscapes, and was constantly surrounded by them. In his " Religion of Geology," speaking of the influence of light upon bodies, and the formation of pictures upon them by means of it, he says: —

" It seems then that this photographic influence pervades all nature; nor can we say where it stops. We do not know but it may imprint upon the world around us our features, as they are modified by various passions, and thus fill nature with daguerreotype impressions of all our actions that are performed in daylight. It may be, too, that there are tests by which nature more skilfully than any human photographist can bring out and fix these portraits, so that acuter senses than ours shall see them as on a great canvas, spread over the material universe. Perhaps, too, they may never fade from that canvas, but become specimens in the great picture gallery of eternity."

Beautiful and true! This conjecture, which was probably suggested by his own experience, accords with many of the facts presented in this volume; some of which go farther, however, than the professor's imagination dared to go, vigorous as was its flight. Thus do the realities of nature constantly outstrip the halting imagination of man.

A son of Professor Hitchcock, Professor Charles H. Hitchcock, State Geologist of Maine, informed me that, during a recent fit of sickness, his father saw spread before him large beds of sandstone, covered with tracks, such as are found in the Connecticut Valley; and that these tracks enabled him to clear up some doubtful points in reference to them, which he had been unable to do by any other means.

As I write this, I am reminded of a vision that Mrs. Denton had while examining a specimen of sandstone from the Connecticut Valley, she knowing its nature :

" I see the whole surface of the rock exposed for acres. There are many footprints, of different sizes, some larger than any that I have seen. In two places I see large jaws and teeth in the rock; they are semicircular, and the teeth flattish and broad. In one place I see a track go round, then it comes to the edge, and I see no farther.

"I do not believe they have opened the richest place yet. There seems a large collection of fossils in one place; I am sure there are bones.

" Now I see a great many feet and ancles. The feet are divided, and the leg is roundish; it has a chubby look, quite unlike that of a fowl."

It is to be hoped that some of these fossils will be found, and the nature of the animals that made the tracks be determined to the satisfaction of all.

Where there is one who possesses the power of seeing psychometrically, there are probably three who possess the power of feeling. For years I have sought to develop in myself the power to see the pictures that all objects contain, but in vain; yet, I am able to feel influences proceeding from substances that had once belonged to organic bodies, and can at times, by this means, from a portion of bone describe the kind of animal to which it originally belonged. In the following case we have, I think, the result of the unconscious exercise of this power:

"In the town of North Walsham, Norfolk, 1788, the *Fair Penitent* was performed. In the last act, where Caliste lays her hand on the skull, a Mrs. Berry, who played the part, was seized with an involuntary shuddering and fell on the stage. During the night her illness continued; but the following day, when sufficiently recovered to converse, she sent for the stage-keeper and anxiously inquired where he procured the skull. He replied, from the sexton, who informed him it was the skull of one Norris, a player, who, twelve years before, was buried in the graveyard. That same Norris was her first husband. She died in six weeks."

Possessed of considerable psychometric power, she recognized the influence proceeding from the skull, and the recognition produced such a terrible shock that her death was the consequence.

Were I disposed to increase the size of this book, I might give many other instances illustrating the unintentional use of the psychometric faculty. All persons doubtless possess and exercise it more or less, and, by proper cultivation, many might make it of the greatest benefit to themselves and others.

CHAPTER VI.

To the geologist psychometry will be of incalculable benefit. There are wide realms of the past that he has never trod; others, that he has visited, are so enshrouded in gloom that his acquaintance with them is extremely limited. How little we know of the land fauna and flora during the Cretaceous period. Trees must have flourished, reptiles must have crawled, and beasts roamed over the surface of the dry land, when the chalk beds of Europe were being deposited in the depths of the ocean, the cream-colored limestones of Texas, and the marls and greensands of the Atlantic States. Yet of these we know hardly anything; the river deltas of that period are yet to be found, and their fossil contents exhumed; and even when that is done, the record will be very incomplete. The advanced psychometer can take a Cretaceous fossil, and, by means of it, not only obtain the forms of marine animals and plants that lived during this period, but, without much difficulty, those also of the land; and thus fill up the great hiatus that at present exists.

What do we know of the commencement of life? True, the *Oldhamia* has been found by the government surveyors in Ireland, below all other fossil remains, and corals in the Taconic formation of the United

States have been discovered below all other organic forms; but it is probable that the traces of life's beginning lie far below these ; not in fossils to be seen, but in influences that the psychometer alone can detect. Forms too small, too soft, or too fragile to leave visible impress upon the rocks, shall be distinguished and described, and vast ages of apparent barrenness be peopled with busy life.

The imperfection of the geological record, especially as a record of organized existences, must be evident from an examination of those parts of the earth where formations are now being deposited and organic remains buried. This age will be geologically represented in the future by those beds that are now forming at the mouths of rivers, such as the Mississippi, the Ganges, and the Nile; by beds of tufa, in the neighborhood of calcareous springs; by beds of peat, as in some parts of Ireland, New York, and Massachusetts; by accumulations of vegetable remains, as in the Dismal Swamp; by coral reefs, such as are now forming in the Pacific Ocean; and by volcanic products similar to the beds near Vesuvius, which contain the works and remains of man. A million years from this, how large a portion of these formations will be dry land trod by human beings? How much of the land thus above the water will be exposed, so that the beds composing it may be examined by the geologist? Among the bones exposed in those beds and examined by geologists, what chance would there be of finding a fossil gorilla? It would not be buried in peat beds, for peat is not formed in countries hot enough for it to exist in. It would not be found in a coral reef, for it is altogether confined to the land. Almost the only chance of discovering the bones of this animal would be in tufaceous deposits, or in beds formed at the mouths of some of the rivers of Western Africa. But how extremely unlikely it would be for any future geologist to exhume the bones of an animal that while living eluded the gaze of naturalists for centuries. So, of course, it must be with many animals that lived millions of years ago. What fishes must have existed of which we have no scale! What reptiles have crawled that have left no track! Had it not been for the enduring character of the dermal skeleton of the ganoids, what should we have known of the strange fishes of the Devonian period? And how many fishes have existed with cartilaginous bodies, of which we have no vestige and are not likely to obtain any! What myriads of beings must have lived and died whose memorial has perished! Of the more than a hundred reptiles, and other animals, whose tracks have been found in the sandstones of the Connecticut Valley, what should we have known if the shore of the estuary on which they wandered had not been composed of material fine enough to retain the impressions made upon it, and conditions had not been exceedingly favorable for their preservation?

The ornithological page of geology is most sadly deficient. A few suspected fragments from the chalk, a few fossils from the London clay and other Tertiary deposits, are the sum total of our acquisitions. Owing to their habits, the lightness of their bones, and the tendency of their dead bodies to float on the water, but few have become fossil, and hence our knowledge of them is extremely limited. Where are the birds that were doubtless the companions of the marsupial quadrupeds of the Oolite, and probably long preceded them? Where the water-fowl that skimmed the Cretaceous seas and fished in their calcareous waters? The number of species of birds at the present time is about five times as great as that of beasts, and their numerical superiority was probably quite as great during the whole of the Tertiary and Secondary periods; and, if so, what revelations are yet to be made in reference to extinct birds! — revelations that, apparently, psychometry alone can make. For, imperfect as the rocks may be in fossils, they are, in my opinion, absolutely perfect in pictorial representations and organic influences; and hence every feather of every wing of every wandering bird has been delineated and may yet be found. Models of these and of all other animals, will be made, and we shall eventually be able to view the great organic procession from the monad to the man. How extravagant! you exclaim. Granted; but the extravagance of one generation becomes the sober reality of the next.

These fossiliferous rocks are a great volume of natural history, illustrated by plates, — how marvellously executed! — of all that has issued from the fertile womb of life. What translators will be needed for centuries to render this volume into our ordinary language, and make its pictures visible to ordinary observers! Over continents, for ages buried in the depths of the ocean, the psychometer shall wander and view mighty Amazons and Mississippis, on which boat never sailed, flowing from mountains that have long been worn down to fertile plains, and sweeping over wide regions, tenanted by stranger monsters than imagination ever conceived.

The geological history of every continent and island may be obtained, and the minutest detail furnished of all the changes to which it has been subjected. Correct maps of the earth will yet be constructed, showing its land and water surface at all periods of its history. Nay, I do not think we need despair of obtaining eventually the absolute date of the formation of all the rocks, and the actual period when the various animals flourished whose fossil remains are found in them. The heavens are a grand chronometer, over whose dial the stars slowly move, and cycles are marked as our clocks mark the hours; and by the position of the stars, as seen by psychometers, the periods of all the great formations may yet be determined, and, in time, the groups in these formations be gradually worked out. Rocks that are now regarded as contemporaneous, because they contain fossil forms that are identical, may be found separated by ages; life having been retarded on some portions of the globe by unfavorable conditions, as it has been advanced on other portions by favorable ones.

Geology is the history of many worlds; the face of the earth having been renewed many times. Mountains have been elevated and degraded, lakes formed and drained, and life in many forms, on land and in water, has spread over wide areas, flourished for countless generations, and then passed away, to give place to others in their turn to flourish and decay. A precipice a hundred feet high may contain the tablets on which are recorded the events that transpired on the surface of many of these successive worlds; and the future psychometers alone can fully understand and correctly translate these for the benefit of those coming after us; who shall read more correctly than we these instructive volumes containing the history of the past.

To the miner, psychometry gives eyes that see through granite almost as readily as through glass; and he shall trace the courses of veins deeply buried under drift accumulations as readily as he does the windings of rivers on the surface.

Frequently, in travelling over the country in the cars, Mrs. Denton will say to me, there is oil under here, or there is lead or copper in this neighborhood; and, in many cases, I have afterward verified the statements, though neither of us, apart from psychometry, knew anything respecting these deposits.

For instance: in passing from Richmond to Quebec, in January last, as we approached Black River Station, Mrs. Denton remarked, "There is considerable copper in this neighborhood." "In what form does it exist?" I inquired. "Some of it appears to be the sulphuret; but there is a good deal of native copper, resembling that which I have seen in the Lake Superior region; it is the first of that kind that I have seen in Canada. I see it distributed in detached, irregular masses."

This surprised me very much, for I had, previous to this, no idea that copper existed in its native form in the eastern townships, unless in very fine grains, one specimen of which I had seen, but from a different locality. But what was my surprise, a few days after ward, at the dinner-table, to hear one gentleman inform another that a piece of native copper had been found in a gravel bank near *Black River*. A few days afterward, Rev. W. L. Thompson, of Stanstead, showed me a specimen from the same locality.

When properly cultivated, what an advantage psychometry will be to the miner and to the world. Digging for metals will be as certain as the reaping of the ripened grain. Mining, at the present time, is a most hazardous business, more than half the mines worked never paying expenses; but it shall not always be. The vast stores of lead, copper, silver, gold, and precious stones, that are lying concealed in the dark recesses of the earth, shall be exposed and obtained. Deep pits need no longer be made to bury the hopes and the money of the men that dig them; nor tunnels made by incredible labor be abandoned when success is nearly certain, by men whose future lives are embittered with poverty and disappointment. These things will become stories of the past, to be repeated no more in the future. Of the wealth of the earth's interior, few beyond psychometers who may have examined it have any idea.

Astronomy will not disdain the assistance of this power. As new forms of organic being are revealed, when we go back to the earlier geologic periods, so new groupings of the stars, new constellations will be displayed, when the heavens of those early periods are examined by the piercing gaze of future psychometers. An accurate map of the starry heavens during the Silurian period may reveal to us many secrets that we have been unable to discover, from the shortness of time that has been devoted to intelligent astronomical observations, and make clearly apparent what is at present but dimly seen. Why may we not indeed be able to read the history of the various heavenly bodies, especially those belonging, to the solar system with which we are so intimately related, — their geological, their natural, and, perchance, their human history? For ages their influences have been rayed upon the earth, for ages they have been relating their stories to their sister worlds, patiently waiting till the intelligent soul should come that could understand their revelations. What books are yet to be written, what histories recorded, and what light to be shed on great problems that have agitated the minds of thinkers for thousands of years! I have good reason to believe that trained psychometers will be able to travel from planet to planet, and read their present condition minutely, and their past history. It may be asked, How shall we be able to know whether the statements that are made are correct or not? The revelations of one may be compared with the revelations of another; and we shall thus be able to judge of their correctness, as we do the statements of astronomers, who see with their sky-piercing tubes what is invisible to the ordinary spectator.

To the physiologist and anatomist it presents a microscope, by which the organs of living animals can be seen as they perform their varied functions; the tissues examined, fresh and beautiful, as they are pervaded by the vital currents; disease traced to its lurking place, and the operation of the appropriate remedy be watched as the system returns to its equilibrium. The secret history of every animal may be obtained, from its birth to its death, and life be made to reveal its most cherished secrets. The great chain of organic existence may be traced, link by link, and the nature of the connection between them be fully understood.

Psychometry has already been employed in the cure of diseases; its principal value having been, hitherto, in giving a correct diagnosis; which can readily be done, in consequence of the sympathy that can be established between psychometers and the diseased; and also by means of that clear vision which has been illustrated in several of our experiments.

I have known persons from letters to give accurate descriptions of the diseases of the persons who wrote them, though having no previous knowledge of the writer. The good that may be accomplished in this way is incalculable.

The artist will find his field almost infinitely extended, as the panoramas of the earlier worlds pass before his eyes. What mountains he shall see in sullen grandeur, as just upheaved they stand, unworn by frosts and rains! What cataracts pouring over immense precipices, long since worn down and swept away! The historical past can be represented by him with all accuracy of surroundings, feature, and costume, and we shall no longer be troubled with the lies on canvas that pass for historical paintings.

Who can estimate the value of psychometry to the historian? "History," said Voltaire, "is a grand lie;" it will be the work of the psychometer to make it a grand truth. The biography of all nations is faithfully recorded somewhere, and all that is needed, I doubt not, can be obtained. What the soul asks for, Nature, in her superabundant fulness, is able and willing to grant. We ask to be delivered from the fables in which the early history of all nations is shrouded, for light to arise upon the darkness of the past; and it shall be done. The history of the early dwellers in Britain, France, Germany, Denmark, and Switzerland shall be read in the light of this power, and the still older histories of the early dwellers in Greece, Asia Minor, Egypt, and India. Man's history on this globe may possibly extend over millions, instead of merely over thousands of years, and we may watch every step of the process by which the brutal savage was eventually transformed into the man. We shall wander along the shore of time, and watch the empires as they rise and fall before us, as rise and fall the waves of a swelling tide. By the aid of psychometry we can tread the sands of Egypt, and see the united multitudes as they drag the ponderous stones and heave the enduring pyramids; walk the streets of Athens in the artistic days of Pericles, and behold it in its wondrous beauty, as adorned by those ancient lovers of art; or when Socrates drops his thoughts in the market-place, like pearls; or when in academic bowers we listen to the voice of his noble disciple, Plato; through the streets of Jerusalem when Solomon sits on the throne of his glory, and the new temple shines in its splendor, "the joy of all the earth;" stand on the Galilean mountain and hear the peaceful lessons that are spoken by the Man of Nazareth, and mark the rapt attention of the multitude as they hear the gracious words that fall from his lips.

The sword that Cromwell used is imbued with his stern spirit, and is prepared to reveal the secrets of its master when a worthy listener shall appear. It is not surprising that relics of Napoleon bring large sums; they are the recipients of the actions and even thoughts of this mighty master of war, and will yet make known what no biographer has written. What a tale a chip of the pyramids might tell, or of the stony-faced Sphinx, that has stared upon a hundred generations as they marched to their destiny over the sands before it! Could the tomb of Mahomet be rifled, what revelations of the private life of the camel-driver it could give us! The history of the world has yet to be written; these accurate, uncorruptible witnesses of the past shall be heard, and their testimony taken.

The history of the *people,* so sadly neglected by historians, shall be sought for and found; for the life of the meanest plebeian is detailed as accurately as the deeds of the proud patrician. The gradual advance of all peoples in language, from the first monosyllabic grunts, to the polished tongues of Europe; in art, from the chipped stone and the rude cave, to the sculptured marble and the stately palace; in religion, from the worship of crawling beetles to the recognition of the Divine Spirit of the universe,— these, and more, will all be traced; and the clouds that now rest over the histories of all nations shall melt away in the beams of the rising sun.

There is a practical, every-day side to psychometry well worthy of consideration. It must be evident to

those who place any faith in the examinations recorded
in this volume, that all bodies, organic bodies more especially, are transmitting influences continually to surrounding objects, the tendency of which is to bring
these objects into a similar condition to their own.
We may readily see how valuable this knowledge is,
and how it explains many facts that are constantly presenting themselves, and are dismissed as mysteries.
Radiant forces pass from us continually, as truly as
light proceeds from the stars; and though they may
be unseen, they are by no means unfelt. "Talk of
the devil, and he will appear," is an old adage, and
made probably in consequence of the vicinity of an
individual directing our attention to him; his atmosphere causing us to think of him, though we perceive
not the reason. Sensitive persons can be influenced
in this way, I am persuaded, at great distances. Husband and wife mutually influence each other, and the
tendency is, though it may fail to secure the object
from the operation of counteracting causes, to bring
both parties to a closer resemblance to each other in
every respect. This has long been noticed, even physically; long-married and lovingly-united couples increase in outward resemblance as year after year passes away. Mentally, this is notorious, and morally not
less so. Where one is on a decidedly inferior plane
to the other, the degrading tendency felt by the higher
and superior may produce great unhappiness and consequent inharmony; hence, the necessity of attending
to the intuitive suggestions which may rise in the soul
previous to an alliance on which so much depends, and
in which the interests of so many may be involved.

To the maiden, who shrinks at the presence of the man who wishes to be her life-companion, I say, let no persuasion of friends, no prospect of wealth, no fear of want, no urgent entreaties or prayers of a lover, induce you to neglect that small voice, which proceeds from woman's wisest instructor and best adviser.

When persons are long and very intimately associated, the life-power of the one seems to become linked with that of the other. Persons have been known to feel a shock caused by the death of a twin brother, though separated at the time by hundreds of miles. Some cases of this kind have occurred during the present war. Long-married people frequently die within a short time of each other; their condition reminding one of the expression of Judah, in reference to Jacob and Benjamin, "His life is bound up in the lad's life."

As the stove parts with its heat to bring all surrounding objects into its own heated condition, so we affect those surrounding us. Not more certainly does a rose diffuse its fragrance than human beings dispense their influence wherever they go. We are each surrounded by an atmosphere, which can convey to sensitives the impression of our character and condition. Wherever the foot touches the ground, the impression of the man is left upon it, so that even the dog, by means of it, can track his master hours after he has passed over the ground; and persons have been known to trace murderers in this way over a large extent of country several days after they had passed.

Not only does a speaker reach his audience by the sounds that strike the ear, and rays of light that pass

from him to the eye, but by invisible rays that reach
the interior sense; and enable him, more than by all
else, to charm and captivate them.   When a speaker
uses a manuscript, that receives it to a great extent
instead of the audience; and hence, such lectures are
pronounced cold and insipid; though the language
may be perfect, the ideas all that could be wished, and
the elocution faultless.   Something is wanting; we
cannot tell what; but all feel it.   Until a speaker has
established a sympathy between himself and his audience, his position is far from being agreeable to himself, or pleasant to them.   Hence, everything that
tends to place a barrier between a speaker and his
audience should be avoided.   All boxes, called pulpits,
all desks and tables, are a hindrance to the free communication that ought to take place between them.
It has long been noticed that preachers give much
better sermons in little country schoolhouses than in
fine churches in the city.   They are nearer the people;
there is less obstruction between them, and a true
sympathy is more readily established.

By the connection existing between speaker and
hearer, he can call up in their minds the feelings existing in his own.   Love, hate, revenge, and even frenzy;
all these are thus communicated, and each one thus
influenced becomes in turn a centre to radiate these
influences to those around.   When the number affected
is large, and the feeling intense, it consumes like a
furnace, and transforms into its own nature whatever
it comes in contact with.   The most indifferent spectator sometimes becomes as rabid as any actor, without
being able to assign a reason.

Where an audience is antagonistic to a speaker, if sensitive, he perceives it; and unless remarkably positive, and his positiveness arouses him to unusual action, he will be so affected by it as to lower the tone of his discourse, or even, as in cases that I have heard of, be compelled abruptly to close it. Where, on the contrary, the audience sympathizes with him, he receives from them as truly as he imparts, and, upborne by their sympathy, he mounts to regions of philosophy that unassisted he could never gain, and pours out his soul in burning eloquence that startles and thrills him not less than his hearers.

Is a man religious? not more truly does the sun shine, imparting its glory to surrounding objects, than that man's religious influence passes from him to all persons and things within its sphere. The house in which he lives, as well as the house in which he worships, becomes a religious house; and the word, thus applied, is by no means as inappropriate as some would have us believe, who see the surface, but not the interior of things. Brutality and lust go forth in like manner, impressing and influencing all within their range. Houses become so imbued with the influence of the people that live in them that sensitive persons can feel that influence as soon as they enter; and if it is unpleasant, they have a feeling of uneasiness, or positive unhappiness, as long as they are subject to it. Many persons feeling this, are entirely unaware of its origin, and suffer the consequences of their ignorance.

It has long been known that the young and healthy impart their health and vigor to the sickly and infirm. Of this, David's advisers seem to have been aware, when, in his old age, they brought the fair Shunamite damsel to " cherish the king."

For this reason, old and young should not unite in matrimony, neither should young children sleep with their grandparents, who by this means prolong their own existence at the expense of the children's health.

" Dr. Copeland relates the following case : —

" 'I was a few years since consulted about a pale, sickly, and thin boy of about five or six years of age. He appeared to have no specific ailment, but there was a slow and remarkable decline of flesh and strength, and of the energy of all the functions, — what his mother very aptly termed " a gradual blight." After inquiring into the history of the case, it came out that he had been a very robust and plethoric child up to his third year, when his grandmother, a very aged person, took him to sleep with her; that he soon afterward lost his good looks, and that he had continued to decline progressively ever since, notwithstanding medical treatment. I directed him to sleep apart from his aged grandparent, and prescribed gentle tonics, change of air, etc., and the recovery was very rapid.' " *

Sickly persons should refrain from kissing and fondling children, and healthy persons alone should be nurses. It is important to know who makes our bread; for the dough necessarily receives the influence of those through whose hands it passes. The baker puts his life in his loaf, and influences persons for good or evil, who eat his bread.

The domestication of animals may have been to a great extent produced by man's influence imparted to

* Millingen's Curiosities of Medical Experience, p. 326.

them; which animals acquainted with man are all glad
to receive. This influence was, of course, more readily imparted to them when man was a savage, and
there exisited a greater familiarity between the beast
and man.

Animals, in their turn, affect human beings. The
influence of healthy horses, cows, dogs, and other animals is beneficial to the sick and the infirm; and much
of the robust health enjoyed by those surrounded by
their influence, in spite of wide departures from correct living, may be attributed to this. Puny children
might play with dogs and cats, and ride on horseback,
to advantage, as far as their health is concerned.

But as animals below man have but little that is
intellectual or spiritual to radiate, and they are con-
santly receiving these from us while we are in contact
with them, we are robbed on these sides of our being
by the association, and receive the brutal in return.
Men who are constantly with hogs, cattle, and horses,
seem to partake of their nature, manifesting the ani-
mality they are constantly receiving.

There is no doubt that the geologic formations of a
country produce some effect on the people who dwell
above them, and who drink the water which has soaked
through them, and is charged with their peculiar influence. I have found the calcareous deposit of a steam
boiler, so charged with the organic influence of the
rocks through which the water had passed, that it could
be instantly perceived on trying it psychometrically.
Certain countries produce certain men. Much is due
to the original stock from which they were derived;
much to the climate to which they are subjected;

much to their habits; but, after all these and other causes are eliminated, there is quite a remainder which may be attributed to the influence that the rocks of a country and their contents have upon its inhabitants. It may be long before we can tell how much effect, and what kind of an effect, the Lower Silurian limestones, so completely filled with fossil forms, may have upon the people of Nashville, Cincinnati, Ottawa, and Montreal, who live above them; but that they do affect them considerably, I have not the slightest doubt.

There is more received by the earth and its inhabitants from the sun than the natural philosopher or the chemist can detect, and the astrologer himself may have had some reason in the nature of things for his belief in the influence of the stars.

As houses receive and retain the influence of the dwellers in them, so cities, aggregates of houses, receive and retain the influence of the people living and walking in them, and then radiate this influence which they have received, so that a stranger, taking up his residence in a city, has this influence brought to bear upon him, the tendency of which is to mould him according to the general character of the place. Who that has travelled does not know that towns have characters just as truly as individuals? and these characters continue, though generation after generation passes away. Louis Napoleon wisely caused the sentry-box to be destroyed, in which three successive sentries had hung themselves. Not more surely did the influence in that sentry-box permeate these men, than influences proceeding from cities permeate the people living in them, and give them a general character. In a feebler degree this is true of a country; the very rocks drink in the character of the people of the country in which they exist, and give this out again, so as to be perceptible to the sensitive psychometer.

Evil associates not only influence by their practices and language, then, but unseen and unheard baleful influences pass from them, as from the fabled stars darkness was rayed forth. The good man, the intelligent man, is a blessing, everywhere and at all times; the man who walks past his house receives his silent benediction, and even when he is dead, the very stones of his hearth spread benign influences around them, and the world is better and more intelligent for his having lived in it. The virtues of mankind outnumber their vices. Their crimes, about which so much is written and said, are but dust in the balance, compared with their good deeds, constantly poured out, and as little regarded as the oft-repeated showers; and in consequence of this, every generation born into the world has a more glorious heritage than the preceding; not only are they the richer and better for the mechanical inventions, the architectural improvements, the scientific advancements, but the world is every year becoming more imbued with intelligence, refinement and virtue, which are silently moulding the masses into more lordly beings, in turn to leave the world better than they found it. Could we psychometrize the planets of our solar system and more distant worlds, as we may do at some time, it is probable that we should find all those that are inhabited having a distinct character impressed upon them by the influences proceeding from their inhabitants, and thus, with their light, these influences may proceed, and they be mutually telegraphing to each other their mental and moral condition, as age after age passes away.

The doctor's presence, if he is healthy and genial, may be of more benefit to the patient than his pills; and mothers, by their soothing manipulations, frequently cure unconsciously their sick children, by imparting to them the health and vigor of their own constitutions. By a knowledge of such facts, much suffering may be removed, and the sum of human enjoyment be greatly increased.

Women are much more susceptible of psychometric impressions than men, probably in the proportion of five to one. And this may be the reason why they are quicker witted, arrive at correct conclusions easier and sooner, and are unable so frequently to give the reason for those conclusions. Ask a woman why she thinks a thing is so, "Because it is," is the answer; and this has been styled "woman's reason." There is a good reason why women employ it. They have such an assurance of the truth of what they say that no doubt exists in their minds; but as they arrived at this assurance intuitively, and by no process of reasoning, they are of course unable to give any other than "woman's reason." While man is toiling up the steep by painful steps, with laboring breath and sweating brow, woman flies to the summit in an instant, and wonders that man should be such a laggard.

When woman shall employ her psychometric power in a scientific direction, as she will ere 'ong, some of our savans may tremble for their laurels. I affirm that by psychometry a woman may have in one year a more correct idea of the condition of the earth and its occupants during the geologic periods than any man without it could in a lifetime. I speak with confidence in reference to geology, for I speak what I know; and I have no doubt that a similar statement in reference to other sciences could be truthfully made.

Woman's superior sensitiveness is frequently manifested, and laughed at by man; and more frequently hidden on account of his ridicule. A lady sees her husband in close conversation with a smooth-spoken gentleman, and, as soon as he is gone, she exclaims, " Oh, John, don't have anything to do with that man!" "What do you know about him?" is the half-angry exclamation of her husband. "Nothing," she replies; "but you will be sorry if you have any dealings with him." The strong-minded man, despising what he calls the "whim" of his wife, only remembers her warning when he finds himself victimized by this artful gentleman. But, of course, it only happened so; and he is no more inclined to heed his wife's "whims" than before.

Psychometry will yet be employed for the discovery and prevention of crime. In its presence, and it is omnipresent, the faintest whisper is loud as the rolling thunder; and there is no cunning that can conceal an evil deed from its eye; its very commission is its publication. It is a mistake, in more senses than one, to suppose that "dead men tell no tales." Their very bone-cells contain the record of every deed committed and every outrage suffered. The dungeon hears and treasures every sigh of tyranny's victim, and the ashes of the martyrs contain the story of their wrongs.

It has been said that the face of the murderer has been found daguerreotyped on the pupil of the eye of his victim. Whether this is true or not, in the sense of ordinary vision, it is certainly so as far as psychometric vision is concerned. When these facts are universally recognized, and the faculty for reading Nature's all-containing book is developed, its influence will certainly be a restraint on the commission of crime, for then: —

> "Man in the sunshine of the world's new spring
> Shall walk transparent, like some holy thing."

CHAPTER VII.

MYSTERIES REVEALED.

PSYCHOMETRY elucidates many mysterious subjects; shedding light upon those departments of Nature whose gloom has deterred almost every investigator.

FORTUNE-TELLING.

It is a notorious fact that many fortune-tellers do tell incidents in the lives of those who visit them; sometimes, indeed, they give an outline of their past histories, though entirely unacquainted with the persons. The reason seems to be, that we carry with us, wherever we go, the history of our lives, which are raying from us continually. Sensitive persons can read this history, when they come into our presence, somewhat as the past history of fossils and pebbles, recorded in this volume, were obtained. In this way we may account for the great success of some fortune-tellers, and the interest taken in them by intelligent persons. Mademoiselle Lenormond, a celebrated fortune-teller of Paris, amassed a fortune of 500,000 francs. She was consulted by Robespierre, Barras, Josephine, Louis XVIII., and Madame de Stael; and this could hardly have been, unless she had possessed some extraordinary power, by which she could in some way satisfy the intelligence of her visitors. Zschokke, the celebrated German author, whom I have previously quoted, seems to have been sensitive enough to receive impressions from individuals in this way. He says : —

"I am almost afraid to speak of this, not because I am afraid to be thought superstitious, but that I may thereby strengthen such feelings in others; and yet it may be an addition to our stock of soul-experience, and therefore I will confess! It has happened to me sometimes on my first meeting with strangers, as I listened silently to their discourse, that their former life, with many trifling circumstances therewith connected, or frequently some particular scene in that life, has passed quite involuntarily, and as it were dream-like, yet perfectly distinct before me. During this time I usually feel so entirely absorbed in the contemplation of the stranger's life, that at last I no longer see clearly the face of the unknown wherein I undesignedly read, nor distinctly hear the voices of the speakers, which before served as a commentary to the text of their features. For a long time I held such visions as delusions of the fancy, and the more so as they showed me even the dress and motions of the actors, rooms, furniture, and other accessories. By way of jest, I once, in a familiar family circle at Kirchberg, related the secret history of a seamstress who had just left the room and the house. I had never seen her before in my life; the people were astonished, and laughed, but were not to be persuaded that I did not previously know that of which I spoke; for what I uttered was the *literal* truth. I on my part was not less astonished that my dream-pictures were confirmed by the reality. I became more attentive to the subject, and when propriety admitted it, I would relate to those whose life thus passed before me, the subject of my vision, that I might thereby obtain confirmation or refutation of it. It was invariably ratified, not without consternation on their part. I myself had less confidence than any one in this mental jugglery. So often as I revealed my visionary gifts to any new person, I regularly expected to hear the answer, 'It was not so!' I felt a secret shudder when my auditors replied that it was true, or when their astonishment betrayed my accuracy before they spoke. Instead of many, I will mention one example, which pre-eminently astounded me. One fair day, in the city of Waldshut, I entered an inn (the Vine) in company with two young student-foresters; we were tired of rambling through the woods. We supped with a numerous company at the *table d' hote,* where the guests were making very merry with the peculiarities and eccentricities of the Swiss, with Mesmer's magnetism, Lavater's physiognomy, &c. &c. One of my companions, whose national pride was wounded by their mockery, begged me to make some reply, particularly to a handsome young man who sat opposite to us, and who had allowed himself extraordinary license. This man's former life was at that moment presented to my mind; I turned to him, and asked him whether he would answer me candidly, if I related to him some of the most secret passages of his life, I knowing as little of him personally as he did of me. That would be going a little farther, I thought, than Lavater did with physiognomy. He promised, if I were correct in my information, to admit it frankly. I then related what my vision had shown me, and the whole company were made acquainted with the private history of the young merchant; his school years, his youthful errors, and, lastly, with a fault committed in reference to the strong-box of his principal. I described to him the uninhabited room, with whitened walls, where, to the right of the brown door, on a table, stood a black money-box, &c. &c. A silence prevailed during the whole narration, which I alone occasionally interrupted, by inquiring whether I spoke the truth. The startled young man confirmed every particular, and even, what I had scarcely expected, the last mentioned. Touched by his candor, I shook hands with him over the table, and said no more. He asked my name, which I gave him, and we remained together talking till past midnight."

Zschokke, referring to this power of his, subsequently adds: — "'What demon inspires you? Must I again believe in possession?' exclaimed the *spiritual* Johann Von Riga, when, in the first hour of our acquaintance, I related his past life to him, with the avowed object of learning whether or not I deceived myself. We speculated long on the enigma, but even his penetration could not solve it." In his last reference to this remarkable power, which enabled him to read the history of individuals, as the psychometers mentioned in this volume read the history of things, he says: — "Not another word about this strange seer-gift, which I can aver was of no use to me in a single instance, which manifested itself occasionally only, and quite independently of any volition, and often in relation to persons in whose history I took not the slightest interest. Nor am I the only one in possession of this faculty. In a journey with two of my sons, I fell in with an old Tyrolese, who travelled about selling lemons and oranges, at the inn at Unterhauerstein, in one of the Jura passes. He fixed his eyes for some time upon me, joined in our conversation, observed that, though I did not know him, he knew me, and began to describe my acts and deeds, to the no little amusement of the peasants, and astonishment of my children, whom it interested to learn that another possessed the same gift as their father. How the old lemon-merchant acquired his knowledge, he was not able to explain to himself, nor to me ; but he seemed to attach great importance to his hidden wisdom."

That some persons are possessed of the power of telling the past history of individuals who are perfect strangers to them, is most evident then; and where the past is told correctly thus, it is easy to become credited with the power of telling the future, though the ability to do the one by no means proves the ability to do the other. I do not deny that this can be done, but I have not had as yet sufficient evidence to satisfy me.

DREAMS.

Into the land of dreams, over whose boundary philosophy never ventures, where the law of gravitation is suspended, over whose fields the living and dead walk and converse, where beggars are kings and queens, and where kings and queens, terror-stricken, flee, pursued by avenging ghosts, boldly marches psy-

chometry, and maps out for us a portion of this enchanted land.   Persons who have been examining
specimens for me have sometimes fallen asleep, and,
on relating their dreams, I have, at times, been able to
trace a direct connection between them and the articles that they were examining.   In some cases they
were evidently a continuation of the psychometric
examination, revealing facts of which previously the
dreamer knew nothing.   Many of the visions seen by
us in our sleeping hours may proceed directly from
the objects we have handled through the day, the persons we have come in contact with, the food we have
swallowed, or the bed we lie upon.   Very sensitive
persons may be affected by influences so slight that it
would appear, to one unacquainted with these matters,
utterly impossible for them to affect an individual.

" Several years ago, during a severe winter, the
Schuylkill River, near Philadelphia, became thickly
bridged over with ice, and thousands of persons re-
sorted thither for the exercise of skating, sliding, etc.
Among other inventions for the amusement of those
visiting the place, there was a post sunk through the
ice, at the top of which there was a pivot and a horizontal revolving arm or shaft attached to it.   To the end
of this the drag-ropes of sleds were attached, so that,
by pushing the shaft, the sleds, with persons on them,
might be made to revolve swiftly in a circle upon the
ice.   Among the rest, a negro got upon the sled, and
the person in charge of the shaft caused it, for sport,
to revolve so violently that the negro was thrown outward by the centrifugal force, and, striking violently
against a large projecting piece of ice, was instantly

killed. This occurrence was witnessed by a physician, a friend of my informant, who happened to be present. On that same evening the physician had occasion to prepare a dose of pills for one of his patients, a lady extremely susceptible to magnetic influences. As he was mixing the ingredients of the pills, and rolling them in his fingers, he related, in all its particulars, to persons in his office, the occurrence he had witnessed on the river during the day. The pills were afterward dispatched to the lady by another person. The next day the physician, seeing one of the lady's family, inquired concerning her health. In the answer that was returned it was stated, among other things, that she had a singular dream the night previous. She dreamed that she was somewhere on the ice, where many people were sliding and skating; that she had there seen a negro thrown from a revolving sled against a cake of ice and instantly killed, etc. Her dream, as related, was an exact reproduction of all the essential statements of facts which had, without her knowledge, been given by the physician while he was preparing the pills, and concerning which fact she had received no information from any quarter." *

As the doctor rolled the pills in his fingers, his influence was communicated to them, and, when swallowed by his patient, a direct psychometric line of communication was established between them. Along that passes the inquiring soul, and receives from his the image so recently and so strongly impressed there, and thus the dream.

There are many facts to show that persons asleep

* American Phrenological Journal.

are much more sensitive to refined influences than when awake; and many remarkable circumstances related to dreaming may be explained when the enlarged powers of the soul, which psychometry familiarizes us with, are taken into account.

When at Canadice, in the State of New York, a gentleman of that place, named A. C. Bishop, informed me of a singular dream that he had. During a snow-storm in the previous March, the stage broke through a bridge about half a mile above the village, was overturned into the water, and the mail-bag swept down the creek. Many persons sought for it day after day, among whom was Mr. Bishop himself. It was all in vain, however, and they came to the conclusion that it must have been washed away and covered up with the gravel carried down by the stream to its mouth. A month after this, when the snow had all melted off the ground, he dreamed that he saw the mail-bag lying in a certain place. So strongly did the dream impress him that he awoke, but slept again and dreamed it a second time. In the morning he told his dream to several persons in the shop, who laughed at the idea of finding the mail-bag then; but on going to the place, which he immediately did, "I found it," said he, "not ten feet from the place where I dreamed that it was."

A Methodist clergyman at Carleton Place, Canada West, informed me that a gentleman of his acquaintance, having on his finger a heavy gold ring, went out in a boat on the Mississippi River, a small stream in the neighborhood, on a pleasure excursion. On his return he discovered that the ring was gone. After searching for some time in vain, all gave it up as lost. A young woman who lived in a house near the river, and who was acquainted with the parties and the circumstance, dreamed that night that she was on the river bank, and, looking into the water, saw the ring by the edge of a particular stone. She told her dream next morning, and, on proceeding to the spot, the ring was found in the identical place where she had observed it in her dream.

As psychometers discover the condition of distant objects that they have never beheld, so dreamers find what in the waking condition they might look for in vain. *How* this is accomplished is not so easy to explain.

RELICS AND AMULETS.

Veneration for relics seems to most educated people absurd enough, and furnishes food for the mirthfulness of some, as it does for the trickery of others. There is said to be as much wood of the "true cross" as would build a man-of-war, and as many teeth of St. John as would fill a peck measure. Yet, despite the superstition that may hide in the love of relics, there is a foundation in truth for it, as indeed there is in almost every superstition, or they could never spring up among so widely distributed peoples and outlast man's most enduring monuments. Belief in relics, charms, and amulets, has its root in the nature of things. A pebble from Jerusalem is very different from one picked up on Dover beach, although no chemical analysis could reveal it. Both are flint, both rounded by the action of the water, and yet they are

as different psychometrically as the history of the
United States is from that of Greece.

An amulet handled by a strong, healthy man, consequently imbued with his influence, and then worn by
a diseased person, might be of great benefit, especially
to very sensitive persons, and in cases of nervous disease.   The laying on of hands is not in all cases
"mere idle mummery," and the belief in the sacred
character of buildings and particular articles is in accordance with many facts that cannot be denied.

What would not a Jew give for some object that
Moses had handled; or a Christian for some undoubted
relic of his Master? While I write this, furniture made
from the Old Elm on Boston Common is advertised for
sale. Would not the wood of some other old elm be
just as good? No. That wood contains the spirit of
Boston, is permeated with the soul of the old revolu-
tionary times, and knows a thousand times more about
the place than the oldest inhabitant. The buyer may
not dream of it, but this unrecognized truth augments
its price, notwithstanding.

HALLUCINATIONS.

Hallucination has been defined as the intellectual
state of a person who believes he sees and hears what
no other person sees or hears; who perceives things
impalpable to the senses. Esquirol defines it "as a
cerebral or psychical phenomenon, acting independently of the senses, and consisting of external sensations, that the patient believes he experiences,
although no external agent acts materially on his
senses." Under this head have been collected a va-

riety of phenomena, some of which psychometry readily explains; thus transferring them from this wilderness to the cultivated fields of science, where they take their place along with other classified facts.

The case of the painter, referred to on page 21, is placed among hallucinations by writers upon this subject; but how readily it takes its place in that of simple psychometric vision. Since a stone takes in the images of surrounding objects and retains them, how much more does the human brain, provided as it is with windows for the very purpose of receiving, and a tablet for recording them. The image of the sitter received into his mind was projected upon the chair at will, some psychometers possessing this power ; and thus he was able to paint him accurately without any farther sitting. As the daguerreotypist needs but one sitting, having during that received an accurate likeness of the sitter, so in this case, where an apparatus was employed as much superior to it as the works of nature are superior to those of art.

Under the head of Hallucinations in febrile and other maladies, De Boismont gives the following case, taken from the *Edinburgh Medical and Surgical Journal:* "I was called in, says Dr. Alderston, to Mrs. ———, a lady eighty years of age, whom I had often attended for the gout. She complained of unusual deafness, with a great distention of the digestive organs, and was expecting an attack. Notwithstanding her great age, this lady enjoyed good health. She confided to me that for some time past she had been disturbed by visions. The first time that she noticed the occurrence, she believed that several uninvited friends visited her. Having recovered from her first surprise, she evinced some regret at not being able to converse with them, and was about to give orders to have a card-table set. For this purpose she rang the bell. On the entrance of the servant, all the party disappeared. The lady expressed much surprise at their abrupt departure, and the servant had great difficulty in convincing her that no one had been in the room.

" She felt so ashamed of the illusion that for several days and nights she suffered, in silence, the appearance of a considerable number of phantoms, some of which represented long-lost friends, and revived thoughts almost entirely effaced. The lady contented herself with ringing the bell, when the entrance of the servant rid her of their presence.

" It was some time before she could make up her mind to confide her sufferings to me. There was nothing either in her conversation or conduct to indicate a derangement of intellect, and she, as well as her friends, were convinced of her perfect sanity.

" The affection was relieved by plasters on the feet, and mild medicines, and was shortly afterwards entirely cured by a regular attack of gout. Since that time both her reason and health have been good." *

The simple explanation that I give of this is, that under the peculiar physiological condition of the lady, her brain was brought to that sensitive condition which is natural to some persons at all times, and that while in this condition she was able to see either the images of persons that had been impressed upon her brain, or the various objects in the house gave out the images

---

* De Boismont, Dreams, Visions, etc., p. 273.

that they had received, and she was able in this state
to perceive them. The most probable explanation is,
that they were the images existing in her own brain,
as the manifestation of these would require a less
degree of sensitiveness than that of the other. The
persons she saw on the first occasion were evidently
persons with whom she was familiar, whose likenesses
she had treasured; and of the other " phantoms,"
some, at least, were long-lost friends — friends that she
had nearly forgotten, as she thought, but whose images
had been ineffaceably stamped upon the soul.

The entrance of the servant caused the disappearance of the images by disturbing the passive condition
favorable to their manifestation, and rendering her too
positive for their impression.

Diseases, which weaken the physical powers of the
patient, seem to produce a condition eminently favorable to the manifestations that we are now considering,
and that are so frequently placed under the head of
hallucination. As the exterior senses are deadened,
and their power to convey impressions to the soul is
weakened, so the interior senses become stronger and
more active ; and what was previously unseen and
unheard, becomes visible and audible, generally to
the great astonishment of the party hearing and observing.

' Mademoiselle N—— was convalescing after a very
prolonged fever, which had reduced her to a state of
extreme weakness. All her family had gone to church,
when a violent storm arose. Mademoiselle N—— went
to the window to watch its effects ; the idea of her
father suddenly struck her, and, under existing cir-

cumstances, she felt much uneasiness. Her imagination soon persuaded her that her father had perished.
In order to conquer her fear, she went into the room
in which she was accustomed to see him in his arm-
chair. On entering, she was much surprised at seeing him in his place, and in his accustomed attitude.
She immediately approached to inquire how he had
come in, and in addressing him, attempted to place her
hand on his shoulder, but she encountered only space.
Very much alarmed, she drew back, and, turning her
head as she left the room, still saw him in the same attitude.

"More than half an hour elapsed from the time she
first saw the apparition until its departure. During
this time, Miss N——, who was convinced that it was
an illusion, entered the room several times and carefully examined the arrangement of the objects, and
especially of the chair." *

The arm-chair, in which her father usually sat, must
have been thoroughly imbued with his influence, radiating from him as influences radiate from all organized
bodies continually. And as these influences are able
to reproduce, to the gaze of the psychometer, the animals from which they passed, and that, millions of years
after they were given forth, what difficulty is there in
conceiving that the influences possessed by the chair
produced the appearance of the father, as seen by the
daughter, when reduced by fever to that passive condition so favorable to the observance of such appearances?

That the image of an object is retained by objects

* De Boismont, p. 276.

contiguous to it, has been noticed by mesmeric opera-
tors repeatedly; and it is doubtless one cause of the
mistakes made by clairvoyants, who see what has been,
instead of what is. I take the following from Cahagnet's Celestial Telegraph : —

"Sometimes the image of a thing remains impressed
in the place where it has stood. M. Teste, in his journal, cites, with respect to this, a curious experiment:
A female somnambulist enters a room and exclaims,
' What a pretty girl is sitting on that chair !' At this
exclamation M. Teste observes to her that she is mistaken; that no pretty girl is there. Far from giving in
to this declaration, she sees one on each chair, and
there were six of them. Unable to account for this
hallucination, M. Teste contented himself with gathering exact details of the dress of these little girls, and
confessed that a little girl precisely similar had been
playing for a moment before the somnambulist entered,
and had jumped on the six chairs, one after the other,
sitting down on them." "I have often recognized,"
says Cahagnet, "that the image of material objects set
in a certain place remained there for a long time."

The excessive use of spirituous liquors seems to
produce a condition that is favorable to the observance
of apparitions such as Nicolai saw, and with which
some psychometers are daily familiar. Dr. Combe
says, "In a case of delirium tremens in an innkeeper
about whom I was consulted, the spectral illusions
continued several days. . . . The man refused to
allow me to look at a blister which had been placed
between the shoulders, because he could not take off
his coat *before the ladies who were in the room.* When

I assured him there was no one in the room, he smiled
at the joke, as he conceived it to be; and, in answer
to my questions, described them as several in number,
well dressed and good-looking. At my request he
rose up to shake hands with them, and was astonished
at finding them elude his grasp, and his hand strike
the wall. This, however, convinced him that it was an
illusion, and he forthwith took off his coat. In a few
days the ladies vanished from his sight." *

Another case is related in the Edinburgh Medical
and Surgical Journal, in which a wine merchant went
into the cellar to draw some liquor for a girl, when he
noticed a quantity of oyster shells on the ground; but
on stooping to pick them up discovered there were
none. On preparing to leave the cellar, he saw a sol-
dier with a forbidding countenance attempt to enter.
He asked what he wanted; but receiving no answer,
attempted to seize him, when he proved to be a phan-
tom. During the whole night he was tormented with
apparitions of living friends, or of those who had long
been dead. He was continually getting out of bed to
assure himself of the truth or falsehood of these visions.

The use of hashish, opium, and the inhalation of
nitrous oxide, or laughing-gas, seem to produce, at
times, and with certain constitutions, a similar effect.

Many persons possess psychometric vision when
dying; and, especially, when dying by drowning. Dr.
Conolly tells us of a person, who, in danger of being
swamped on the Eddystone rock, saw the phantoms of
his family passing distinctly before him. The English
opium-eater says, "I was once told by a near relation

* Life and Correspondence of Andrew Combe, p. 177.

of mine, that having in her childhood fallen into a river, and being on the very verge of death, but for the critical assistance which reached her, she saw in a moment her whole life, in its minutest incidents, arrayed before her simultaneously, as in a mirror, and she had a faculty developed as suddenly for comprehending the whole and every part."

"Dr. Binns says, 'We are acquainted with a gentleman, who, being able to swim but little, ventured too far out, and became exhausted. His alarm was great, and after making several but ill-directed efforts to regain the shore, he shouted for assistance, and then sank, as he supposed, to rise no more. . . . Then he saw, as if in a wide field, the acts of his own being, from the first dawn of memory to the moment when he entered the water. They were all grouped and ranged in the order of the succession of their happening, and he read the whole volume of existence at a glance; nay, its incidents and entities were photographed on his mind, limned in light, and the panorama of the battle of life lay before him.'" *

Numerous examples of this kind might be given. They afford us glimpses of man's mighty powers, all but unused in this condition of existence. "We are," indeed, "wiser than we know."

* Sleep, Sensation, and Memory,—Fosgate, p. 43.

CHAPTER VIII.

CONCLUSION.

LITTLE knows the fish of the ocean of air above it, in which the bird swims; still less of the starry realm that lies beyond; and we, with all our boasted powers, hold a similar relation to unknown realms. Like clams in a sand-hole, who know nothing of the flying clouds, the tinkling rills, the sunshine so glorious, and all the busy world of beautiful women and brave men, so we, deepening our holes with each returning tide, know hardly anything of the great worlds surrounding and interpenetrating our own.

I believe that psychometry, as displayed in this volume, and in varied phenomena, generally called "mysterious," which are continually taking place around us, is but the exercise of those faculties which belong to the soul, and are not dependent upon the body for their exercise. Thus the psychometer sees without the use of physical eyes, — sees the past as readily as the present, the far-off as easily as the nigh-at-hand; hears sounds that are inaudible to physical ears, and travels without the ordinary powers of locomotion.

In sleep, as I have shown, persons may learn what they never could in the waking condition; for the body, the soul's master as well as its servant, being powerless, the soul is able to exercise, to some extent, its native powers. In somnambulism, when the senses are doubly locked, so that the loudest voice makes no impression, and the sense of feeling is so completely suspended that what at other times would produce intense pain is not felt at all, — in this condition " the somnambulist can see with his eyes closed and bandaged; he can then even see what waking men in his place cannot see with their open eyes. He can read the contents of letters unopened; he can see through clothing, wood, and metal boxes, and walls of brick and stone; he can tell what is going on in the room above him or in the room below." All this is equally true of persons in a mesmeric condition, as I had abundant opportunities of satisfying myself in England, nearly twenty years ago.

Fasting, the use of narcotics and stimulants, sickness, in which the powers of the body are gradually weakened, loss of sleep, and drowning, are all favorable to the manifestation of the soul's peculiar powers, so different from those of ordinary sensation. The rule is, apparently, that whatever weakens the body, and unfits us for ordinary sensation, in the same ratio strengthens these internal powers, or gives them an opportunity for exercise.

May we not infer from these facts our conscious existence after what is called death? the continued being and activity of the spirit, with a perfect remembrance of all its experiences, and able to travel at will over the wide realm of the past, gathering knowledge at every step, and preparing for the great hereafter that shall still await it?

Our researches and discoveries have been made in

but a small portion of a great and unexplored domain. The very difficulty we have found, in explaining what has come before us in the course of these experiments, convinces me that we have been but coasting along some headland in an unknown ocean; and that great continents yet lie beyond, to be discovered by future explorers.

PART II.

QUESTIONS, CONSIDERATIONS, AND SUGGESTIONS.

BY ELIZABETH M. F. DENTON.

QUESTIONS,

CONSIDERATIONS, AND SUGGESTIONS.

INTRODUCTORY.

THERE are, perhaps, few persons who are by nature more thoroughly skeptical than I; and, though I cannot remember the time when I did not behold objects or their representatives, by night as well as by day, in darkness as well as in light, with closed as well as with open eyes, I was very far from believing such vision other than in every respect illusive. Instructed from infancy to accept nothing as true which failed to address itself to my reason, or which could not be substantiated by facts, I was by no means ready to accept any theory which should give to these illusive forms, as I then regarded them, a character of reality; and it was not until some years after I had commenced to examine specimens by means of this vision that I was prepared to acknowledge it the natural result of forces subject to law, and those laws deserving of investigation. I have, therefore, no word of reproach for those who hesitate to accept the statements contained in this volume until they shall have investigated the subject for themselves. I am certain I should have been one of their number had the evidence been presented by another to my understanding only, instead of having come home with its facts to the recognition of my senses. It was no one examination which convinced me of the error in my former conclusions, but the accumulated evidence of hundreds of experiments, all pointing with significant unanimity to the existence of this faculty in the human economy.

To the minds of such as shall have felt an interest in the perusal of the foregoing pages, and yet have never recognized in their own experience, nor observed in their intercourse with others, any of the phenomena therein described, a long array of inquiries have, no doubt, many times presented themselves, and now clamor for a hearing. Some of these inquiries I will endeavor to answer; to some I can only respond, *I have no answer.* In attempting to present the conclusions at which I have arrived, and the facts and reasonings by which such conclusions have been reached, I must ask permission to draw largely from my own experience. I would gladly avoid this, but at present have not in my possession, from other sources, the requisite material for the purpose, and hence proceed at once to the consideration of those inquiries.

QUESTION I.

" *In the first place, then, (granting the correctness of the statements and the accuracy of the descriptions,) how is this thing done? Are these objects seen as we behold the flowers in the field, the stars in the sky, the lines in the hand?* "

Much, yet not, as a general rule, precisely the same. In some instances they pass before the observer as a

panorama, moving with the velocity of lightning. In
such instances it is, of course, impossible to catch
even the outline of an object, however strikingly peculiar. Partial outlines may, indeed, be traced, but
the object has passed from sight long before the outline is complete. For some time I regarded these
views as merely fragmentary; and it was not until I
learned that, by a powerful effort of the will, these
flying scenes could be made to pause, that I discovered they were not fragmentary, as I had heretofore
supposed, but many, perhaps all of them, objects, or
their representatives, entire in their outline, and as
real, apparently, as are any with which we come in
contact in this every-day world.

At other times, everything around one seems immov-
ably fixed. There is, perhaps, only a small area visible; but, however protracted the observation, this
area, its lights and shadows, its boundaries, the objects, if any, within it—in short, all its features, remain
precisely the same as when the eye of the psychometer first fell upon it, while curtains of impenetrable
darkness close around all beside.

Again, there are times when the psychometer is
no longer a silent observer. Gravitation has lost its
force; his own will is powerless or inactive, and he
finds himself an inhabitant of space instead of a
dweller upon earth. His surroundings are worlds,
and he, cut loose alike from earth and heaven, is moving with a velocity that laughs the lagging winds to
scorn. On, on, on he flies, tireless, fetterless, free;
emphatically free from all that in any respect would
check his speed.

But in these instances we must regard the psychometer as being in a state of utter passiveness. Ignorant of the power in his possession, he spends hours, it may be, in gazing at the various forms of beauty or of horror that flit before his vision when all around him is quiet and his own mind is at rest. Knowing nothing, really, of the nature of these results, he knows not where to look for the cause. Such was my own experience in childhood. Often have I amused myself until a late hour of the night with the scenes which came sweeping past, not my fancy, *but my vision*, as clear and as distinct as were any that greeted my sight by day.

The cause of this phenomenon I then supposed to be the pressure of the lids upon the eye, causing its humors so to arrange themselves as to present these numerous and changing views. My mother gave me this in reply to my inquiries respecting them, and I accepted it with the trust of childhood. Very naturally supposing the eyes of all persons to have been arranged on a plan quite similar to that of my own, and that, consequently, every individual must realize the same or a similar experience, and thinking, farther, that, had there been anything of interest or of value connected therewith, it would long since have been sought out and acknowledged, on approaching the years of discretion I treated this faculty as we naturally treat that to which we attach no value. Occasionally, it is true, I would return to the folly of my childhood, and occasionally I was startled by some seemingly remarkable coincidence between the appearances recognized by this, as Aristotle terms it, "*internal action of the sense of vision*," and the realities of the outer world, as I would *afterward* find them to have existed at the time when I had observed them. But life was of too much practical value to be wasted in idle dreaming, and hence I allowed myself only an occasional visit to this ethereal land of ethereal forms; and to-day, I have no doubt, there are multitudes of persons who have known such experiences from infancy.

We come now to the time when the psychometer begins to feel an assurance that pressure of the lids upon the eye is not the only cause of this phenomenon; to the time when a succession of coincidences leads him to inquire if there be not some relation between these singular visions and the realities of external life. Are you that psychometer? You look the matter over, and wonder if the open eye cannot also behold objects in darkness. You try the experiment, and find that such is, indeed, the fact. Still, there is a difference; and although that difference is in favor of the closed eyes, yet it is evident that the pressure of the lids is not the only cause. Again and again you shut the light from your room and look around you in astonishment. True, you are obliged to sit longer, much longer, perhaps, than would be needful with closed eyes, before you discern aught but the darkness. After waiting, however, until your anxiety has somewhat subsided, here and there a form, in part, is visible. It is, perhaps, a horrible face, or a beautiful flower. It may be a *fac-simile* of something with which you are familiar; it may be utterly unlike anything you have ever seen before. A moment more,

and the darkness rolls over it. Indeed, it seemed little
other than an outgrowth of that darkness, so perfectly
did darkness envelop the larger portion of what you
consider its proper dimensions. Each succeeding experiment gives you a more satisfactory result, and you
find at last that pressure upon the eye has nothing
whatever to do with the matter, and you must look for
some other method of solving the problem, or the
cause must remain a mystery. But, whither can you
go? Books are silent on the subject. The anatomist
does not even recognize an organ in the human economy capable of such vision, much less give you its
anatomy. The optician makes no mention of it, and
would, no doubt, regard it as an abnormal action of
the eye which he makes his study; and whither can
you go? True, Mesmerism has induced something
analogous, but you are not Mesmerized. You are as
perfectly conscious of all that is passing in your presence now as at any other time, and, so far as you are
capable of judging, your condition is not in any respect an abnormal one, the only requisite being that
of mental and physical quiet. You at length take up
Dr. Buchanan's Journal of Man, Vol. i., No. 2. There
is a sudden start of your nerves — your eye kindles —
you turn the pages rapidly, catching here a word and
there a sentence. *"Psychometry!"* you exclaim, "what,
what is this?" You turn back and commence the
paper, reading carefully and devouring eagerly every
line of that startling article. Your cheeks are flushed
—your eye is aglow—there is a tremor in every limb.
What now? Has Dr. Buchanan solved your problem?
Not exactly, but he has, at least, endeavored to trace

to a cause some of the phenomena which seem to you
inseparably linked with this inner sense of sight. You
take courage, and at once resolve to experiment. Is
there not some one whose coöperation would greatly
assist you in these experimental researches? Nay,
rather, you are fortunate if there be one among your
associates who would not think you a fit subject for
the insane asylum should you even manifest an interest in so wild a fancy as is the Doctor's theory. But
you are resolved to experiment. With your eyes closed
you select from your letter-trunk a package, which you
convey, under cover, to the drawer of your dressing-
table, and at night, when all have retired, still wakeful,
anxiously waiting for such an opportunity, you abstract
a letter from that package and place it upon your
brow. With joy unspeakable you realize the various
sensations to which the Doctor has alluded. More
than this, you see — see the face and bust, perhaps, of
a friend who has found in your affections the place of a
brother. You look around you, and you are in his
room; now you see his entire figure. He sits beside
his table writing — "perhaps writing this very letter,"
you think. You allow your fancy a moment's range,
and you are ready to exclaim, "I believe it is from
him; I cannot doubt this influence; it is the same that
ever thrills me when I read his letters!" But you
must have some other evidence — the testimony of the
chirography and of the signature. Noiselessly as possible you arise, your confidence in the identity of the
authorship of this with that of the thrilling letters
you have so frequently received from your friend dur
ing the past few years increasing with every added

grain that falls in the hour-glass. You draw a match
and convey it to your burner, that you may be certain
of the success of your experiment. *I* can appreciate
the depth of your chagrin when the light reveals to
your astonished gaze the signature of an individual as
utterly unlike your friend as darkness is unlike day.
Your friend is all spirit, all nerve, all life; the author
of the sheet before you is, comparatively, a moving,
breathing clod. Your friend writes you because he
must — because the thoughts are there burning in his
brain and he is compelled to give them expression;
and, as he traces the characters by which they are
represented, "they breathe in every line" and gleam
on every page. By some unaccountable freak in nature, the author of the sheet before you has fancied
you, or you would never have had his letter with
which to experiment. You are pained beyond expression. "Bah!" you exclaim, as you bring down the
letter upon the table with a force which a moment
before, judging from your caution in moving, would
have startled the whole house. You turn off the gas
and return to your pillow. How thankful you feel
that no one but yourself has known of your folly. A
reaction has come, and on the breast of Morpheus you
gladly forget your vexation.

Morning dawns. The first note of the robin falls
upon your ear and arouses you to partial consciousness. In this condition a cold, damp weight seems to
hang heavily about your heart. Slowly returning consciousness brings to your mind the cause of this de-
pression, and at once you are awake. Sadly you run
over the events of the preceding evening, — the slum-

bering hopes which had been kindled to a flame, the experiment, and — the failure. Was it a dream? Hopefully you turn to the table, but the package of letters, and the same identical sheet that lies open beside it, convince you that it was all too real. You murmur that hopes so bright in their dawning are doomed so soon to fade, and so ingloriously. You think the subject over once more, and wonder if there is nothing for the race but this continual groping in darkness. With a sigh for humanity, you ask, "Is this then all? Has Nature, with unceasing toil, during all these millions of ages, been fitting up this planet for the reception of her sovereign, Man, and, after her prolonged apprenticeship, with the accumulated wisdom of cycles instead of years, and the united skill of unnumbered forces ready to do her bidding, must her last and crowning effort prove only a stupendous failure?"

The morning bell rings! You must stop moralizing, and take your place with the stupid throng you now feel mankind to be. You arise, but before leaving your room, you must replace those letters in your trunk. With a feeling of mingled shame, vexation and discouragement you take up the package, when, lo! there lies a letter from the very friend you had seen in your evening's experiment. A thought flashes through your mind, and if a thunderbolt had fallen at your feet, you could not have been more thoroughly electrified. For a moment you are powerless. There lie those letters as they have lain for weeks, — the one all inanity, — empty as the space beyond the spheres; the other full of the fire of thought, — the earnestness of a great mind, and the glow of an affectionate heart.

Happening to have been in haste when you filed them away, you had attended to nothing but the order of their dates, and this from your friend, folded, it may be, inside out, had lain pressed upon that wanting all character, until the very spirit of your friend was stamped upon the one as well as upon the other. May it not be possible, then, that your experiment has, indeed, been a success? You think it more than possible, and resolve to repeat it at the earliest opportunity, and with little fear for the result. You try again. Fortunate in your selection, your success more than realizes your highest anticipations, and you tremble with a joy you hardly dare to cherish. Is it strange that you begin to feel a measure of confidence in its reliability? What an extended field for future exploration now opens before you! "Where," you ask, "have been the sages of all past time? What hand can have lain so heavily on the eyelids of a slumbering world as to have deprived it of the knowledge even of so wonderful a possession?" Your first impulse is to publish at once an account of your experiment, and the result. A little reflection determines you to keep your own counsels, at least for the present, and by a course of experiments, which you can yourself conduct, to gain some information relative to the nature of this new-found faculty, and the extent of its real practical value to mankind. Circumstances, no doubt, have more than indicated the wisdom of that determination.

QUESTION II.

"Are these objects seen in daylight, or in darkness?"

They may be seen in both. Usually, however, and it seems to me for valid reasons, darkness is preferable. No one will ask me to prove that to the human eye a weaker may, by the presence of a stronger light, be rendered altogether imperceptible. Any one who has, in the dark, drawn a common match over a rough surface, has observed a line of bright light following in its path, only visible, however, until the match becomes thoroughly ignited, when it is apparently extinguished. That such, however, is only its apparent condition, may be readily ascertained by extinguishing the match, when the former, which is a weaker, and in some respects a different light, will at once reappear. So with that under consideration. Usually the psychometer sees by a weaker, and it may be, a very differently derived light from that which renders visible the tangible objects by which we are surrounded. Hence, it seems reasonable to conclude that the more perfect the darkness that shadows the outward sight, the more perfect will be this interior vision, if I may be permitted thus to designate it.

Again, who of us but has been so blinded by the sunlight on the snow, for example, as to be quite incapable of discerning even the outlines of objects in a room we may have suddenly entered, when that room was as full of daylight as a common uncurtained window could make it? Yet to us, for the time being, even this daylight has been darkness, and we have found ourselves incapable of using it until the organs

of vision have become accustomed to the change.
How materially would the difficulty be increased,
should we continue to stand in the sunlight thus reflected by the snow, and examine minutely the contents of a room but dimly lighted by a taper of the
olden time. Many of us would find ourselves physically incapable of any such examination, while perhaps there are none among us to whom the task would
not be indeed 'a difficult one. In many respects the
sensations of the psychometer, when in the presence
of any strong light, whether natural or artificial, are
analogous to those above indicated, and hence, when
vision only is required, one is often compelled to wait
not only until the organs become adjusted to the new
or changed condition, *but until the eye has been wholly
relieved from any sensible impression made by ordinary light,* before these objects become distinctly visible, or the brain is capable of taking cognizance of
their peculiarities.

May it not, then, with even more propriety, be said
that in this, as in common sight, the ability to use the
weaker is negatived by the presence of other and
stronger light? Be this as it may, the effect is the
same.

Farther than this, there are times when, either from
some peculiar physical condition of the psychometer,
or from some peculiarity of the atmosphere, or of both
combined, the light by which objects are thus made
visible vies in strength, or illuminating power, even
with daylight. Of several instances, analogous in
character, the following will, no doubt, sufficiently illustrate the peculiarity to which I refer.

At one time, while travelling in the West, during the summer of 1861, we were compelled to wait a weary time for the train which was to convey us to Peru, Ill., it having been delayed considerably beyond the usual hour. We had walked with our children through town until they were too weary to appreciate the little beauty left by the previous frosty night. They had exhausted the novelties of the station, consisting of railroad charts and a few dusty as well as rickety seats, and now began to watch earnestly for the coming of the iron horse. At length, his unearthly scream gave warning of his approach, and he came thundering past, as if resolved to visit utter ruin on those who would chain his spirit to the sluggish will of man. "Twenty minutes for dinner!" sang out the brakeman, after announcing the name of the place, while a general rush of the passengers, some to the eating-room, and others to the various places to which they were destined, either for business or pleasure, soon gave me my choice of a seat in any one of the vacant cars. Taking the children each by the hand, while my husband gave orders in reference to baggage, etc., I selected a car and walked leisurely in, very naturally expecting myself and children to be, for a few moments at least, its only occupants. Judge of my surprise, on glancing around, as I entered the car, to find it already crowded with passengers! Many of them were sitting perfectly composed, as if, for them, little interest were attached to this station; while others were already in motion (a kind of confused motion), as if preparing to leave. I thought this somewhat strange, and was about turning to find a vacant seat in another car, when a second glance around showed me that the passengers who had appeared so indifferent to the arrival of the train at Joliet, were rapidly losing their apparent entity, and in a moment more they were to me invisible. I had had sufficient time to note the features, dress, and personal appearance of several, and, taking a seat, I awaited the return of the passengers, thinking it more than probable I might find in them the prototypes of the faces and forms I had a moment before so singularly beheld; nor was I disappointed. A number of those who returned to the car I recognized as being in every particular the counterparts of their late but transient representatives.

But the question arises, how could these individuals be seen in the car, when, in fact, they were not in the car at all, but in the dining-room of the station?

We know there are peculiar conditions of the atmosphere which render it, like the polished plate of the skilful artist, capable of receiving and of reflecting the images of objects occupying positions favorable for such reflection of their images. Of this we have ample evidence in the various species of mirage. That there may be conditions of the atmosphere fitting it not only to receive and reflect, but also to retain these images, after the objects have been themselves removed, appears to be a conclusion not altogether unwarranted by facts. That, in the above instance, the persons or images seen were indeed the individuals who at that moment were in the station, I do not believe. That the persons who had so lately been sitting in the car, some of them, doubtless, for several hours, had radiated to the surrounding atmosphere that ethereal fluid which stamps upon it these images, it being in a condition to receive, to retain, and to render them visible in open day, I regard as a simple, safe, and natural conclusion.

Again, may we not suppose that every particle of this fluid, like the particles of all other matter, is subject to the laws of attraction and repulsion? — that the particles radiating from each individual, would, unless prevented by some exterior force or interference, continue to attract each other, if not with the same power, yet by virtue of the same or similar laws as those by which their union had from the first been effected and sustained? Let us then suppose the condition of the atmosphere favorable for, or at least not in any way opposed to, the free arrangement of these particles in accordance with these laws, and I can see no valid objection to the idea of their continuing for a time to preserve the form they have so long worn. This view of the matter of course supposes that the objects thus seen, however ethereal they may really be, are, nevertheless, material, tangible forms; and in some instances I have no doubt that such is the case. With many persons the sudden appearance of shadowy forms, now here, now there, which by the time the eye is adjusted to observe objects of so aerial a nature are no longer visible, is an almost every-day occurrence. Of course they conclude their eyes have been at fault, — that no form was there, — that the appearance was due to some condition of the eye which they do not understand, which cannot be of any earthly consequence, and to observe which would, therefore, be folly in the extreme. At other times there are sensations accom-

panying these appearances, and seemingly so connected with them that one can but inquire if after all
they are not worthy of consideration. And again
there are times when the shadowy forms assume to
the *inner* senses all the characteristics of animated
life. At such times their presence may not be recog
nized by the outward sense of sight, and yet to the
individual who perceives them, that presence is none
the less a reality. Was it to this internal recognition
that Professor Longfellow referred when he wrote of

" PHANTOMS.

" All houses wherein men have lived and died
     Are haunted houses.   Through the open doors
The harmless phantoms on their errands glide
     With feet that make no sound upon the floors.

" We meet them at the door-way, on the stair,
     Along the passages they come and go,
Impalpable impressions on the air,
     A sense of something moving to and fro.

" There are more guests at table than the hosts
     Invited ; the illuminated hall
Is thronged with quiet, inoffensive ghosts,
     As silent as the pictures on the wall.

" The stranger at the fireside cannot see
     The forms I see, nor hear the sounds I hear ;
He but perceives what is ; while unto me
     All that has been is visible and clear.

" We have no title-deeds to house or lands ;
     Owners and occupants of earlier dates,
From graves forgotten, stretch their dusky hands,
     And hold in mortmain still their old estates."

And this is true not only of houses and lands, but

     " Owners and occupants of earlier dates "

than the human period still hold in mortmain the dust
once animated by their life.

QUESTION III.

" *Are the eyes open or closed?* "

They may be either.   More frequently, however,
when only vision is required, it is perhaps better to
close them, as the objects which meet the eyes, if
open, especially in the light, become mingled with, or
wholly crowd out of sight the views under consideration.   Some, no doubt, are better able to distinguish
between the two methods of sight when the eyes are
open than are others, yet I believe, judging from my
own experience, and from my observation of others
with whom we have experimented, that, under ordinary
circumstances, the psychometer is able to give more
accurate descriptions with closed than with open eyes.
When the object of the experiment is not vision, but
the exercise of some other sense, there may be less
necessity for shutting from sight the objects by which
we are surrounded.   Still I find that whatever serves
to disturb the mind, or in any way to call it from the
recognition of phenomena for which the experiment is
being conducted, in just so far serves to render it a
fruitless effort.   In my own case, this rule applies to
any unhappy condition of the mind, whether induced by
any outward unpleasant circumstance, or by thoughts
having a tendency to produce dissatisfaction, or even
unrest.

It should not be inferred from the preceding observations that all mental activity, or even intense mental

excitement, is opposed to the development of these phenomena. On the contrary, the mind of the psychometer was, perhaps, never more thoroughly active or more intensely excited than during some of the experiments recorded in this volume. In some instances, as, for example, in the case of the oil-bearing coral, the facts observed were, at the time, so at variance with all received opinion on that subject among our savans, that the mere discovery of its true origin might be considered of itself sufficiently startling; while combined as it was with the discovery of the enormous quantities underlying extensive districts, both in the eastern and western hemispheres; and not only so, but with the feeling that one stood in those ancient seas, while, extending to the right and left many, many miles away, and stretching before one for many leagues, was the glow and quiver of every rainbow hue, flashed back by the contents of unnumbered millions of cells; and with the reflection that every one of those cells had been the many-sided habitation of a minute animal whose very pulsations were throbs for the benefit of humanity, and whose life was a willing charity reserved for man whenever intellect should teach him its great value, — was to realize emotions that language fails to portray. But I must return to your inquiries.

QUESTION IV.

" But why designate this faculty ' sight,' if the eye is not the medium by which these impressions are conveyed to the brain?"

Simply because the one is no less sight than is the other. Apparently the same organ of the brain which recognizes the delicate tints of a beautiful flower, plucked to-day by the hand of innocent childhood, also recognizes the gorgeous hues of those ancient garlands with which our mother earth so lavishly adorned herself in the ages of her girlhood. That the power of vision in the one case differs materially from the same power in the other, is sufficiently evident; for while the one requires, as a positive necessity, that the lids be open in order to a correct perception of the object by which the impression is made, they may be in the other, according to circumstances, either open or closed. While one requires light, either direct, or reflected from some luminous body, to enable it to distinguish the objects within its range, the other finds in a pebble no larger than a common pea a sufficiency to light up a world, while we read the myriad pages of its thrilling history.

But there are times when the closed eyes of the psychometer cannot see, and yet perhaps the true condition of that with which he is in communication is as accurately perceived as if the eye took cognizance of all connected therewith. In such instances the impression appears to be made directly upon the brain; and when the individual has learned to discriminate between these direct impressions and the creations of fancy, or the workings of the imagination, they may be considered equally reliable with true vision. To those who have never cultivated this faculty, the above statement may appear somewhat incomprehensible; but it is none the less a fact, only wanting proper conditions to render it evident to any understanding of ordinary capacity. The statement of Professor Agassiz, which may be found in his " Tour to Lake Superior," may not be altogether inappropriate in this connection. He says, speaking of a certain fish, " I can distinguish the European species by a single scale; but this not from any definite character, but rather by a kind of instinct." He does not here claim to have seen them, it is true, but what *"kind of instinct"* is that which enables him to distinguish the European from any other species, by a single scale? Professor Agassiz has, no doubt, been too much absorbed by the investigations to which he has given the energies of a great mind, to permit him to analyze the sensations to which he so pleasantly alludes. Were he to do so, I can but believe he would find himself possessed of a faculty, compared with which, in the scope of its comprehension, instinct, as defined by our lexicographers, is but as the limited sphere of the coral polyp compared with that of the free, intelligent man. On the other hand, a person of very imaginative nature should be exceedingly careful in reference to trusting these sensations, and believing them to be genuine impressions, with which neither fancy nor imagination has anything to do. Especially should great care be exercised where the supposed impression relates to, or may in any way affect, any other than the individual impressed. A world of mischief has, in my estimation, resulted from our ignorance of the origin of thoughts which, springing to life within the brain, assume at once the character of legitimacy, and demand of us an acknowledgment of their claims to our consideration. Though there is no doubt that, at times, these thoughts are the offspring of influences existing exterior to,

readily acting upon, and sensibly affecting, that delicate organ, the brain, but influences of a nature so refined that the outward senses have as yet no power to
take cognizance of their presence, yet at other times
they are, as the experience of all will testify, neither
more nor less than distorted fancies, resulting from
disturbances in the electrical or nervous forces of
one's own system, and no more worthy of trust than
are the changing breezes of an April morn. By a
want of this knowledge, how many loving hearts have
been sundered forever! Over how many families has
it permitted some deadly upas to spread its branches
of blight, until the cup of joy, once brimming with a
healthful harmony, a kindly sympathy, a tender affection, has been turned to the gall of bitterness, and until the peace-loving olive has been changed to the
wormwood of woe! Throughout how many neighbor-
hoods has it scattered the seeds of dissension, and
nourished the roots of strife, until the beautiful plants
of friendly, social intercourse have been robbed of
their sustenance and uprooted from their place! The
effects are none the less terrible that any lack of care
on this point may have been due to our ignorance of
their nature or of their source. Like all things else,
they must be studied to be known. Persons have said
to me, "I can never understand my impressions. At
one time a matter of which I had previously known
nothing has been vividly impressed upon my mind, and
I have afterward found it to have been in strict accordance with the facts. Again, an impression would be
made, fully as strong, in every particular as distinct as
the first, and I would feel certain of its correctness,

when I have afterward learned that in this instance it was without any foundation in fact, and perhaps directly opposed to the true state of the matter to which it had referred. Sometimes, several instances occurring successively would prove to be in accordance with the facts to which they related, and I would conclude that, of a truth, my impressions had at last come to be reliable, when, lo! perhaps the succeeding instance playing me wholly false, I would find myself acting the part of a dupe of my own credulity. With a cheek ever ready to crimson at the naked remembrance of these instances, I have long since resolved never to heed impressions more, let their origin be what it may."

But, my friend, is there any wisdom in thus summarily disposing of a power, the possession of which, when you have learned its use, and understand the laws of its modifications, may be found of incalculable value? Depend upon it, these phenomena are not due to chance. They are governed by law, as the wandering stars are governed by law, and it is our business to observe and compare the facts of our being, and of our relation to the inner as well as to the outer world, if we would learn the laws upon which depend the development of that being and the harmony of those relations. To my mind, the folly consists, not in the failure of an honest endeavor to give to any fact its appropriate niche in the universe of facts, but in henceforth refraining from all effort to do so, because, forsooth, a previous effort has proved unsuccessful.

QUESTION V.

" *Is no Mesmeric influence needful to induce the required degree of sensitiveness of the brain, and of those organs which convey these impressions to the brain?* "

None whatever! Except in very rare instances this influence should never be accepted by the psychometer immediately previous to an experiment. To those who have studied the subject, the reasons for this will appear sufficiently obvious without further elucidation. For the benefit of those who have given little or no attention to the subject, I will endeavor to explain. That there are individuals so sensitive to the Mesmeric influence as to give back, for the time being, mere reflections of the mind or will of the Mesmerizer, is a fact too well established to require argument in this connection. Now, let us suppose you wish an experiment in psychometry. You Mesmerize your subject, and give to him or her, as the case may be, a fragment, perhaps of some rock, or a chip from some structure, or a bone from some animal, with the nature and much of the history of which you are already familiar. The description coincides perfectly with the facts, so far as you know them. " What a wonderful phenomenon!" the credulous bystander is ready to exclaim. But, *how* wonderful? Is not the result in strict accordance with the known laws of Mesmerism? You have proved nothing, either for or against psychometry. The whole matter rests on precisely the same basis now as before the experiment. " But," you say, " suppose that, while in a Mesmeric condition, the psy-

chometer is handed a specimen by a third individual,
of which, both in its nature and history, I am wholly
ignorant, and the description of which is, as in the first
instance, perfectly correct?" Though such a phenomenon has never come under my own observation, I do
not deny its possible occurrence. But suppose such a
result can be obtained, the same accuracy of description may be had without any such previous preparation; and if it might not in all, it certainly would in
numbers of instances, wholly· invalidate the experiment; for, while we know that by the establishment
of a certain electrical relation between Mesmerizer
and subject, the latter, for the time being, lives, as it
were, in a world prepared and peopled by the mind of
the former, may we not suppose that by consent of the
operator a secondary relation, if I may use the term,
may be established between the subject and another
individual, which shall give, if not equally perfect, at
least similar results to those developed by the primary
relation, or the relation between operator and subject?
And may not this be done by the subject simply coming within the electrical atmosphere of this third individual, who is supposed to be cognizant of the facts
connected with the specimen examined? If so, what
right have we to conclude that the effect is not due to
Mesmerism, as a consequence of this same electrical
relation? The fact is, it is not to prove that mind
can read mind, that the experiment is instituted. It
is to ascertain, if possible, whether mind, unassisted
by the outward senses, can read the sealed-up records
of the ages from the merest fragment of that volume,
on the pages of which are daguerreotyped all the por-

traits of the past; and to do this the mind of the observer should be as free as possible from every influence that could weaken the testimony in reference to
the result. Recollect, the question is not whether
this knowledge can be obtained, but whether it can be
obtained by this particular means. The faintest tinge
of light, then, that greets the eye of the psychometer,
unassisted by any influence save that of the specimen
you are supposed to have given him, is worth infinitely
more in this experiment than would be the brightest
sunshine that has ever blessed the world, if, for him to
behold it, it must first be discerned by another; and
the softest sound his ear is capable of receiving and
distinguishing as such, is of more value than the thun-
ders of a thousand cannon, if, to be recognized by his
sense, they must be conveyed thereto by the force of
your will. Nor can I believe that, as a rule, this influence is of greater value subsequent to an experiment
of the kind under consideration, than would be the
same influence subsequent to the healthful exercise
of any other faculty, whether mental or physical.

QUESTION VI.

"*Is the gaze directed into space, or is it directed upon some
object out of which these various forms appear to arise?*"

As soon expect the anatomist in a charnel-house,
dissecting-knife in hand, and invested with full authority to select his own subject, to direct his gaze into
space for bone and muscle, for nerve and fibre, when
the objects of his search are within his very grasp.
As soon expect the connoisseur to look for figures of

beauty on the unstained canvas, while he is literally
surrounded by that on which the artist has, as it were,
kindled the quenchless fires of very life. I fear I
shall fail to answer this inquiry fully, and to the satisfaction of those who have in all apparent honesty propounded it. To an individual having any conception
of the nature of this faculty the question is simply
absurd. We do not look into space for the tangible
objects by which we are surrounded; why should it
be expected of us in the instances under consideration? Nor do we in common life direct the gaze or
fix the attention upon one object in order to behold
another, or with any expectation of seeing other objects take the place of the first, under the influence
of our gaze. Are we more likely to do so when the
entire range of vision is crowded to excess with forms
heretofore, perhaps, as utterly unknown to us as they
could have been had they never had an existence, and
forms, too, as startling as they are new? No; the psychometer has little need to *look for* objects. In nine-
ty-nine cases out of every hundred he sees infinitely
more than he can describe. He has little need to hunt
up views; they crowd themselves into his presence,
not as if endowed with life and its attribute of locomotion only, but as if they read the mandates of the mind
and hasted to obey.

QUESTION VII.

*" But why, then, as in numbers of instances recorded in this
volume, talk of inability to see objects distinctly? If the power
of vision is, in one instance, so acute that the finest particles of*

matter, as they arrange themselves in various forms under the
influence of electrical currents, are clearly visible, why is it that,
perhaps in the same experiment, there is an acknowledged ina-
bility to discern distinctions which even to common sight would
be strikingly apparent?"

Did these scenes hang silent before us, as do the
pictures in the gallery of the artist, — were they fixed
and immovable as are the landscapes of a country village, — inert as are the granite hills of our own New
England, — then might be expected of us a careful
delineation of all their characteristics, so far, at least,
as the time given to the examination would permit us
to observe them in the minutiæ of detail. But when
it is remembered that to prevent these scenes passing
with the velocity of light an energetic action of the
will is required, and required continually, it will be
understood that the difficulties are of no ordinary character, and are, perhaps, peculiar to this sight alone.

Beside, the value of this vision depends, in a great
measure, upon the ability of the individual to distinguish between the nature of two influences, or rather
the source of each, and at the same time to render
himself positive to the one influence and passive to
the other. It is, perhaps, needless to add that, in the
ability to do this, people differ, and differ esssentially,
as does the same individual differ at different times. I
will endeavor to render this idea more lucid by illus-
tration. Let us imagine, then, for example, that you
have composed yourself for the examination of some
specimen. The field of vision is, as may not be unfre-
quent in your case, crowded with forms which you

recognize as being wholly independent of any influence derived from the specimen. Their appearance is
involuntary, and their disappearance, without a change
in yourself from the negative or passive to the positive condition, is entirely beyond your control. But
you cannot, at this time, pass to the positive condition
without rendering yourself equally incapable of discerning the forms or scenes resulting either from the
one influence or the other. In other words, you cannot now render yourself positive to this first influence,
whatever it may be, and thus banish from sight its
resulting images, or passive to the influence of the
specimen, and thus bring before you the scenes with
which it may hitherto have been associated, while at
another time to do this might be but the work of a
moment.

Again, we must remember that even in common
sight the image of any object presented to the eye
must be recognized by the brain, or there can be no
true vision. Without this recognition, the object may
be there, it is true, and its image may rest on the
retina, but so far as your knowledge of the fact is concerned, it is simply invisible. If this may be true of
the brain in reference to common sight and the gross
materials by which we are everywhere surrounded,
how much more so in reference to that subtle sense,
and to those excessively refined materials to which we
are directing our attention! And if true of the brain
as a whole that it may remain passive to one influence
and positive to another, why may it not be true of the
brain in its several parts? I believe it may be so;
and that in this fact lies the secret of those irregulari-

ties and seeming inconsistencies to which our seventh
inquiry especially alludes. It is not to be denied,
however, that there are sensations connected with this
interior vision, which are not common to the outer
sense of sight; but as I shall have occasion to allude
to this subject hereafter, I proceed to the consideration of

QUESTION VIII.

"What is the nature of this light, and whence is it derived?"

To this inquiry I frankly confess my inability to give
any definite reply. There are doubtless numbers of
persons who will feel satisfied that the answer is altogether too evident to admit of any controversy; and yet,
were the answers of these several individuals to be
obtained, they would be found to differ as widely as
do the color of their eyes, or as their various methods
of thought. To one it seems a necessity that this
light, derived, as he supposes, from all bodies radiating
light, whether natural or artificial, as well as from all
objects reflecting such light, has, as it were, been drunk
in and treasured up by the very elements of which
the specimen is composed, and from the earliest date
of its existence, only to be given off now, when the
magnetism of the human brain shall have induced sufficient activity in the infinitesimal particles of the hitherto latent mass. "While," he would contend, "to assume that all things, everywhere, are continually repro-
ducing themselves or their images upon the face of all
else, is, at most, but a step in reasoning from the known
to the unknown, and one that may be taken with appa-

rent security; we have then," he will add, "only to
admit that these daguerreotyped images are visible to
the sensitive eye of the psychometer, and we have
the whole matter before us, with outlines so well defined that a few experiments would be quite sufficient
to set at rest at once and forever all questions of
doubt." To another, however, this method of account-
ing for these phenomena is the veriest folly. He believes that the human being combines two distinct natures. That the outer—the physical—is simply the
medium through which the inner — the spiritual —
sustains to the more gross materials of the outer world
that relation which nature evidently regards as of vital
importance in the perfecting of the highest workman-
ship of her hands. That, while an intimate organic
relation between these two natures is a positive necessity to the continued exercise of that functional power
which is dependent upon the will, there may be, and
often is, a partial and temporary suspension of that
union or relation, granting to the spiritual nature comparative freedom from the dead weight of the inert
physical. That the spirit, in this semi-independent
existence, assuming a measure of its native force, is,
as it were, capable of annihilating time and space, and
living over in an hour the countless lives of the ages.
That the office of the specimen, which, by being
placed upon the forehead, is brought as nearly as possible to the brain itself, is merely, by its magnetic
influence, to direct the spirit, or rather, perhaps, to
lead it in the pathway of its own experience, when
thus comparatively free from its earthly moorings.
This, to his understanding, is a satisfactory solution of
the entire problem.

While, however, I would most willingly accord to each of these views any merit it may justly claim, I cannot accept either the one or the other as the only legitimate answer to this inquiry, until the facts bearing upon this question have been carefully collected and critically compared. There may be truth in both these propositions; but that a sufficient number of facts from the various departments of this science have been collected to furnish the needful materials for building a theory that shall prove perfect in all its parts when the dimless eye of research shall have pierced the last shadow, and shall have discovered the last treasure in the realm of inquiry, is, of course, not to be presumed. Indeed, that life will have been well spent which at the close of " threescore years and ten," can lay claim to the accomplishment of so masterly an endeavor. That, however, sufficient material has already been gathered together to justify the commencement of so wonderful a structure, when the several parts shall have been fitted to their places, is not, perhaps, an assumption without basis.

Let us recapitulate; and among the apparent facts bearing upon the question of the nature and source of this light we find, —

1st. That in this, as in ordinary sight, light is indispensable to the recognition of objects in the manner under consideration, — that is, by sight.

2d. That in this, as in ordinary sight, light appears to be either direct or reflected, or it may appear generally diffused, as is the case with daylight when the sky is overcast with clouds.

3d. That the light by which objects are thus seen

is overpowered, dissipated, or rendered imperceptible by the presence of ordinary light, if strong. Especially is this the case when the rays are permitted to fall directly in the face of the psychometer, unless, as is sometimes the case, he can render himself positive to ordinary light, and passive to that under consideration. But, whether this light be of the same nature as common light, differing only in intensity, or whether they be two distinctly differing elements or principles, it is, perhaps, more difficult to preserve toward them this twofold — this positive and negative or receptive — relation than toward any other influences by which we are surrounded, and which is so readily recognized by both the exterior and interior faculties.

This light, unperceived by the outward sense of vision, at least under ordinary circumstances, and hence not generally recognized as a subject for scientific investigation, I take the liberty to designate *Latent Light*, until some name shall be substituted more clearly expressive of its several characteristics.

4th. That latent artificial light (see experiment No. 22, and others of a kindred character) is more readily radiated than is latent natural light; at least, that such is the case under certain conditions or circumstances. Whether such would be apparent to all individuals, or to the same individual under all circumstances, is, of course, as yet an unestablished, though seemingly a probable, conclusion. If such be the case, and I am inclined to the opinion that it may be, then, whether this difference in radiation be the result of some difference in the chemical or electrical forces of the two substances, if substances they may be called, or whether, from some other cause, the one becomes apparent while the other remains *in statu quo*, and, if so, the cause to which this result is due, I leave, for the present at least, to the consideration of those who have made light and its properties a subject of investigation.

5th. That if the light which reveals to us this inner world be derived from the specimen, there are abundant reasons for presuming that the latent light of the past, that of the present, as, also, that of all intervening time, may exist together in the same specimen, and, when conditions are favorable, may become apparent to the psychometer.

6th. That in the examination of each particular specimen, the light by which its surroundings are observed corresponds to the light of the locality from which it was obtained, and the period to which the examination may be confined. To illustrate : — I am given a specimen I have never seen, and all knowledge of which is carefully concealed by the experimenter. I take it with my eyes closed, that I may form no idea of its nature from its appearance. When in a suitable condition for an experiment there is no seeing "through a glass darkly." There is, perhaps, the glowing light of day, or the more dim rock-light of underground; there may be the fierce glare of the volcano, or the soft water-light under the wave ; there is the glittering light of golden sands, or the sparkling glimmer of silvery seams; the clear, pure, life-giving atmosphere of the present, or the atmosphere of the long ago, laden with steam and heavy with the vapor of minerals and metallic substances; the direct and searching beams of a southern sun, forever multiplied by gorgeous bloom, while they are softened by the fadeless verdure of luxuriant foliage, or the weak and scattered rays of a chilled and snow-capped mountain peak, or of a no less chilled and ice-bound Arctic plain. Nor is this all. It may be observed, further,—

7th. That with many of the great changes to which the specimen, the globe, or that portion of the globe in which the specimen has existed for ages, has been subjected, there is a corresponding change in the quantity, the quality, and, perhaps, in the very nature of the light which becomes present to the sight of the psychometer.

Such are some of the facts; but the question, "What is the nature of this light, and whence is it derived?" is still unanswered. I do not pretend to answer it; but, in turn, I ask, Does the psychometer, in any instance, see only by the light contained in or radiated by the specimen examined? I do not deny it; still, granting such to be the case, between the light which renders visible this outer world and its multitudinous forms, and that under consideration, there exists, it appears to me, a wide and, as yet, an unbridged chasm. True, by its discoveries science is gradually narrowing this abyss, and we may, perhaps, hereafter find that at their extremes the boundary lines of these two realms melt into one, or, possibly, that no boundary save the measure of our capabilities ever existed between them. Let us calculate, if we can, how nearly these two limits already approach each other.

It is well known that, for some time after exposure to the direct rays of the sun, the diamond and other gems will radiate a brilliant light, especially if placed in darkness. We have seen, page 29, that, even in the most perfect darkness it is possible to secure, the image of one object may become stamped upon the very elements of another, and that without contact. And in view of these facts we may ask, without effrontery, Who shall say that the radiation of the gem has ceased when its brilliancy is no longer visible? If, then, the gem is capable of such radiation, — if a coil of string may, without light and without contact, leave its image upon the metallic plate, — is there any absurdity in supposing that the commonest objects by which we are surrounded are continually radiating that light, or those forces which, when collected, if not themselves visible, produce at least visible results? For years I have occasionally noticed, in rooms that no external light could enter at the time, a radiation from wall and ceiling which sometimes for an instant would flash with electrical brightness. At other times a quivering, wavy light, somewhat resembling the Aurora Borealis in some of its appearances, would float, perhaps, from one end of a wall to the other before it would wholly disappear. Of late I have observed these appearances more frequently; and sometimes, in rooms that have during the day been open to sunlight, I have found it no longer a fitful flash remaining visible only for an instant, but of such even, steady strength, that, before any artificial light has been introduced for the evening, I have been able to read and write by it after daylight had become altogether insufficient to enable me to perform such labor. In such instances, may it not be inferred that, by exposure to the light of day, the active principle of this element, be it what it may, becomes excited and its effects greatly intensified? And yet, except as in the case of the gem, it may be doubted whether even this intensified radiation would be observed by the outward eye in its normal condition. So closely, however, is the sensation in these instances allied to that of common sight, that only the fact that persons, whose external organs of visions are even stronger than my own, have been unable to discern it has led me to suppose it possible the recognition may be due to some other than the outward faculty of sight.

Thus far the facts appear in favor of the supposition that the psychometer sees only the daguerreotyped images of past or present forms. But there is another class of facts to which I must call attention, and which may, I fear, be regarded as even more incomprehensible than is that class already considered. I refer to those sensations which seem to indicate actual existence in the locality whence the specimen was obtained, and not only so, but existence in the locality *at the time* of the occurrence to which the examination relates; for, instead of being at all times seen directly before the face, as it seems to me we might reasonably expect were these images contained in the specimen, the psychometer is not unfrequently compelled to look up, or down, or at either side of his own position, to look near by him, or afar off, as the case may require, to turn round, or change his position, so that scenery which was at one time in the rear of that position may now be before his face, in order to obtain a clear view of it, as any one would find it needful to do were he actually in the same locality and desirous of beholding all that might come within the sphere of his vision in every direction. In short, the entire sensation is as if he lived and moved, perhaps in the light and atmos- phere of to-day, perhaps in that of a million years ago, himself a living, sentient being amid living forms; not merely beholding their daguerreotyped images upon the flinty fragment, but an observer of the *life and habits* of those beings, as if they swarmed the waters of the present seas, or roamed the earth to-day, rather than centuries agone. And this sensation is not unfre- quently so absolute, the consciousness of an existence in the *then and there* is so perfect, so vivid, that a *sud- den* return to the *now and here*, to a recognition of the occurrences of the present, may be attended by a shock, with nervous derangements that are some- times felt for hours afterward. This sensation is some- what analogous to that produced by the galvanic bat- tery, though it may be, perhaps, more refined in its nature, and, if possible, more thoroughly diffused through the system. There are times, it is true, when none of these sensations are realized — when the views have all the appearance of daguerreotypes, all the fixedness of the painted portrait. There are other times when all that is seen appears objective, indeed; but so diminutive are the objects, you feel yourself at a loss for a criterion by which to judge of their real or approximate size. These are, however, the exceptions, being of comparatively rare occur- rence. But you ask, —

QUESTION VIII.

" By what means does the psychometer appear to himself thus suddenly to become a denizen of some other locality than that of which he is really the inhabitant?"

We may ask, by what means does the mind project that thought which, in a moment of time, sweeps the boundary of the known universe, and returns to us again, before we are aware it has fled, or even that it has been fully formed? Who is able to point out to us the operations of our minds in connection with any phenomenon of thought? Philosophers have, for centuries, puzzled their brains, and puzzled each other, with the inquiry, "How, or by what means, does the mind of the human being reach out, as it were, from himself and grasp the finite, or even grapple with the Infinite?" But men and women have not ceased to think, nor yet is the speed of thought denied, because the philosopher has thus far failed to answer the inquiry. Life itself is, as yet, an unfathomable mystery, but who, on that account, would cease to live? The means by which we thus exchange the one place for the other, or it may be, perhaps, exist in two distinct and distant places at one and the same moment, I do not profess to understand; nor do I assert that such is really the case; only this, that so far as all the sensations of existence are concerned, I can distinguish no difference between that which appears to me, at the time, to be my life or existence on one side of the globe, and that which is my acknowledged existence on the other. Certainly, the senses—hearing, seeing,

smelling, tasting, and feeling — are as acute in the former as in the latter case; while, in the comprehensive-
ness of vision, the power and speed of transit, and in
much to which all our senses are keenly alive, the latter can bear no comparison with the former.

Again, *Can* MOTION *be daguerreotyped?* for it must
be remembered that these objects are seen, not at rest
nor in one position only, as if the uplifted arm of man,
or wing of bird, had been caught by the artist, and, being thus arrested, remained uplifted still, but each successive movement reveals itself, as would be the case
were the being before you instinct with life.

It may perhaps be answered, "The motions or occurrences impressed upon an object, between two
given points of time, have, of necessity, an order of
impression; the image of the being which was the
subject of the motion, is fixed upon the specimen or
object impressed, in all the various attitudes it exhibited at the time, *and in the order of that exhibition;*
and in that same order, or, if not the same, at least in
an order that renders the apparent motion equally perfect, and the apparent subject of the motion equally
substantive in all its parts, these images become visible to the psychometer." There is much in my own
experience that greatly favors this view of the matter,
and it may, perhaps, be the correct method of account-
ing for these phenomena; still, there is much which,
as it appears to me, remains wholly unaccounted for on
this hypothesis.

But, again, you ask, "Does every grain of sand on
the wave-washed shore, every atom composing the
rocky ribs of this old earth, contain within itself the

likeness, the photographic image of every object, the
shadow of which may have reached it, even from a distant sphere? and does it retain a record of every act
that has produced a vibration in some ethereal fluid, by
which it and the subject of that act are alike surrounded?" I grant the idea seems strangely monstrous! Still, the fragment examined may be divided
and subdivided, until the dust of its cleavage alone remains, and yet that dust will give you back the same
extended views, — the same entirety of objects, in the
infinitely varying positions consequent upon the activity due to life, or upon changes resulting from the conditions to which, at least on our own planet, matter is
subject; and who shall limit the extent to which this
reduction may descend, and ever with the same result?

But if only daguerreotype or photographic images
are seen, how is it that we appear to ourselves to stand
within this vast circle of ever-active and ever-changing
forms? If these objects and these scenes have their
only existence on or within the specimen, by what
means, by virtue of what law, do the movements of
the psychometer in any way affect the condition of
that which he beholds? I admit that instances of this
kind are comparatively rare; still, it has been, and can
be done. When, for example, I stood, or seemed to
stand, upon that immense accumulation of vegetable
matter, in one of those extensive fields of the Carboniferous age, and by a slightly springing motion shook
acres of the spongy mass, the motion of that mass was
as really, to my senses, the result of my own motion,
as could have been the case had my physical being occupied a similar relation to a genuine mass of the same

material, were such to be found existing on the globe
to-day.   Now the question is, could we thus bring ourselves into contact with that which only exists as an
image of the real? or is there somewhere in this infinite universe, not the image only, but the positive, the
actual, the continued existence of all that has ever
been?   If, as philosophers contend, "the slightest
movement of the smallest body produces results which
diffuse themselves through all space and all time," may
we not go still farther, and conclude that any impulse,
however metamorphosed it may have become in its effects, exists forever, in all its original purity?

But to proceed directly to the consideration of your
inquiry.   In the examinations of Mrs. Taylor, of Lockport, and of Mrs. DoViel, of Pultneyville, both of New
York State, I observe the psychometer not unfrequently designates her course from the present to the
former locality of the specimen, by descriptions of various places and objects which would be met by the
common traveller in passing by the same route from
one place to the other.   Other individuals with whom
we have experimented may have done the same, but
if so, I do not, at this moment, recall the circumstance.
Mr. Denton tells me, that of the thirteen specimens
examined, at his request, by Mrs. DoViel, during his
stay in Pultneyville, he does not remember that she
once failed thus to indicate her course.   This I do not
remember to have accomplished in a single instance;
and by what means they succeed in doing so, I have
little or no idea.   I may, at times, by the force of my
will-power, after having reached the locality from
which the specimen was obtained, move in any direc-

tion, and to almost any distance, either on the surface
or below it; and in the same way I may go backward
in time almost indefinitely; I may examine, with considerable minuteness, objects that would seem to bear
no relation whatever to the specimen; I may name
with tolerable accuracy, and at times with, perhaps,
exact precision, the locality from which the specimen
was obtained; but I do it by a *sense* of the position I
then occupy, instead of judging of my whereabouts
by any knowledge of the course by which my position
has been reached. Indeed, I seem, as it were, to close
my eyes on that which immediately surrounds me, only
to open them on that by which the specimen has been
surrounded at some other time and in some other
place, and by which I then seem to myself to be also
surrounded. Of course, this is not always the work
of an instant. My condition is not naturally passive
or receptive,— far otherwise; and at times I find it not
only difficult but nearly or quite impossible to become
so. For this reason I do not consider myself a naturally ready psychometer. Though by cultivation of this
faculty I can now make examinations more readily,
and with far less fatigue, than I could do at the commencement of our experiments, I have no doubt that
hundreds of persons could "begin where I leave off;"
that is, that in their first examinations the descriptions
would be not only more full, more elaborate, than are
my own, even now, but that they would be conducted
in less time, and with far greater ease. I have spoken
of these visions as having been of frequent occurrence in childhood, but have said nothing of fatigue as
a consequence, for the simple reason that I felt none;

at least no more than one would naturally feel in looking at any panorama of interest. Of course, in time,
one will weary even of sight-seeing. But the fatigue
to which I have elsewhere alluded is the result, not
of *beholding*, but of those efforts of the will by which
one influence is refused, while another is received; by
which one object is retained in view, while others are
prevented from taking its place; those by which I
move from place to place, or by which I force myself
to remain in one position; those mental efforts by
which, while the will is thus actively engaged in one
direction, — perhaps in more than one, — I am at the
same moment comparing objects then seen with objects
familiar to common sight; examining structures and
parts of structures, hesitating and examining again,
that I may be certain I am making no mistake; comparing the size of one object with that of another;
measuring distances, calculating forces, and estimat-
ing, so far as is practicable, causes and effects, conditions and their consequences.

When these views are spontaneous, — when the psychometer is merely a passive spectator, as I was in
childhood, and as I may become at almost any hour of
the night or day, there is little cause for fatigue. The
scenes may be pleasing and, if in health, I may observe
or dismiss them, as I choose. They may be unpleasant,
and I have but to render myself positive to the influence by which they are produced, which, in my case,
unless ill, or over-exhausted, it is not difficult to do,
and dissipate them at pleasure. It is when the experiment is conducted for a purpose, and it becomes needful to control the influence of different objects, — to

distinguish between them, — to examine one object, while others are, as it were, held in abeyance until that is accomplished, etc., etc.; or when illness renders one passive, and lack of strength prevents a return to the positive condition, that these examinations exhaust the nervous energies of the system, and that with a rapidity to which physical labor can bear no comparison.

QUESTION IX.

" *But how is it possible, on any scientific or philosophic principle, to account for the hearing of sounds, when the atmosphere has for ages ceased to vibrate to the causes by which they were originally produced?* "

If it be proven that we live only in the outward; that we hear only by means of vibrations in the atmosphere; that the duration of a given vibration is dependent upon a given amount of force; and that, when the sound is heard, the time elapsed since the force which produced it was exerted, precludes a possibility of the continuance of the vibrations, then, of course, there is no room for controversy. But have we, as yet, arrived at the *ne plus ultra* of knowledge in this direction? Are we absolutely certain that sounds can be conveyed to the human ear *only* by the atmosphere, or by some outward, tangible substance, as for instance, a block of wood, or a bar of iron? My own outward sense of hearing is far from being acute, and has been so for years, yet within that time I have distinctly heard conversations between individuals who at the moment were distant from the spot where I then was, between forty and fifty miles. Will any one pretend that this was the result of vibrations in the atmosphere? I do not believe it. Yet, if you accept the fact, by what means do you account for the occurrence, but by supposing either that we may exist in two distinct places at one and the same moment, or that some fluid, infinitely more refined than is our atmosphere, conducts to our interior sense of hearing vibrations which the atmosphere fails to convey to the ear? And who shall say when, in this fluid, these vibrations cease? or that they may not extend outward in time as well as outward in space? Or will you go still farther, and suppose that all matter retains in a latent condition whatever force may hitherto have been applied to it, and that, by the perception of these latent conditions, the psychometer may, when this faculty shall become developed in the fulness of its strength, arrive at the facts of all past time?

Usually, in my own case at least, these sounds are *perceived* rather than *heard*. Sometimes they are as clear and distinct to the internal sense of hearing as are common sounds to the outward ear; and there have been times when I could not, and cannot yet, tell whether they were heard by the external or only by the internal ear, so like were they in all respects to sounds produced by outward, tangible forms. In respect to the inability, in some instances, to distinguish between recognition by the external, and recognition by the internal senses, hearing and sight stand, I believe, alone. I do not remember that smelling, taste, or feeling — though when in the psychometric condition they may be acute as are hearing or sight, —

have ever so closely approached the boundary between these external and internal realms as to render it impossible for me to say by which they were really addressed.

QUESTION X.

" *But what is meant by ' going backward in time ' ? Do you wish to convey the idea that the spirit leaps, as it were, from the present to the past ?* "

I do not assert anything in answer to this inquiry, save that the sensation is in all respects that of closing the eyes on the present, and opening them on the past; or, where the effort is made to do so, that of going from the present to the past by force of the will. But by what means this is accomplished, — what is the cause of this sensation, — whether the sensation be a true or a false one, or what may be the philosophy of the whole matter, I can form no idea. I state only the fact, desiring that others may direct their attention to the subject, and arrive, if possible, at the true solution of the problem.

QUESTION XI.

" *But, if this faculty be common to humanity, why have I no knowledge of my inheritance ?* "

Can you tell me, my friend, why it is that the room in which the loved one breathed out the last ray of earthly, organic life is still so very dear to you? What it is you so distinctly feel within those walls that reminds you of the loved and lost? Why, when you pass within its portals, your eye instinctively turns toward sofa, bed, and chair, as if you expected the same fond gaze to greet you now as it has often done before? Why you feel, to throw open that room to the sunlight, and the air, and to all the influences of busy life, would be to scatter to the elements a something which, however undefinable, is yet a *something* that unites you to that past in which your friend, though with ebbing life, still thought and spoke and loved? Nor are these sensations confined to the room alone. The clothing our loved ones have worn, the books they have handled, and, I may add, even the objects on which they have gazed with fondness and pleasure, have all a kindred power to reproduce sensations of their presence. Who believes that the ideas so finely embodied in the following lines by Wm. C. B., (I regret that I cannot give the entire name, but my efforts to find it have been unavailing) live only in the fancy of the poet?

"BABY'S SHOES.

" Oh, those little, those little blue shoes !
Those shoes that no little feet use.
   Oh, the price were high
   That those shoes would buy ;
Those little, blue, unused shoes !

" For they hold the small shape of feet,
That no more the mother's eyes meet,
   That by God's good will,
   Years since grew still,
And ceased from their totter so sweet.

" And, oh, since that baby slept
So hushed, how the mother has kept,
   With a tearful pleasure,
   That dear little treasure,
And over them thought and wept !

"For they mind her forevermore
 Of a patter along the floor;
   And blue eyes she sees
   Look up from her knees
 With the look that in life she wore.

"As they lie before her there,
 There babbles from chair to chair
   A little sweet face
   That's a gleam in the place,
 With its little gold curls of hair.

"Then, oh, wonder not that her heart
 From all else would rather part,
   Than those tiny blue shoes,
   That no little feet use,
 And whose sight make the fond tears start."

Ay, mother, and have not "those little blue shoes"
a charm for thee independent of the *remembrance*
merely that thy darling once wore them? Art thou
at all times satisfied merely with beholding them? Is
there not a greater pleasure in clasping them in your
own warm palms? a sensation as of the little feet within,
upon which you have so often fastened them? And
the hat that hangs against the wall, soiled by the little
fingers, tell me, mother, do you ever take it from its
place, but you feel the "little gold curls," as they
cluster around your own fingers?

Did we never realize their presence thus, save when
our friends have passed "the shadowy vale," we might,
perhaps, conclude that to the still-existing spirit, these
objects form, as it were, that

　　　·　·　·　,　·　　"bridge of light,
O'er whose unsteady floor, that sways and bends,"

they come again to meet and mingle with their friends. But such is not the case. Our friends may have left us for a few months, or for a few weeks only. Day after day we visit the room they so lately occupied, and, with that same sense, we recognize the presence of the absent. How many times, since the little one went home with grandmamma, only last week, have you seen the laughing eyes peep from beneath the little hat, and heard the pattering of the little feet! And is this all fancy? Trust for once, fond mother, to the answer of your throbbing heart. In a sense, the little one is with you still; and when you shall have become sufficiently sensitive to these influences, there will be no wall so thick, and no distance so great, as to preclude the possibility of your holding daily communion with those you love.

We perceive like causes producing like effects when, standing in the presence of some old ruin " that Time hath made," while the " ivy green " was gathering in its close embrace the scattered fragments of the lonely representative of ancient art, we run backward in our sympathies to the brain that designed, and the taste of a people which made possible this outward expression of those interior creations; and this we do instinctively, and without pausing to call to our remembrance the written record of its time. So with all our relics, — the products of whatever clime or age. From the tumuli of Great Britain, from the mounds of America, from the tombs of Egypt, from the sepulchres of Judea, from the burial-places of every tribe among the ancients, wherever it is practicable, we gather these treasures of the past, and cherish them

with religious care. And why do we do this? They
have a value, it is true, inasmuch as they furnish, so
far as they go, evidences of the habits and customs of
the people of those olden times. So have the histories
of those times a kindred value, — histories written by
men who have devoted years to the investigation of
these subjects, — yet with what widely differing sensations do we take into our hands a printed volume on
Egypt and her once powerful inhabitants, or on India
and her wonderful Cave Temples, for example, and the
long fringed cloth, heavy with emanations from the
dead, in which the mummy was wrapped for inter-
ment, and in which it has lain for centuries; or one of
those implements of flint, by which the slender records
of forgotten tribes have been handed down the steep
of unknown centuries. The air in our museums —
both public and private — is laden with disagreeable
effluvia from these silent hosts, that so unerringly repeat the stories of their age; and in your answer,
"*It were sacrilege to wash them!*" there is a volume
of the richest meaning, — of the highest import. I
can believe that a true warrior may derive inspiration
from the sword worn by a brave and daring comrade,
while that of a coward can be redeemed from its curse
only by the hand of courage. I can fancy that a man's
religious zeal and devotion may be intensified by the
possession of a copy of the Bible, worn with frequent
use by some heroic martyr, while had he received the
same inheritance, minus the influence, from some hea-
then or infidel, he might have been less devotional,
and perhaps far more critical. I can conceive it not
only possible, but probable, that a natural tendency to

aberration of the mental faculties may be developed into actual madness by continued association with places and objects which have previously received the influence of the insane, unless counteracting influences or agents be greatly in preponderance; and it has frequently been remarked that in places where one individual has committed a crime, another, perhaps more than one, has fallen a victim to the same temptation.

In view of these considerations, how many of us can claim exemption from all experimental knowledge of our strange inheritance?

QUESTION XII.

" But among all these ethereal forms, so vividly present to the senses, do you never recognize spirits of the departed?"

I have frequently been asked this question, but I cannot answer it satisfactorily, even to myself. So far as all my theories, bearing upon this subject, are concerned, I frankly confess they do not admit even the possibility of such an occurrence. Still, had I never thus seen images of any save of those who had previously departed this life, I should, no doubt, have concluded that if the question of spirit-existence and of spirit-intercourse with the living were not already settled, I had, at least for myself, strong testimony in favor of its affirmative. But when I see those who are still in life, though separated from them many, many miles; when, though thus separated and thus seen, I hear them speak as distinctly as I hear the sound of my own voice; when I see those who departed this life centuries ago, engaged in the same

pursuits, dealing with the same facts, and living essen‧
tially the same lives which the habits and customs of
the times warrant us in believing they must of neces‧
sity have lived; when I see animals of which, for ages
past, the earth has borne no living representatives,
and see all these as vivid realities, — the question be‧
comes to my understanding, at least, exceedingly com‧
plicated, and I confess myself unable to perceive that
any theory with which I am acquainted can be made
to cover all the facts.

QUESTION XIII.

"*But, granting the correctness of your own deductions, we
ask, how is it that with a given specimen the attention of the
psychometer is arrested by some* ONE *circumstance recorded in
the great volume of its history, — why some* ONE *condition, or
some* ONE *epoch, in that history stands out from all the others,
bold and distinct in its every outline, — while that same speci‧
men, or, at least, every particle of which it is composed, has re‧
ceived its share of the modifying influences of all time?*"

Permit me to submit, first, that though all matter
may, as it would seem, retain the influences of all
time, and may communicate these influences to the
sufficiently sensitive, still those of organic are more
marked, or more marked in their effects upon certain
organisms, than are those of inorganic matter; second,
that of organic forms the influences of the animal
kingdom are more active or more marked than are
those of the vegetable kingdom; third, that there is
observable, so it seems to me, a gradual increase of

activity or force in these permeating influences as we
ascend in the scale of organization from the animal-
cule to the man; fourth, that we may go yet farther,
and trace a corresponding increase in the force or
radiation of these influences as we ascend from the
lower to the higher developments of the human species; fifth, that, farther still, we may find that, by
perhaps the same law, whatever serves to increase the
radiation of these influences, as, for example, great
grief, great fear, great gladness, or intense activity of
any one or all of the mental faculties, serves, also, to
render more effective their results, both primary and
secondary. If this be so, and so it seems to me, then
a specimen of any geological era, however saturated
it may be with the influences of its own age, from exposure to the stronger influences of the human period,
and the still stronger influences of some particular
portion of that period of more lively interest than another, may yet more readily yield to the psychometer
the influences of that particular time. And may not
the same be true in a corresponding ratio of any unusual activity or disturbance among the bodies of inorganic matter, or even in the primary elements of all
things? It has been suggested that a specimen yields
to the psychometer the influences it has received in
the same order as that in which they were impressed
upon it; but in my own case this is not, or at least
does not appear to be, an invariable rule. Sometimes,
beginning with past conditions, I seem to trace the
events forward in time, and, to a great extent, in the
order of their occurrence. At other times, beginning
with more recent conditions, I seem to trace the events

backward in time, preserving here, also, in a great measure, a like regard for the order of their occurrence; while on still other occasions all relation between one view and another is wanting, and it is nearly or quite impossible to give anything like a connected account of the scenes or objects which so suddenly dart into sight and are as suddenly lost to sight again.

CONCLUSION.

Such are some of the inquiries which seem to me likely, on reading the body of this work, to arise in the minds of those who have never investigated the subject for themselves. Granting the facts herein presented, are we too enthusiastic if we indulge the belief that, with the general cultivation of this faculty, there will dawn a brighter day than humanity shall ever before have witnessed? May we not reasonably hope for less of wrong and more of right, when men and women shall have learned that all on which their shadows rest — every ray of light which they reflect — become, emphatically, "recording angels," faithfully transcribing their words, their deeds, their thoughts, nay, the very motives of their hearts? Alas for the peace of the evil-doer, when, from every object by which he is surrounded, his own image stares him back in every attitude requisite for the consummation of that crime, and with a persistency that time cannot affect! Alas for the plotter of mischief, when he sees in every flag in the pavement, every pebble in the street, his thoughts indelibly recorded, and learns that the record may be "known and read of all men"!

When the slanderer learns that "there are tongues in trees" which still rehearse his truthful words with the lying accent, will he hasten to repeat the falsehood? When the highwayman and the murderer shall hear the voice of their victim ring out on the evening breeze to every passer-by, and when they can no longer wash from their own sight, or from that of the avenger, the gore with which their hands are crimsoned, will they be likely to enlarge the stains, or to add another to the voices that already cry against them? I am not dealing in fancies. If the influence of the suicide who falls a victim to insanity may be so treasured by the wooden walls of the room in which he expires as to present the psychometer, years afterwards, with a faithful representation of the sad, sad scene (and this has come within my own experience), are these suppositions unfounded — these conclusions but over-wrought fancies?

No doubt, when this subject shall have been more thoroughly studied, and its various bearings more carefully observed, other questions will arise every way equal in interest and importance to those already considered. Certainly, as I contemplate it, there open before me fields for investigation that seem to know no boundary. If we have correctly interpreted this "*hand-writing on the wall*," what is there desirable which the future does not promise us? What records are here from which the historian may gather without stint! What domains for the naturalist! What limitless realms for the natural, the mental, and the moral philosopher! And how, to the utmost extent of his capabilities, may each revel in the field of his choice without fear of exhausting his supplies! Truly, its ultimate and inevitable results to science are grand beyond comparison; its benefits to humanity, in every department of life, of incalculable value! "He who runs may read" the promise of the future!

INDEX.